SOURCEBOOK ON POPULATION

1970-1976

Compiled and edited by

TINE BUSSINK
JEAN VAN DER TAK
CONNIE S. ZUGA

A publication of the

POPULATION REFERENCE BUREAU, INC.
Washington, D.C. 20036

1976

Z
7164
D3
B878

Published in 1976 by

Population Reference Bureau, Inc.
1754 N Street, N.W.
Washington, D.C. 20036

Publications of the Population Reference Bureau are not copyrighted. They may be copied or reproduced without specific permission provided that the appropriate bibliographic citation is given.

Library of Congress Cataloging in Publication Data

Bussink, Tine.
   Sourcebook on population, 1970-1976.

   Continues Bibliography on population and Source book on population, which were issued in Population bulletin, the former in 1966 as a supplement to v. 22, no. 3, and the latter in 1969 as v. 25, no. 5.
   1. Population—Bibliography. I. Van der Tak, Jean, joint author. II. Zuga, Connie S., joint author. III. Population Reference Bureau, Washington, D.C. IV. Title.
Z7164.D3B878   [HB871]   016.30132   76-27595
ISBN 0-917136-01-2

Library of Congress Catalog Card Number: 76-27595

International Standard Book Number: 0-917136-01-2

Additional copies of this *Sourcebook on Population 1970-1976* are for sale by the Population Reference Bureau at the rates quoted on the inside back cover.

Table of Contents

Introduction 1

Glossary 3

      BIBLIOGRAPHY 4

   I. Introduction to Demography and Population Studies 4
      A. Textbooks 4
      B. Readers: Collections of articles to use with texts in a
         general study of population 5
      C. Early Population Thought and Historical Demography 5
      D. Studies in Related Fields: Anthropology, Ecology,
         Geography, Genetics 6

  II. Demographic Methods 7

 III. Demographic Data 9
      A. United States 9
      B. International Data 11

  IV. Fertility 12
      A. General and National Fertility Studies 12
      B. Biological, Cultural, Psychological and Socioeconomic
         Determinants and Consequences of Fertility 14

   V. Marriage, Family, and Non-Familial Roles of Women 16
      A. Cross-Cultural and National Studies of Marriage and
         the Family 16
      B. Variant Family Styles and Illegitimacy 17
      C. Non-Familial Roles of Women 18

  VI. Mortality and Morbidity 19

 VII. Migration and Population Distribution 20
      A. International Migration 20
      B. Internal Migration 21
      C. Urban, Suburban, Rural Distribution and Characteristics 22

VIII. Population Characteristics 24
      A. Age, and Population Structure 24
      B. Labor Force Participation and Socioeconomic Status 24
      C. Ethnicity and Religion 25

  IX. Causes and Consequences of Population Growth 27
      A. General Works on Current Population Problems 27
      B. Population, Nutrition, and Food Supply 29
      C. Population, Resources, and the Environment 31
      D. Culture, Ethics, Education, and Population Change 32

X. Population and Economic Development 33
    A. Developed Countries 33
    B. Less Developed Countries 33

XI. Population Policies and Laws 35

XII. Fertility Control 37
    A. Family Planning 37
    B. Abortion 40

XIII. International, Regional, and National Studies 42
    A. International 42
    B. Africa 43
    C. Asia 44
    D. Europe and the U.S.S.R. 48
    E. Latin America and the Caribbean 49
    F. Middle East 50
    G. North America 51
    H. Oceania 52

XIV. Population Education 52

XV. General Bibliographies and Computerized Information
    Retrieval Services 54

XVI. Periodicals 57

POPULATION PROGRAMS AND ORGANIZATIONS 61

I. Graduate Training Programs in Demography and
   Population Studies in the United States 61

II. Major Private Organizations in the Fields of Population
    and Family Planning Located in the United States 64

III. Population and Family Planning Programs of the U.S.
    Government and of Multilateral Agencies Headquartered
    in the United States 65

IV. Population Libraries and Information Sources Around the World 67

V. Population Research and Training Programs and Sources
   of International Assistance Around the World 68

Author Index 69

Introduction

With the publication of this third *Sourcebook on Population,* the Population Reference Bureau attempts the well nigh impossible—to cover in one reasonably sized volume the major population-related books, monographs, reports and bibliographies issued in the English language between 1970 and the summer of 1976, to cite the chief English-language periodicals now being published in the field, and to list the principal demographic training centers, and population and family planning programs currently operating in and from the United States, with a look at such programs and sources of information available around the world.

In the seven years since our 1969 *Sourcebook on Population* the world's population explosion appears to have crested; growth rates in the developed world are in many cases nearing the magic zero, and there is increasing evidence that the hoped-for turning point in alarmingly high fertility rates may also have been reached in many parts of the Third World. The population information explosion, however, continues unabated. All to the good. To cope with it, the past few years have been marked by the appearance of many bibliographies focused on special areas within the population-family planning field and computerized information retrieval services (some of which are listed in Section XV of our *Bibliography).* Nevertheless, this very wealth of guides to information may defeat the non-professional but concerned layperson and even many population students and specialists. It is to these readers that this *Sourcebook* is dedicated.

Like the Population Reference Bureau itself, this *Sourcebook* is intended, as stated in the introduction to our 1969 *Sourcebook,* "to bridge the gap between the demographic researcher and the public, between the scholar in one corner of the population-ecology-economics field and his counterpart in another." Not all highly technical works and data sources have been excluded from the bibliographic listings, but the emphasis is on the more general, and more accessible. The focus is further on population and demography, rather than fertility control and family planning. However, the bibliographic sections on "Fertility Control," "Periodicals," and "General Bibliographies and Computerized Information Retrieval Services," and the sections on programs and organizations operating in the United States contain listings of general interest in these fields.

This 1970-76 *Sourcebook* is an update rather than replacement of the Bureau's *Sourcebook* of 1969 (*Population Bulletin,* Vol. 25, No. 5, November 1969), which contained some 430 annotated literature citations, and our 20-page, non-annotated *Bibliography on Population* of 1966 (A Reference Supplement to *Population Bulletin,* Vol. 22, No. 3, August 1966). These predecessors retain their merit for the time periods they covered. The present bibliography contains over 900 annotated citations, including 62 periodicals. (The many series count as single citations.) To keep it within manageable proportions we continue to exclude individual journal articles, while recognizing these as generally the first public airing for new developments and findings in the population-demographic world, as in all scientific fields. To keep abreast of these, the reader can best refer regularly to the periodicals listed in Section XVI of the Bibliography and the quarterly *Population Index,* published for the Population Association of America by Princeton's Office of Population Research.

We also confine ourselves to the printed word, eliminating—with a few exceptions—sources of data tapes, microforms and audiovisual materials. For a comprehensive listing of population-related films, we recommend *Population Education: Sources and Resources,* published in 1975 by the Bureau's population education department (free for single copies; $1.00 each for bulk orders. A revised edition is planned for 1977.)

Further caveats. The many works relevant to more than one category within the population-demography field have been placed where we felt it most appropriate. The *Table of Contents* should help the reader to locate sections which may contain relevant listings. The retail prices listed should be taken as approximations only, given our inflationary times. Also, only paperback prices have been listed (and noted as such) for books available in both paperback and hardback.

The *Sourcebook* is divided into two major sections: a *Bibliography,* (pages 4 through 59) preceded by a glossary of common demographic terms, and including listings of general bibliographies, computerized information retrieval services, and periodicals; and a guide to *Population Programs and Organizations* (pages 61 through 68), followed by an *Author Index.*

The first part of the *Bibliography* (Sections I-VIII) consists of the more purely demographic categories except for Section V on "Marriage, Family, and Non-Familial Roles of Women." The second part deals with general concerns about population growth, its interaction with related areas, and with population policies and programs (Sections IX-XII). The selection of entries in Section XIII on "International, Regional, and National Studies" was made from works in the English language with particular emphasis on the developing world. These are meant to serve as an introduction to research and programs focused more narrowly on specific geographical areas. The new section on "Population Education" (Section XIV) will introduce the general reader to important materials in this rapidly expanding field.

In the second major portion of the *Sourcebook,* "Population Programs and Organizations," we refer readers to the several useful guides to sources of such information that have appeared since our last *Sourcebook,* e.g., the *International Directory of Population Information and Library Resources* of the Carolina Population Center, and the two-volume guide to *Population Programmes and Projects,* recently issued by the United Nations Fund for Population Activities. However, we again list names and addresses for U.S. graduate training programs in demography and population studies and for the major private and public organizations involved in population and family planning, if located in the United States (greatly expanded from the listings of 1969).

Tracking down the materials cited in the *Bibliography* may take some persistence. *Books in Print,* published annually by R. R. Bowker Company, lists addresses of U.S. publishers and is available at most libraries and bookstores. Your local library may have some titles or be able to obtain them through interlibrary loan arrangements. For non-commercial and foreign sources of works cited, we have occasionally listed appropriate addresses. Please note that only Population Reference Bureau publications can be ordered through our Circulation Department.

In compiling this *Sourcebook* we have received help and advice from many people. Within the Bureau these have been Vera Gathright, Milton Fairfax, Amara Bachu, Judith Seltzer, Carol Fletcher, Laurence Mase, Richard Kirchberger, Susan Nichols, Leon Bouvier and Robert Worrall. Conrad Taeuber and Joan Helde, Director and Librarian of the Center for Population Research, Kennedy Institute, Georgetown University, Larry Long of the Population Division, U.S. Bureau of the Census, David Radel and Lynn Yoshimoto of the East-West Communication Institute, Honolulu, Helen Kolbe, Director, and Martita Midence, Rita Bergman, Inara Gravitis, and Robert Updegrove of the staff of the Population Information Program, George Washington University, and H. Neil Zimmerman and Stephen Viederman, Librarian and former Assistant Director, Demographic Division, of The Population Council, have kindly read, commented on, and added to various versions of the manuscript. To all of these we are most grateful.

We realize that imperfections and oversights are unavoidable in the extensive search that this has been.

To keep up to date on later major publications in population, we draw the reader's attention to the annotated listing of "Current Readings" carried in each issue of the Bureau's monthly population newsletter *Intercom.*

Tine Bussink
Jean van der Tak
Connie S. Zuga

Glossary

Age-Sex Structure. The composition of a population as determined by the number or proportion of males and females in each age category.

Age-Specific Fertility Rate. Yearly number of live births by age of mothers, usually shown per 1,000 women in each of seven age groups (15-19, 20-24. . . ., 45-49).

Cohort Fertility. The number of births experienced over time by a group of women or men born in the same period (a birth cohort) or married in the same period (a marriage cohort). (See *Period Fertility* for a contrasting measure.)

Crude Birth Rate (or simply "birth rate"). Yearly number of live births per 1,000 population.

Crude Death Rate (or death rate). Yearly number of deaths per 1,000 population.

Demographic Transition. An historical shift of birth and death rates from high to low levels; the decline in mortality usually precedes the decline in fertility, thus resulting in rapid population growth during the transition period.

Demography. The scientific study of human populations, including their size, composition, distribution, and characteristics, and the causes and consequences of changes in these factors.

Dependency Ratio. Number of persons aged 0-14 and 65 and over, divided by number aged 15-64 (multiplied by 100 to give a whole number). Assumes that the latter generally provides support for the former two groups, and hence is a rough measure of the economic burden carried by those in prime working ages.

Fecundity. Physiological capacity of a woman, man, or couple to produce a living child.

Fertility. Actual reproductive performance, or the bearing of a live child by a woman.

General Fertility Rate. Yearly number of live births per 1,000 women of childbearing age (defined as ages 15-44, or 15-49).

Gross Reproduction Rate. Average number of daughters a woman would have if she were to bear children at the prevailing age-specific fertility rates and to live through the entire reproductive span from age 15 to age 50. Equals total fertility times the proportion of births that are daughters.

Infant Mortality Rate. Number of deaths among children under one year of age in a specific year per 1,000 live births in the same year.

Life Expectancy at Birth. The average number of years a newborn child would live if the current age-specific death rates were to prevail throughout his or her lifetime.

Migration. Movement of people across a specified boundary—within or between countries—for the purpose of establishing a new permanent residence.

Morbidity. The frequency of disease and illness in a population.

Mortality. Death to members of a population.

Net Reproduction Rate. Gross Reproduction Rate adjusted to take mortality into account; i.e., some girl babies do not survive to reproductive age and other women die during the reproductive age span.

Period Fertility. The current reproductive performance of a group of women or men, or their fertility during a particular period of time. (See *Cohort Fertility* for a contrasting measure.)

Rate of Natural Increase. Yearly net relative increase in population size due to excess of births over deaths (equals *Crude Birth Rate* minus *Crude Death Rate*). Usually expressed as a percent.

Rate of Population Growth. Yearly net relative increase (or decrease, in which event negative) in population size due to natural increase and net migration. Usually expressed as a percent.

Replacement Fertility. Level of fertility at which childbearing women on the average have only enough daughters to "replace" themselves in the population. *(Net Reproduction Rate = 1.0.)* A population which has reached replacement or below-replacement fertility may still continue to grow for some decades, since past high fertility may have led to an unusual concentration of women in the childbearing ages and hence total births continue to exceed total deaths.

Sex Ratio. Number of males per 100 females in a population.

Stable Population. Population whose rate of growth or decline is constant, and in which the birth rate, death rate and age-sex structure are also constant.

Stationary Population. Stable population which does not increase or decrease in size.

Total Fertility Rate. Number of children a woman would have if she were to bear children at the age-specific rates prevailing during a given year while living from age 15 to age 50.

Zero Population Growth. The stage at which annual births plus net migration exactly equal annual deaths.

Bibliography

I. Introduction to Demography and Population Studies

A. TEXTBOOKS

Cox, Peter R. *Demography*. 5th ed. New York: Cambridge University Press, 1976. $8.95 paper.
  Latest edition of a standard British text on principles and methods of demography; includes extensive international data.

Goldscheider, Calvin. *Population, Modernization and Social Structure*. Boston: Little, Brown, 1971. 345 pp. $10.95.
  A textbook for advanced students in demography. Special attention to African migration and differential mortality in the U.S.

Hartley, Shirley F. *Population: Quantity vs. Quality*. Englewood Cliffs, N.J.: Prentice-Hall, 1972. 343 pp. $9.95.
  Textbook that can serve as a reference on a wide variety of population-related issues, e.g., density, food supply, natural resources, and consequences of overrapid population growth in the developing world.

Heer, David M. *Society and Population*. 2nd ed. Englewood Cliffs, N.J.: Prentice-Hall, 1975. 155 pp. $3.50 paper.
  New edition of an introductory college text with emphasis on biological rather than social composition of the population.

Hellman, Hal. *Population*. New York: Lippincott, 1972. 192 pp. $5.95.
  A simple general introduction to socio-demographic determinants of population growth and its consequences. Recommended for high school and junior college.

Hernandez, Jose. *People, Power and Policy: A New View on Population*. Palo Alto, Cal.: National Press Books, 1974. 287 pp. $5.95 paper.
  A simple introduction to population studies from an interdisciplinary and sociological perspective.

Kammeyer, Kenneth C. W. *An Introduction to Population: Sociological Perspectives*. Scranton, Pa.: Chandler, 1971. 196 pp. $4.00 paper.
  An easy-reading short introductory textbook which summarizes basic knowledge on population processes and offers conceptual frameworks for the study of migration and fertility.

Matras, Judah. *Populations and Societies*. Englewood Cliffs, N.J.: Prentice-Hall, 1973. 562 pp. $12.95.
  Undergraduate text on demography in its sociological and ecological contexts.

Nam, Charles B. and Susan O. Gustavus. *Population: The Dynamics of Demographic Change*. Boston: Houghton Mifflin, 1976. 360 pp. $10.95.
  An introduction to the fundamentals of population study for undergraduates.

Petersen, William. *Population*. 3rd ed. New York: Macmillan, 1975. 784 pp. $13.95.
  New edition of a classic for advanced undergraduate sociology courses linking demographic variables with historical, economic, biological and sociological factors and situations in primitive, pre-industrial and totalitarian societies.

Pressat, Roland. *Population*. Baltimore: Penguin Books, 1971. Translated from French. 152 pp. Out of print.
  Paperback edition of a standard introduction to demography for undergraduates by a leading French demographer.

Smith, T. Lynn and Paul E. Zopf, Jr. *Demography: Principles and Methods*. 2nd ed. Port Washington, N.Y.: Alfred Publishing, 1976. 615 pp. $12.50.
  Updated demographic text which provides a general frame of reference as well as latest data and demographic trends.

Spengler, Joseph J. *Population and America's Future*. San Francisco: Freeman, 1975. 260 pp. $3.95 paper.
  A text for advanced students on the demographic and historical determinants of population growth and its impact on environment, population composition and distribution, and public policy.

Thomlinson, Ralph. *Population Dynamics: Causes and Consequences of World Demographic Change*. 2nd ed. New York: Random House, 1975. 653 pp. $12.95.
  Revised edition of a classic text for undergraduates on all aspects of population.

United Nations. Department of Economic and Social Affairs. *The Determinants and Consequences of Population Trends*. Vol. 1. Population Studies No. 50. Sales No. E.71.XIII.5. New York: United Nations, 1973. 661 pp. $24.00.
  Exhaustive summary of scientific studies on the relationships between population trends and socioeconomic development. Replaces and updates similarly entitled 1953 classic. Bibliographical supplement forthcoming.

B. READERS: COLLECTIONS OF ARTICLES FOR USE WITH TEXTS IN A GENERAL STUDY OF POPULATION

Callahan, Daniel, ed. *The American Population Debate*. New York: Doubleday, 1971. 380 pp. $2.50 paper.

Twenty-three articles by Ehrlich, Coale, Bogue and others with opposing views on whether the U.S. has a population problem, and, if so, what might be done about it.

Davis, Wayne H., ed. *Readings in Human Population Ecology*. Englewood Cliffs, N.J.: Prentice-Hall, 1975. 251 pp. $9.95.

Thirty-one provocative articles on population growth and policy implications in relation to economic development.

Ford, Thomas R. and Gordon F. DeJong, eds. *Social Demography*. Englewood Cliffs, N.J.: Prentice-Hall, 1970. 690 pp. $12.95.

A reader based on a social demographic framework for analyzing the relationships between demographic and socioeconomic processes and variables.

The Human Population. A *Scientific American* Book. San Francisco: Freeman, 1974. 147 pp. $3.95 paper.

Eleven articles by leading U.S. and European scholars from the September 1974 *Scientific American* on the genetics and physiology of populations, demographic history, migration, population in developed and developing countries, the family, changing status of women, food and population, and transfer of technology from developed to developing countries.

International Union for the Scientific Study of Population (IUSSP). *International Population Conference, London 1969*. 4 vols. Available from IUSSP, 5 rue Forgeur, 4000 Liège, Belgium, 1971. 3,050 pp. $64.00.

Proceedings of the 16th IUSSP general conference, with 240 papers printed in full, 32 summarized; organized into 41 sessions on all aspects of demography and population.

International Union for the Scientific Study of Population (IUSSP). *International Population Conference, Liège 1973*. 3 vols. Available from IUSSP, 5 rue Forgeur, 4000 Liège, Belgium, 1973. 1,379 pp. $45.00.

Ninety-five expert papers covering the full range of population issues.

Johnson, Stanley, ed. *The Population Problem*. New York: Halsted Press, 1974. 231 pp. $9.95.

A collection of 40 articles, reports and statements on the international implications of population growth, official policies and ideological "obstacles to action."

Kammeyer, Kenneth C. W., ed. *Population Studies: Selected Essays and Research*. 2nd ed. Chicago: Rand McNally, 1975. 509 pp. $7.95 paper.

Revised edition of readings for undergraduate course on demography with a special revision of population politics and policies.

Petersen, William, ed. *Readings in Population*. New York: Macmillan, 1972. 483 pp. $6.25 paper.

A reader supplementary to the author's demographic textbook *Population*, with emphasis on population policies and a comparative cross-cultural approach.

Pohlman, Edward, ed. *Population: A Clash of Prophets*. New York: Mentor Books, 1973. 490 pp. $1.95 paper.

Eighty-five quotations from the international literature revealing similarities of concern about population decline in the 1930s and population growth in the 1970s.

Reid, Sue and David Lyon, eds. *Population Crisis: An Interdisciplinary Perspective*. Glenview, Ill.: Scott, Foresman, 1972. 220 pp. $4.95 paper.

Thirty-three papers used in a course on population and ecology at Cornell College, Iowa, representing opposing points of view from a variety of disciplines.

Reining, Priscilla and Irene Tinker, eds. *Population: Dynamics, Ethics, and Policy*. Washington, D.C.: American Association for the Advancement of Science, 1975. 184 pp. $4.95 paper.

Thirty-one population-related articles, research reports, and policy debates that have appeared in *Science* since 1966.

Stanford, Quentin, ed. *The World's Population*. New York: Oxford University Press, 1972. 346 pp. $6.95 paper.

An introductory reader to the demographic causes of population growth, its biological and socioeconomic implications, plus population policies and programs.

United Nations. Department of Economic and Social Affairs. *The Population Debate: Dimensions and Perspectives: Papers of the World Population Conference Bucharest 1974*. Population Studies No. 57. 2 vols. Vol. 1: Sales No. E/F/S.75.XIII.4. Vol. 2: Sales No. E/F/S.75.XIII.5. New York: United Nations, 1976. 676 and 726 pp. $30.00 each.

Compendium of background papers and documents from the 1974 World Population Conference and pre-conference symposia. Volume 1 contains the basic conference documents on the four main agenda items, the World Plan of Action, and 40 demographic background papers. Volume 2 contains 62 background papers presented under five broad topics relating population to resources and the environment, the family, human rights, family planning, and policies and programs.

C. EARLY POPULATION THOUGHT AND HISTORICAL DEMOGRAPHY

Chambers, J. D. *Population, Economy and Society in Pre-Industrial England*. New York: Oxford University Press, 1972. 162 pp. $7.25.

Describes and analyzes changes in English patterns of marriage, mobility, fertility and mortality from 1086 to 1801.

Cogswell, Seddie. *Tenure, Nativity, and Age as Factors in Iowa Agriculture, 1850-1880*. Ames, Iowa: Iowa State University Press, 1975. 70 pp. $5.00 paper.

Uses manuscript census records for over 12,000 farms to analyze the extent to which tenancy, age and place of birth shaped farmers' adaptation to demands of prairie agriculture.

Cook, Sherburne F. and Woodrow Borah, eds. *Essays in Population History: Mexico and the Caribbean.* Vol. 2. Berkeley, Cal.: University of California Press, 1974. 472 pp. $16.50.

Eight essays examine the history of the Yucatan population and Mexico's racial mixture from the early 16th century to the 1960 census.

Glass, David V., ed. *Pioneers of Demography Series.* Cambridge Group for the History of Population and Social Structure. Farnsborough, U.K./Lexington, Mass.: Gregg International/D. C. Heath, 1973.

Key British documents and essays in the early development of demography presented in their original format. Includes the following:

The Earliest Classics: John Graunt and Gregory King (£8.50).
Numbering the People (£3.00).
The Eighteenth Century Population Controversy (£7.50).
The Development of Population Statistics (£10.50).
Rates of Mortality (£4.50).

Glass, David V. and Roger Revelle, eds. *Population and Social Change.* New York: Crane, Russack, 1972. 520 pp. $24.75.

Papers from two international conferences of 1966 and 1967 on historical population studies, chiefly in the West, with three papers on Japan and India.

Laslett, Peter, ed. *Household and Family in Past Time.* Cambridge Group for the History of Population and Social Structure. Cambridge, U.K.: Cambridge University Press, 1972. 623 pp. $39.50.

Comparative studies on the size and structure of the domestic group over the last three centuries in England, Serbia, Japan, North America and parts of Western Europe.

MacLeod, M. J. *Spanish Central America: A Socioeconomic History, 1520-1720.* Berkeley, Cal.: University of California Press, 1973. 554 pp. $20.00.

An analysis of population decrease in Central America in relation to the availability of land before the arrival of the Spaniards and the effect of the introduction of European diseases.

Nickerson, Jane S. *Homage to Malthus.* Port Washington, N.Y.: Kennikat Press, 1975. 150 pp. $7.95.

Examines Malthus' theories of population growth, the problems and solutions he saw, and demonstrates their validity for the world today.

Overbeek, J. *History of Population Theories.* Rotterdam: Rotterdam University Press, 1974. 232 pp. Dutch guilders 49.50.

Evolution of population theories from Greek philosophers to the present, emphasizing effect of population factors on economic resources and prosperity.

Sex, Marriage and Society Reprints Series. *Abortion in Nineteenth-Century America,* 90 pp., and *Birth Control and Family Planning in Nineteenth-Century America,* 70 pp. New York: Arno Press, 1974. $14.00 and $20.00, respectively.

Collections of original writings reveal contemporary U.S. 19th century attitudes: favorable towards "regulating reproduction by controlling conception," but disapproving of abortion.

Tranter, N. L. *Population Since the Industrial Revolution: The Case of England and Wales.* New York: Barnes and Noble, 1973. 206 pp. $13.50.

Discusses ways to obtain population statistics for the years before 1837. Demographic change as both a determinant and consequence of social and economic change.

van de Walle, Etienne. *The Female Population of France in the Nineteenth Century.* Princeton, N.J.: Princeton University Press, 1974. 483 pp. $21.50.

Statistical reconstitution of the 19th century French female population, undertaken in order to understand the phenomenon of early French fertility decline; a preliminary work to emerge from the study of historical European fertility decline by Princeton's Office of Population Research.

Wells, Robert V. *The Population of the British Colonies in America before 1776: A Survey of Census Data.* Princeton, N.J.: Princeton University Press, 1975. 342 pp. $18.50.

Demographic history of the American colonies based on 124 recently discovered censuses covering 21 colonies between 1623 and 1775.

D. STUDIES IN RELATED FIELDS: ANTHROPOLOGY, ECOLOGY, GEOGRAPHY, GENETICS

Benjamin, Bernard et al, eds. *Population and the New Biology.* New York: Academic Press, 1974. 188 pp. $10.00.

Proceedings of a Eugenics Society symposium in 1973 on increased life span, oral contraception, voluntary sterilization and population policies in developing countries.

Berry, Brian J. L., Edgar C. Conkling, and D. Michael Ray. *The Geography of Economic Systems.* Englewood Cliffs, N.J.: Prentice-Hall, 1976. 529 pp. $13.95.

A college textbook which examines the spatial interdependencies of population, resources, land use, industrial location, prices and demand within the economic system.

Boughey, Arthur S. *Ecology of Populations.* Riverside, N.J.: Macmillan, 1973. 175 pp. $3.95 paper.

Systems analysis applications, behavior of human populations, and the principal concepts of population ecology.

Cavalli-Sforza, L. L. and W. F. Bodmer. *The Genetics of Human Populations.* Series of Books in Biology. San Francisco: Freeman, 1971. 965 pp. $29.50.

Comprehensive treatment of the genetics of human populations and their relationship with demographic processes.

Clarke, John I. *Population Geography.* 2nd ed. New York: Pergamon Press, 1972. 175 pp. $5.25 paper.

Introduction to population study for young geographers.

Clarke, John I. *Population Geography of the Developing Countries.* New York: Pergamon Press, 1971. 282 pp. $5.00 paper.

Discusses demographic variables, ethnic composition, and rural-urban distribution of six regions of the developing world.

Etzioni, Amitai. *Genetic Fix: New Opportunities and Dangers for You, Your Child, and the Nation.* New York: Macmillan, 1973. 276 pp. $7.95.

Genetic engineering and its private and social implications.

Harrison, G. A. and A. J. Boyce, eds. *The Structure of Human Populations.* New York: Oxford University Press, 1972. 447 pp. $12.75 paper.

Anthropological, genetic and ecological aspects of demographic variables and processes.

Jones, Owen H. and Elizabeth A. Jones. *Index of Human Ecology.* Detroit: Gale Research Co., 1974. 169 pp. $16.00.

Provides a ready means for retrieving cross-disciplinary information on this topic in all languages and countries.

Nag, Moni, ed. *Population and Social Organization.* Paris: Mouton, 1975. 376 pp. $16.50.

Twelve articles by anthropologists interrelating population and such social phenomena as kinship and marriage.

Polgar, Steven, ed. *Culture and Population: A Collection of Current Studies.* Cambridge, Mass.: Schenkman, 1971. 196 pp. $8.95.

An anthropological study of family structures, ecological adaptation and family planning in traditional cultures.

Polgar, Steven, ed. *Population, Ecology, and Social Evolution.* Paris: Mouton, 1975. $16.50.

A collection of anthropological studies on the role of population dynamics in cultural evolution.

Quick, Horace F. *Population Ecology.* Indianapolis: Pegasus, 1974. 187 pp. $3.25.

The interrelationships of natural and human ecology, demography and geography, and discussion of the concept of optimum population.

Spooner, Brian, ed. *Population Growth: Anthropological Implications.* Cambridge, Mass.: M.I.T. Press, 1972. 425 pp. $17.00.

The non-Malthusian model of population growth as a direct cause of agricultural development examined as a primary explanatory factor in anthropology.

Weiss, Kenneth M. and Paul A. Ballonoff, eds. *Demographic Genetics.* New York: Halsted Press, 1975. 414 pp. $25.00.

Twenty-four benchmark papers, with editorial comments, on the interrelationship of demographic characteristics and population genetics.

II. Demographic Methods

Bogue, Donald J. *Demographic Techniques of Fertility Analysis.* Family Planning Research and Evaluation Manual No. 2. Chicago: Community and Family Study Center, University of Chicago, 1971. 116 pp. $2.00.

A practical manual on the most generally used techniques for analyzing fertility data from vital statistics, censuses, and surveys.

Bogue, Donald J. and Louise Rehling. *Techniques for Making Population Projections: How to Make Age-Sex Projections by Electronic Computer.* Family Planning Research and Evaluation Manual No. 12. Chicago: Community and Family Study Center, University of Chicago, 1974. 174 pp. $3.00.

Explains the methodology involved in population projections and provides practical instructions on how to compute them.

Carrier, Norman and John Hobcraft. *Demographic Estimation for Developing Societies.* London: London School of Economics, 1971. 204 pp.

A practical manual for both students and professional statisticians who work with defective demographic data.

Demographic Research Institute, University of Gothenburg, Sweden. *Reports.*

A series of brief (approximately 50 pp.) monographs mostly on the use of models for measuring demographic change. Sw.Cr. 15 each, from Almquist and Wiksell, 26 Gamla Brogatan, S-111 20 Stockholm. For complete listing, write the Institute, Viktoriagaten 13, S-411 25 Gothenburg, Sweden.

Frejka, Tomas. *The Future of Population Growth: Alternative Paths to Equilibrium.* New York: Wiley-Interscience, 1973. 268 pp. $12.00.

Applies traditional demographic theory in a nontraditional way to explore trends that can realize the goal of a nongrowing population. A summary of selected parts of this book was published by the Population Reference Bureau in "World Population Projections: Alternative Paths to Zero Growth," *Population Bulletin,* Vol. 29, No. 5, 1974. 31 pp. $1.00.

Grebenik, E. and A. Hill, eds. *International Demographic Terminology: Fertility, Family Planning and Nuptiality.* IUSSP Papers No. 4. Available from IUSSP, 5 rue Forguer, 4000 Liège, Belgium, 1975. 53 pp. $3.00.

Draft of the first completed section of a projected new international dictionary of demographic terminology designed to replace and update the U.N. *Multilingual Demographic Dictionary* of 1958, to appear eventually in English, French, Spanish and Russian versions.

Greville, T. N. E., ed. *Population Dynamics.* New York: Academic Press, 1972. 445 pp. $13.00.

Fourteen papers applying mathematical models to demographic and contraceptive events.

Henry, Louis. *On the Measurement of Human Fertility: Selected Writings of Louis Henry.* Translated and edited by Mindel C. Sheps and Evelyne Lapierre-Adamcyk. New York: American Elsevier, 1972. 256 pp. $15.00.

Classic papers by the distinguished French originator of a new approach to fertility measurement and analysis—mathematical models of the sequence and timing of such events as marriage, first and second birth.

Keyfitz, Nathan and Wilhelm Flieger. *Population: Facts and Methods of Demography.* San Francisco: Freeman, 1971. 613 pp. $15.00.
: Applies mathematical models to the processes of birth and death, differentiated by age and sex, for all countries with usable vital statistics.

Marks, Eli S., William Seltzer, and Karol G. Krótki. *Population Growth Estimation: A Handbook of Vital Statistics Measurement.* New York: The Population Council, 1974. 418 pp. $4.95 paper.
: Details a variety of ways for coping with the difficulties of demographic measurement, particularly where civil registration systems function poorly.

McGranahan, D. V. et al, eds. *Contents and Measurement of Socioeconomic Development.* New York: Praeger, 1972. 178 pp. $11.00.
: Guide to the measurement of social and economic development.

Pittenger, Donald B. *Projecting State and Local Populations.* Cambridge, Mass.: Ballinger, 1976. 246 pp. $15.00.
: Presents various practical methods for projecting small area populations.

Pollard, J. H. et al. *Demographic Techniques.* Elmsford, N.Y.: Pergamon Press, 1974. 200 pp. $11.25 paper.
: Introduction to demographic techniques by Australian college professors. Deals with life tables, stationary population models, demographic sample surveys, etc.

Pollard, J. H. *Mathematical Models for the Growth of Human Populations.* New York: Cambridge University Press, 1973. 186 pp. $17.50.
: Particular emphasis is on stochastic models. Includes exercises and solutions.

Pressat, Roland. *Demographic Analysis: Methods, Results, Applications.* Translated from the French by Judah Matras. Chicago: Aldine Atherton, 1972. 498 pp. $14.50.
: A comprehensive textbook on methods of demographic analysis.

Rogers, Andrei. *Introduction to Multiregional Mathematical Demography.* New York: Wiley, 1975. 203 pp. $18.00.
: Technical analysis of migration and its contribution to projections of the growth and distribution of multiregional population systems; suitable for a graduate course in mathematical demography.

Seltzer, William. *Demographic Data Collection: A Summary of Experience.* New York: The Population Council, 1973. 50 pp. $2.00 paper.
: Concise explanation of the methodology of taking censuses and surveys.

Sheps, Mindel and Jane Menken. *Mathematical Models of Conception and Birth.* Chicago: University of Chicago Press, 1973. 427 pp. $18.50.
: A manual which uses mathematical models to explain physiological variations in human reproduction; includes bibliography on analytic and computer models.

Shorter, Frederic C. *Computational Methods for Population Projections: With Particular Reference to Development Planning.* New York: The Population Council, 1974. 158 pp. $6.75.
: Convenient manual for development planners, researchers and teachers designed for use with a computer package program available on tape or cards from The Population Council for $25.00.

Shryock, Henry, Jacob S. Siegel, and Associates. *The Methods and Materials of Demography.* 2 vols. 3rd rev. printing. Washington, D.C.: Government Printing Office, 1975. 880 pp. $15.75 paper. Condensed edition published by Academic Press, New York, forthcoming 1976. $16.50 (hardbound).
: The most comprehensive text and reference on how to gather, classify, summarize, and analyze demographic data, with copious examples and extensive reading lists.

United Nations. Methodological studies by U.N. staff are included in several series. Recent publications are as follows (available from the U.N. Sales Office, New York, N.Y. 10017 or U.N. branch sales offices around the world):

United Nations. Department of Economic and Social Affairs. *Manuals on Methods of Estimating Population.*
: V. *Methods of Projecting the Economically Active Population.* Population Studies No. 46. Sales No. 70.XIII.1. 1971. 119 pp. $1.50.
: VI. *Methods of Measuring Internal Migration.* Population Studies No. 47. Sales No. E.70.XIII.3. 1970. 72 pp. $1.50.
: VII. *Methods of Projecting Households and Families.* Population Studies No. 54. Sales No. E.73.XIII.2. 1973. 100 pp. $5.00.
: VIII. *Methods for Projections of Urban and Rural Population.* Population Studies No. 55. Sales No. 74.XIII.3. 1974. 142 pp. $7.00.

United Nations. Statistical Office. *Statistical Papers, Series M.*
: No. 19, rev. 1. *Principles and Recommendations for a Vital Statistics System.* Sales No. E.73.XVII.9. 1973. 220 pp. $6.00.
: No. 51. *Methodology of Demographic Sample Surveys.* Sales No. E.71.XVII.11. 1971. 311 pp. $5.00.

United Nations. Statistical Office. *Studies in Demography, Series F.*
: No. 9. *Short Manual on Sampling.* 2 Vols. and Add. 1.
: Vol. 1. *Elements of Sample Survey Theory, Rev.* Sales No. E.72.XVII.5. 1972. 325 pp. $7.00.
: Vol. 2. *Computer Programs for Sample Designs.* Sales No. E.71.XVII.4. 1970. 77 pp. $1.50.
: Add. 1. Contains a set of computer programs for each of the ten additional processes described in Vol. 1.
: A manual for statistical authorities regarded as non-mathematicians who are aware of statistical shortcomings in their countries which could be made good by the sample survey method.

: No. 15: *Methods and Evaluation of Population Registers and Similar Systems.* Sales No. E.69.XVII.15. 1969. 66 pp. $1.50.
: No. 16: *Handbook of Population and Housing Census Methods.* 6 parts.
: Part 1. *Planning, Organization and Administration of Population and Housing Censuses.* Out of print.
: Part 2. *Topics and Tabulations for Population Censuses.* Out of print.
: Part 3. *Topics and Tabulations for Housing Censuses.* Sales No. E.70.XVII.7. 1969. $2.00.
: Part 4. *Survey of Population and Housing Census Experience: 1955-1964.* 2 sections. Section 1: Sales No. E.70.XVII.7. 1972. 99 pp. $3.00. Section 2: Sales No. E.70.XVII.7/Add. 1974. 95 pp. $5.00.
: Part 5. *Methods of Evaluating Population and Housing Census Results.* Out of Print.
: Part 6. *Sampling in Connection with Population and Housing Censuses.* Sales No. E.70.XVII.9. 1971. 34 pp. $1.00.
: No. 18: *Towards a System of Social and Demographic Statistics.* Sales No. E.74.XVII.8. 1975. 187 pp. $9.00.
: Proposal for organizing a worldwide system for collecting and reporting social and demographic statistics which clearly defines the kinds of information and social aspects to be covered and the links between the two.

University of North Carolina at Chapel Hill. *International Program of Laboratories for Population Statistics (POPLAB)*. A program begun in 1967 "dedicated to research on improved methods for the measurement of population change and to the analysis of demographic data." Has since published or reprinted many technical and scientific manuals by recognized authorities, grouped under the following four series titles, which are invaluable to workers in the fields of demographic data collection and analysis, particularly in developing countries. For individual titles, write Population Laboratories, Dept. of Biostatistics, School of Public Health, University of North Carolina, Chapel Hill, N.C. 27514. Single copies are free to qualified institutions and persons.

Scientific Report Series

Reports on systems of demographic measurement, including data collection and especially the "dual record" system, and their application in selected developing countries, plus proceedings of international POPLAB conferences.

Manual Series

Manuals on design, processing and analysis of demographic censuses and surveys.

Reprint Series

Reprints of key works on various methodological approaches to the collection and measurement of demographic statistics.

Occasional Publications

Includes the following four to date:

Research Topics for the Measurement of Population Change: A Catalogue of Study Protocols, by Anders S. Lunde (1974).

A Glossary of Selected Demographic Terms (1974).

A Handbook for Population Analysts, by Joan W. Lingner (1974).

Methods for Estimating Fertility and Mortality from Limited and Defective Data, by William Brass (1975).

U.S. Bureau of the Census. *Procedural Reports*. Series PHC (R). Washington, D.C.: Government Printing Office. Dates of publication, page numbers and prices vary.

Irregular reports, each consisting of one or two chapters to be included in the forthcoming *1970 Census of Population and Housing: Procedural History,* on design, methodology, evaluation, and publication of the 1970 census. For individual titles see U.S. Bureau of the Census *Catalog of Publications* below.

U.S. Bureau of the Census. *Evaluation and Research Program*. Series PHC(E). Washington, D.C.: Government Printing Office. Dates of publication, page numbers and prices vary.

Irregular reports dealing with the accuracy and efficiency of specific methodologies used in the 1970 Census. For individual titles see U.S. Bureau of the Census *Catalog of Publications* below.

U.S. Bureau of the Census. *Census Methodological Research: An Annotated List of Papers and Reports*. First list 1963-1966; annually since then. Latest year covers 1974. Washington, D.C.: Government Printing Office, 1975. 18 pp. $0.85.

Annually updated annotated listing of methodological research papers and reports by Census Bureau staff, whether or not issued by the Bureau itself.

U.S. Department of Health, Education, and Welfare. National Center for Health Statistics (NCHS). *Vital and Health Statistics. Series 2: Data Evaluation and Methods Research*. Issued periodically. Single copies free from the Scientific and Technical Information Branch, NCHS, 5600 Fishers Lane, Rockville, Md. 20852.

Methodological studies based on experience with surveys of the NCHS. For individual titles write above address for *Current Listing and Topical Index to the Vital and Health Statistics Series*.

Willis, Kenneth G. *Problems in Migration Analysis*. Lexington, Mass.: Lexington Books, 1974. 247 pp. $16.00.

Technical guide to the measurement and projection of labor migration.

III. Demographic Data

A. UNITED STATES

Congressional Information Service. *American Statistics Index, 1974*. Consists of an *Index* (840 pp.) and two volumes of *Abstracts* (638 and 1,232 pp.). Covers 1973 and major statistical material 1960-72.

First Annual Supplement, 1975. Covers publications in 1974. *Second Annual Supplement, 1976.* Covers publications in 1975. Updated by continuing quarterly accumulations of the *Index* and monthly supplements of *Abstracts*. Annual subscription rates vary $310.00-$790.00 depending on type of library and institution; $50.00 extra for overseas subscribers. Available from Congressional Information Service, 7101 Wisconsin Ave. N.W., Washington, D.C. 20014.

These publications provide an index, comprehensive guide and abstracts of all statistical publications of the U.S. government. Publications are arranged under the issuing Department and its bureaus and subdivisions, which include: Executive Office of the President, Executive Departments (including the Department of Commerce which incorporates the Bureau of the Census, and the Department of Health, Education, and Welfare which incorporates the National Center for Health Statistics), Independent Agencies (including the Environmental Protection Agency), special boards, committees and commissions, U.S. courts, U.S. Congress (Senate, House of Representatives, and Joint Committees). Two indexes serve to locate statistical data and abstracts on a particular subject: *Index by Subject and Names,* and *Index by Categories.*

U.S. Bureau of the Census. *Catalog of Publications: 1790-1972.* Washington, D.C.: Government Printing Office, 1974. 911 pp. $7.10.

This volume comprises two parts, listing in Part 1 all materials issued by the Bureau of the Census starting with the first census report of 1790. Part 2 describes over 60,000 publications issued from 1946 through 1972. Includes subject and geographical index. Population materials per se comprise only a small proportion of the materials listed.

Supplementary *Bureau of the Census Catalogs* are issued on a continuing basis each quarter and cumulated to an annual volume. Latest available annual volume covers 1975 (249 pp; $3.40). In addition, there are *Monthly Supplements* to the *Catalog*, listing new publications. Subscription price $14.40 for four consecutive quarterly issues cumulative to annual volume, including 12 issues of the *Monthly Supplement;* $3.60 additional for foreign mailing. Single copies vary in price. Available from U.S. Government Printing Office, Washington, D.C. 20402.

Each *Catalog* is divided in two parts of annotated listings: (1) Publications; (2) Data files and special tabulations, and unpublished materials such as maps and computer programs available for cost of reproducing, transcribing, or tabulating. Again, population materials per se comprise only a small part of the Census Bureau materials listed.

U.S. Bureau of the Census. *U.S. Census of Population: 1970.* Data from the 1970 Census of Population have been published since that time in a variety of formats identified below. All publications are available from the U.S. Government Printing Office, Washington, D.C. 20402, at the prices indicated.

Vol. I. *Characteristics of the Population.*
Data covered in this section have been published in three different formats as follows:

(1) Parts 1 to 54-58. Fifty-four books (hardbound). Pages and prices for individual parts vary. Total cost: $712.25.

Part 1 presents U.S. summary information. Parts 2 through 52 refer to the 50 states and the District of Columbia. Part 53 is Puerto Rico. Parts 54-58 (bound together) cover Guam, Virgin Islands, American Samoa, Canal Zone and Trust Territory of the Pacific Islands. Each of these Parts (i.e. geographical areas) contains data presented under four general chapter headings, previously issued as separate reports. These are:

Chapter A. Number of Inhabitants (Total numbers for the states, counties, Standard Metropolitan Statistical Areas, incorporated places, etc. within each state).

Chapter B. General Population Characteristics (race and sex, age, household and family characteristics by areas within the state).

Chapter C. General Social and Economic Characteristics (education, occupation, income, etc. by areas within the state.)

Chapter D. Detailed Characteristics. (Detailed cross tabulations of all data collected in the census by areas within the state.)

(2) Chapter A from each of these 58 parts, i.e. Number of Inhabitants, has been reassembled into a two-volume publication called: *U.S. Census of Population: 1970. Volume 1. Characteristics of the Population: Number of Inhabitants.* 2,194 pp. Sold only as a set: $20.75.

Chapters B, C, and D from each of these 58 parts have not been reassembled in this way.

(3) Part 1 described in (1) above, i.e. the summary information for the U.S. as a whole under the four chapter headings, has been reassembled into a summary volume in two parts called: *U.S. Census of Population, 1970. Summary Volume.* 1,782 pp. $33.40.

Vol. II. *Subject Reports.*
Consist of 40 cardstock-covered reports identified as Series PC(2). Each has an individual title. Prices and number of pages vary. The *Subject Reports* cover the following ten general subject areas: ethnic groups, migration, fertility, marriage and living arrangements, education, employment, occupation and industry, income low income, and geographic areas.

A useful guide to finding specific 1970 Census published data (except for *Subject Reports PC [2]*), is:

U.S. Bureau of the Census. *Index to Selected 1970 Census Reports.* By Paul T. Zeisset. Washington, D.C.: Government Printing Office, 1974. 354 pp. $3.70.

U.S. Bureau of the Census. *County and City Data Book, 1972.* Washington: Government Printing Office, 1973. 1,020 pp. $11.25.

Latest in a series published every four or five years. Compact presentation of numerous statistical data for counties, Standard Metropolitan Statistical Areas, cities, urbanized areas, and unincorporated places.

U.S. Bureau of the Census. *Current Population Reports.* Listed below are the eight series published under this general title, with descriptions of the five of most interest to general demographers. Most data presented in these Reports are derived from the Current Population Survey (CPS) conducted by the Census Bureau, a monthly sample survey of approximately 47,000 households interviewed across the United States. Primary purpose of the CPS is to obtain monthly labor force statistics for the U.S. Department of Labor. However, supplementary questions (particularly in the CPS for March of each year) provide current demographic data between the decennial population censuses. The eight series of *Current Population Reports* published throughout the year can be obtained as a subscription package for $56.00/year from the U.S. Government Printing Office (GPO). Individual reports within a series (except P-28) are available from the GPO, but subscriptions to separate report series are not available. For individual titles within series see Bureau of the Census *Catalog of Publications* (above). All new titles in Series P-20, P-23, and P-25, and selected titles in series P-28, are also cited in the "Official Statistical Publications" section of *Population Index* (see p. 55).

P-20. *Population Characteristics.*

Approximately 15 reports each year regularly covering current data for the total U.S. and metropolitan-nonmetropolitan population on school enrollment, educational attainment, characteristics of persons, families, and households (e.g. "Persons of Spanish Origin in the U.S.: March 1975", P-20 No. 290; "Marital Status and Living Arrangements: March 1975", P-20 No. 287), fertility (e.g. "Fertility History and Prospects of American Women: June 1975", P-20 No. 288), and mobility status, with an annual summary "Population Profile of the United States" (latest is for 1975, P-20 No. 292). P-20 also includes occasional reports on, e.g., ethnic origin, voters, college students, illiteracy.

P-23. *Special Studies.*

Several each year. Subjects vary, recent ones have been a five-part series on the black population (P-23 Nos. 29, 38, 42, 46, 48), reports on American youth (P-23 Nos. 40, 44, 51), and one report each on the aging, survival rates, population in metropolitan and nonmetropolitan areas, fertility indicators, and female family heads.

P-25. *Population Estimates and Projections.*

Appear monthly and annually, presenting estimates and projections for the U.S., states, Standard Metropolitan Statistical Areas and Outlying Areas (Guam, etc.) prepared by Census Bureau personnel by, e.g., age, race, sex, households, school enrollment, educational attainment.

P-26. *Federal-State Cooperative Program for Population Estimates.*

P-27. *Farm Population.*

P-28. *Special Censuses.*

Special Bureau area censuses conducted at the request (and expense) of local governments on age, sex, race, and population changes since the last decennial census. Findings published in two summary reports each year, plus individual reports for places of 50,000 or more.

P-60. *Consumer Income.*

Several each year covering data for the U.S., metropolitan-nonmetropolitan, and rural farm-nonfarm population on money income of families and persons, household money income and selected social and economic characteristics of population, characteristics of the low-income population, and occasional reports on, e.g., lifetime and annual mean income.

P-65. *Consumer Buying Indicators.*

U.S. Bureau of the Census. *Historical Statistics of the United States: Colonial Times to 1970.* 2 vols. Washington, D.C.: Government Printing Office, 1976. 1,290 pp. $26.00.

Replaces earlier editions. A statistical history of U.S. demographic, social, economic, political and geographical development, from 1610 to 1970.

U.S. Bureau of the Census. *Statistical Abstract of the United States.* Published annually since 1878. Latest edition covers 1975. Washington, D.C.: Government Printing Office, 1976. 1,050 pp. $8.00.

An annual summary of data on demographic, social, political and economic characteristics of the U.S. A useful condensation of the *Statistical Abstract* is published every other year as the *Pocket Data Book, U.S.A.* Latest edition covers 1973, available from the Government Printing Office. 352 pp. $2.80.

U.S. Bureau of the Census. *Status: A Chartbook of Social and Economic Trends.* Publication begun with July 1976 issue, for sale by Subscriber Services Section, Bureau of the Census, Washington, D.C. 20233. 96 pp. $3.60.

Collection of full-color charts, maps and tables, launched as a regular publication in July 1976 in "an attempt to breathe life into the many numbers which spill daily from the diverse agencies of the U.S. Federal Statistical System." Publishing schedule not yet fixed.

Note re Bureau of the Census materials. The Bureau of the Census publishes only the most essential and widely useful data in its printed reports of censuses and surveys, but much more information is available to the public. The Bureau maintains machine-readable data files which can be processed to yield almost unlimited cross-classified subject and area tabulations. Some of these tape and punchcard files may be purchased. All can be used by the Bureau to prepare tabulations specified by customers. A nine-page listing of *Computer Tape Files Available from the Bureau of the Census,* by Larry Carbaugh, and specific information regarding tapes from the 1970 Census of Population are available from Data User Services Division, Bureau of the Census, Washington, D.C. 20233. Listings of new data files and special tabulations appear in part 2 of each quarterly issue of the *Bureau of the Census Catalog* (above).

In addition to the Bureau of the Census, some 100 private organizations scattered across the U.S. can provide data tapes from the 1970 Census of Population. Numbers of tapes available and prices vary among the organizations, which are referred to as "summary tape processing centers." For an address list of such centers, write Data Access and Use Staff, Data Users Services Division, Bureau of the Census, Washington, D.C. 20233.

U.S. Department of Health, Education, and Welfare. National Center for Health Statistics (NCHS). *Monthly Vital Statistics Report.* Single copies free from the Scientific and Technical Information Branch, NCHS, 5600 Fishers Lane, Rockville, Md. 20852.

Regular issues provide monthly provisional data on births, deaths, marriages, and divorces in the U.S. Supplements are used for final vital statistics and for the release of preliminary data from surveys of the NCHS.

U.S. Department of Health, Education, and Welfare. National Center for Health Statistics (NCHS). *Vital and Health Statistics Series.* Issued periodically. Single copies free from the Scientific and Technical Information Branch, NCHS, 5600 Fishers Lane, Rockville, Md. 20852.

Publications of varying lengths presenting data from the surveys and analytical studies conducted by the NCHS. For individual titles, write above address for *Current Listing and Topical Index to the Vital and Health Statistics Series.* Most useful for students of U.S. population characteristics are:

Series 10. Data from the Health Interview Survey.
Series 20. Data on Mortality.
Series 21. Data on Natality, Marriage, and Divorce.
Series 22. Data from the National Natality and Mortality Surveys.
Series 23. Data from the National Survey of Family Growth (beginning fall 1976).

U.S. Department of Health, Education, and Welfare. National Center for Health Statistics (NCHS). *Vital Statistics of the United States.* Vol. 1: *Natality;* Vol. 2: *Mortality,* Parts A and B; Vol. 3: *Marriage and Divorce.* Published annually since 1937. Latest available set covers 1972. Washington, D.C.: Government Printing Office. Prices vary per volume.

Final natality, mortality, marriage and divorce statistics with tabulations by demographic variables and for geographic divisions.

B. INTERNATIONAL DATA

With one exception (The Population Council. *Country Prospects*), this section includes only international compilations of primary data. For official publications covering census and sample survey data, vital statistics, yearbooks and other primary data by individual countries, see the section on "Official Statistical Publications" in each issue of *Population Index* (p. 55).

Blake, Judith and Jerry J. Donovan. *Western European Censuses, 1960: An English Language Guide.* Population Monograph Series No. 8. Berkeley, Cal.: Institute of International Studies, University of California, 1971. 421 pp. $3.25 paper.

A compendium in English of the contents of all Western European censuses for the 1960 period, and a guide to their location in U.S. libraries.

Inter-American Statistical Institute. *America en Cifras.* Published biannually since 1960. Spanish with English explanatory notes. Latest edition covers 1974. Vol. 1: *Situacion Demografica.* Washington, D.C.: Inter-American Statistical Institute, Organization of American States, 1974. 231 pp. $3.00.

A multi-volume statistical document for 26 countries of the Americas, including the U.S. and Canada. Demographic data assembled from official census publications and various other national statistical services. Other volumes present data on social, political, economic, geographic and cultural aspects of the region.

Organisation for Economic Co-operation and Development (OECD). *Demographic Trends 1970-1985 in OECD Member Countries.* Paris: OECD, 1974. 454 pp. $17.00.

Fourth in a series presenting detailed data and projections for 19 mainly European developed countries based on 1960-61 census data.

The Population Council. *Country Prospects, 1973.* New York: The Population Council. English, French, or Spanish. Free.

Series of short papers, published 1974-75, presenting population projections in a standardized format for 29 individual countries.

Population Reference Bureau. *World Population Data Sheet.* Published annually. Latest edition, 1976. Washington, D.C.: Population Reference Bureau. 1 p. $.50, less for bulk orders.

Large, two-color wall chart listing latest available demographic and income data for world, regions, and some 160 individual countries.

United Nations. Department of Economic and Social Affairs. *World Population Prospects, as Assessed in 1968.* Population Studies No. 53. English/Russian. Sales No. 72.XIII.4. New York: United Nations, 1973. 167 pp. $4.00.

Population projections to 2000 for world regions and to 1985 for each country.

United Nations. Population Division.
World Population Prospects, 1970-2000, as Assessed in 1973, 10 March 1975. Working Paper No. 53.

Selected World Demographic Indicators by Countries, 1950-2000, 28 May 1975. Working Paper No. 55.

Single-Year Population Estimates and Projections for Major Areas, Regions and Countries of the World, 1950-2000, October 1975. Working Paper No. 56.

Three working papers giving results of revised population projections as assessed in 1973. All free on request to the Population Division.

United Nations. Department of Economic and Social Affairs. Statistical Office. The following four regular U.N. publications, assembled and issued by this Office, are the most comprehensive sources of official population-related data for the world, regions, and individual countries. All are available from the United Nations Sales Office, New York, N.Y. 10017 or U.N. branch sales offices throughout the world.

Demographic Yearbook. Published annually since 1949. English/French. Latest edition covers 1974. Sales No. E/F.75.XIII.1. 1,108 pp. $42.00.

Basic demographic statistics for over 200 countries and territories assembled from official publications and from data transmitted in monthly and annual questionnaires by national statistical services or similar offices in these countries. Each annual volume includes detailed tables on a special topic; topic for 1974 is mortality.

Population and Vital Statistics Report. Published quarterly as Statistical Papers Series A, English only. Annual subscription $10.00. $3.00 per copy.

Worldwide coverage of basic demographic series for the current year.

Statistical Yearbook. Published annually since 1949. Latest edition covers 1974. Sales No. E/F.75.XVII.1. 877 pp. $30.00 paper.

A wide range of demographic, economic and social data for over 200 countries and territories.

Monthly Bulletin of Statistics. Published monthly as Statistical Papers Series Q. English/French. Annual subscription $70.00. $7.00 per copy.

Provides monthly statistics for over 200 countries and territories together with special tables illustrating important economic developments.

U.S. Bureau of the Census. International Statistical Programs Center. *World Population 1975: Recent Demographic Estimates for Countries and Regions of the World,* Washington, D.C.: Government Printing Office, 1976. 270 pp. $3.90.

In tabular form with notes, 1975 estimates of 16 demographic measures and 1950-1975 annual population and growth rates for 201 countries and regions, prepared by the International Statistical Programs Center of the U.S. Bureau of the Census.

World Bank. *Trends in Developing Countries.* Washington, D.C.: World Bank, 1973. 72 pp. Free.

Dramatic socioeconomic differentials between developed and developing countries about 1970 demonstrated by statistical tables and charts. (Formerly an annual publication. Now discontinued.)

World Bank. *World Bank Atlas: Population, Per Capita Product, and Growth Rates.* Published annually. Latest edition, 1975. Washington, D.C.: World Bank. 30 pp. Free.

Latest available data on population totals, per capita income, and growth rates by regions and individual countries.

IV. Fertility

A. GENERAL AND NATIONAL FERTILITY STUDIES

Acsádi, György T. *A Selected Bibliography of Works on Fertility.* World Fertility Survey Occasional Papers No. 10. The Hague: International Statistical Office, 1974. 98 pp. Free.

Well-organized, annotated listing of over 100 books, articles, etc. in English, French and Spanish up to 1973, designed for World Fertility Survey trainees but useful for others interested in fertility.

Acsádi, György, András Klinger, and Egon Szabady. *Family Planning in Hungary: Main Results of the 1966 Fertility and Family Planning (TCS) Study.* Budapest: Demographic Research Institute, Central Statistical Office, 1970. 212 pp.

Findings and analysis of Europe's first major national KAP survey.

Balakrishnan, T. R., J. F. Kantner, and J. D. Allingham. *Fertility and Family Planning in a Canadian Metropolis.* Montreal: McGill-Queen's University Press, 1975. 233 pp. $14.50.

Findings and analysis of Canada's first comprehensive fertility survey, conducted in Toronto in 1968.

Bernhardt, Eva. *Trends and Variations in Swedish Fertility: A Cohort Study.* Urval No. 5. Stockholm: National Central Bureau of Statistics, 1971. 227 pp. Sw. Crs. 20.40.

An analysis of fertility in Sweden based on records of the country's population register which dates back to the mid-18th century.

Bumpass, Larry and Charles F. Westoff. *The Later Years of Childbearing.* Princeton, N.J.: Princeton University Press, 1970. 168 pp. $7.50.

Final volume of the Princeton Fertility Survey presents findings of the third and final round of interviews conducted 1963-67 with 814 U.S. women first interviewed in 1957 shortly after giving birth to a second child.

Cho, Lee-Jay, Wilson Grabill, and Donald J. Bogue. *Differential Current Fertility in the United States.* Chicago: Community Family Study Center, University of Chicago, 1970. 420 pp. $6.75.

The "own children" method of measuring fertility is shown to be a powerful tool for the study of fertility differentials, using 1960 U.S. census data.

Cicourel, Aaron V. *Theory and Method in a Study of Argentine Fertility.* New York: Wiley, 1974. 212 pp. $12.95.

Examination of forces working for and against population control in Argentina and explanation of ethnomethodological approach to fertility research.

Grier, George. *The Baby Bust.* Washington, D.C.: Center for Metropolitan Studies, 1971. 76 pp. $2.50.

Implications of declining U.S. fertility, such as changing population age structure and zero growth.

International Migration Review. Vol. 9, No. 2, Summer 1975. Staten Island, N.Y.: Center for Migration Studies. Pp. 111-297. $5.00.

Special issue devoted to relationships between migration (international and internal) and fertility in the U.S. and Latin America, with an extensive bibliography.

International Statistical Institute. *World Fertility Survey (WFS).* An international research program begun in 1972 to assess the current state of fertility throughout the world, principally through promoting and supporting nationally representative, internationally comparable and scientifically designed and conducted sample surveys of fertility behavior in as many countries as possible.

The WFS is being conducted by the International Statistical Institute in cooperation with the International Union for the Scientific Study of Population, with the collaboration of the U.N. and principal support from the U.S. Agency for International Development and United Nations Fund for Population Activities.

An extensive and useful program of publications includes the following to date. For free copies and further information write the International Statistical Institute, 428 Prinses Beatrixlaan, The Hague-Voorburg, Netherlands.

The World Fertility Survey. The First Three Years: January 1972–January 1975. 1974. 66 pp.

Covers activities of the two-year development phase and first year of project implementation.

The World Fertility Survey: January 1975 December 1975. 1976. 67 pp.

First annual report and second WFS progress report.

Basic Documentation Series

Prepared by the WFS staff. Covers survey design and methodology.

Occasional Papers Series

Expert discussions of many issues related to fertility surveys. Includes the following as of mid-1976.

1. *Fertility and Related Surveys,* by William G. Duncan.
2. *The World Fertility Survey: Problems and Possibilities,* by John C. Caldwell.
3-6. *World Fertility Survey Inventory: Major Fertility and Related Surveys, 1960–73,* by Samuel Baum et al. *Asia, Africa, Latin America, Europe, North America and Australia.*
7. *The Study of Fertility and Fertility Change in Tropical Africa,* by John C. Caldwell.
8. *Community-Level Data in Fertility Surveys,* by Ronald Freedman.
9. *Examples of Community-Level Questionnaires,* by Ronald Freedman.
10. *A Selected Bibliography of Works on Fertility,* by György T. Acsádi.
11. *Economic Data for Fertility Analysis,* by Deborah S. Freedman (with Eva Mueller).
12. *Economic Modules for use in Fertility Surveys in Less Developed Countries,* by Deborah S. Freedman and Eva Mueller.
13. *Ideal Family Size,* by Helen Ware.
14. *Modernism,* by David Goldberg.
15. *The Fiji Fertility Survey: A Critical Commentary,* by M.A. Sahib et al.
16. *The Fiji Fertility Survey: A Critical Commentary—Appendices,* by M. A. Sahib et al.
17. *Sampling Errors for Fertility Surveys,* by L. Kish, et al.

Kiser, Clyde V., ed. *Forty Years of Research in Human Fertility: Retrospect and Prospect. Milbank Memorial Fund Quarterly,* Vol. 49, No. 4, October 1971, Part 2. New York: Milbank Memorial Fund. 254 pp. $3.00.

Proceedings of a conference including ten papers by leading demographers.

Peel, John and Griselda Carr. *Contraception and Family Design: A Study of Birth Planning in Contemporary Society.* New York: Churchill Livingstone, 1975. 180 pp. $11.50.

Report on the first round of a pioneering national longitudinal survey of the fertility history of a sample of British women, married 1970-71, who will be reinterviewed at five-year intervals throughout their childbearing years.

Ryder, Norman B. and Charles F. Westoff. *Reproduction in the United States, 1965.* Princeton, N.J.: Princeton University Press, 1971. 419 pp. $16.00.

Comprehensive analysis of findings from the 1965 National Fertility Study.

Social Forces. "Part 1: Fertility Models and Measurement." Special editor: N. Krishnan Namboodiri. Special issue, Vol. 54, No. 1, September 1975. Chapel Hill, N.C.: University of North Carolina Press. Pp. 1-138. $5.00.

Critical examination of the nature, use and effectiveness of a variety of theoretical models for the study of fertility dynamics by eight noted demographers.

United Nations. *Human Fertility and National Development: A Challenge to Science and Technology.* Sales No. 71. II.0.12. New York: United Nations, 1971. 140 pp. $2.50.

One of the U.N.'s most comprehensive and readable publications on the entire range of issues involved in human fertility and fertility control.

United Nations. Department of Economic and Social Affairs. *Interim Report on Conditions and Trends of Fertility in the World, 1960–1965.* Population Studies No. 52. English/French/Russian/Spanish. Sales No. E.72.XIII.3. New York: United Nations, 1972. 89 pp. $3.00.

Summaries of global findings on 1960–65 changes in fertility levels.

United Nations. Economic and Social Commission for Asia and the Pacific (ESCAP). *Fertility Studies in the ECAFE Region: A Bibliography of Books, Papers, and Reference Materials.* Asian Population Studies Series No. 6. Bangkok: ESCAP, 1971. 54 pp. Free.

Partly annotated listing of 584 items for 1965–1970 covering all items relevant to fertility research and findings in this region.

Westoff, Leslie Aldridge and Charles F. Westoff. *From Now to Zero: Fertility, Contraception and Abortion in America.* Boston: Little Brown, 1971. 358 pp. $4.25 paper.

Differential fertility, fertility control, and Catholic attitudes to birth control, based in part on data from the 1965 U.S. National Fertility Study.

Yaukey, David. *Marriage Reduction and Fertility.* Lexington, Mass.: Lexington Books, 1973. 115 pp. $10.00.

Poses a conceptual framework for reviewing and analyzing the impact of periods of non-marriage on fertility, particularly that of delayed first marriage.

B. BIOLOGICAL, CULTURAL, PSYCHOLOGICAL AND SOCIOECONOMIC DETERMINANTS AND CONSEQUENCES OF FERTILITY

Askham, Janet. *Fertility and Deprivation.* New York: Cambridge University Press, 1975. 188 pp. $14.50.

Presents a model to analyze differences in fertility between unskilled and other manual occupational groups in Aberdeen.

Ben-Porath, Yoram. *First Generation Effects on Second Generation Fertility.* Report No. R-1259-NIH. Santa Monica, Cal.: Rand, 1973. 30 pp. $3.00.

Explores the relationship between number of children and socioeconomic and familial background of husband.

Ben-Porath, Yoram and Finis Welch. *Chance, Child Traits, and Choice of Family Size.* Report No. R-1117-NIH/RF. Santa Monica, Cal.: Rand, 1972. 26 pp. $3.00.

Technical discussion of the effect of inborn traits of children on subsequent family size.

Bernard, Jessie. *The Future of Motherhood.* New York: Dial, 1974. 426 pp. $10.00.

Discusses population problems, personal choice, and individual responsibility as they relate to motherhood.

Bouvier, Leon F. and S. L. N. Rao. *Socioreligious Factors in Fertility Decline.* Cambridge, Mass.: Ballinger, 1975. 204 pp. $14.95.

A cross-sectional panel study of fertility behavior in Rhode Island between 1967–1971 with special focus on Catholics and their changing attitudes and behavior regarding birth control.

Butz, William P. and Julie DaVanzo. *Economic and Demographic Family Behavior in Malaysia: A Conceptual Framework for Analysis.* Report No. R-1834-AID. Santa Monica, Cal.: Rand, October 1975. 24 pp. $1.50.

Describes a research design for identifying and evaluating key relationships between socioeconomic and biological factors and fertility.

Chung, Bom Mo et al. *Psychological Perspectives: Family Planning in Korea.* Seoul, Korea: Korean Institute for Research in the Behavioral Sciences, 1972. 532 pp. $10.00.

A pioneering fertility survey of 1,883 Korean women which stressed psychological factors, finding these to be as important as sociodemographic factors in explaining fertility and family planning behavior.

Committee for International Coordination of National Research in Demography (CICRED). *Proceedings of the Seminar on Infant Mortality in Relation to the Level of Fertility, Bangkok, Thailand, May 1975.* English/French/Spanish. Paris: CICRED, 1975.

Discussion of the "child survival" hypothesis, i.e., that reduction of infant mortality in developing countries could remove one heretofore important barrier to voluntary fertility reduction.

Coombs, Lolagene C. *Are Cross-Cultural Preference Comparisons Possible? A Measurement-Theoretic Approach.* IUSSP Papers No. 5. Available from IUSSP, 5 rue Forgeur, 4000 Liège, Belgium, 1976. 77 pp.

Methodological approaches to the measurement of preference for number and sex of children and test findings with the Coombs preference scale in Korea, Hungary, Malaysia, the Philippines, Taiwan and the U.S.

Dixon, Ruth. Special Rapporteur, United Nations Commission on the Status of Women. *Status of Women and Family Planning.* New York: United Nations, 1975. 148 pp. $7.00.

A specially commissioned, comprehensive review of relationships between the status of women and fertility. Based on U.N., government and nongovernmental data, special surveys in Egypt, India and Indonesia, and papers from three 1972–73 U.N. seminars; with recommendations for action.

Dixon, Ruth. "Women's Rights and Fertility." *Reports on Population/Family Planning,* No. 17. New York: The Population Council, 1975. 20 pp. Free.

Evidence presented from a number of countries to show the strong relationship between women's rights, their public and private status, and their reproductive behavior.

East-West Population Institute. *The Value of Children: Cross-National Study.* 7 vols. Honolulu: East-West Center. Vol. 1, $2.75; other volumes, $3.00 each.

Cultural, socioeconomic, and psychological differences in the perceived satisfactions and costs of children, based on findings from exploratory studies among young middle class and lower class urban couples, and rural couples in six countries. Volume 1 (1976) is entitled *Introduction and Comparative Analysis.* Volumes 2 through 7 present findings from: The Philippines (1976), Hawaii (1976), Korea, Taiwan, Japan and Thailand (latter four forthcoming). A readable summary of these findings, together with their implications for population policy, appears in James T. Fawcett et al, *The Value of Children in Asia and the United States: Comparative Perspectives.* Papers of the East-West Population Institute No. 32. Honolulu: East-West Center, 1974. 69 pp. Free.

Fawcett, James T., ed. *Psychological Perspectives on Population.* New York: Basic Books, 1973. 522 pp. $15.00.

A "state of the art" report on the new field of population psychology.

Fawcett, James T. *Psychology and Population.* New York: The Population Council, 1970. 149 pp. $3.95 paper.

A concise introduction to the population field for psychologists and other behavioral scientists.

Francoeur, Robert T. *Utopian Motherhood: New Trends in Human Reproduction.* Cranbury, N.J.: A. S. Barnes, 1973. 292 pp. $2.95 paper.

Discusses the future technology of human reproduction and the potentially associated psychological, emotional, and religious repercussions.

Freedman, Ronald. *The Sociology of Human Fertility: An Annotated Bibliography.* A Population Council Book. New York: Halsted Press, 1974. 283 pp. $14.95.

Classified and annotated bibliography of 1,657 items on human fertility published from 1962 to 1970 plus 430 non-annotated listings for 1970–72, with an introductory essay on major research trends, findings and unsolved problems.

Freedman, Ronald and Lolagene C. Coombs. *Cross-Cultural Comparisons: Data on Two Factors in Fertility Behavior.* New York: The Population Council, 1974. 94 pp. $3.95.

Comparative analysis of findings from recent fertility surveys in Asia, Europe and the U.S. on sex preferences for children and the prevalence and correlates of wanting no more children but not using contraception.

Groat, H. Theodore and Arthur G. Neal. *Social Psychological Correlates of Urban Fertility.* Rockville, Md.: Center for Population Research, National Institutes of Health, 1975. 286 pp.

A study of alienation and fertility based on a 1963–1971 panel survey of a sample of mothers in Toledo, Ohio.

Kaplan, Bernice A., ed. *Anthropological Studies of Human Fertility.* Detroit: Wayne State University Press, 1976. 146 pp. $8.95.

Anthropologists examine social and environmental factors affecting fertility in a number of small closed populations around the world.

Kocher, James E. *Rural Development, Income Distribution and Fertility Decline.* New York: The Population Council, 1973. 105 pp. $3.95.

Argues that without rural modernization in low-income countries, rural fertility will not decline unless effective demand is created by more equal income distribution.

Llewellyn-Jones, Derek. *Human Reproduction and Society.* New York: Pitman, 1974. 547 pp. $14.95.

Describes principles of population dynamics, birth control technology (emphasizing older methods), and socioeconomic and demographic factors which affect pregnancy outcome.

Marshall, John F., and Steven Polgar, eds. *Culture, Natality and Family Planning.* Chapel Hill, N.C.: Carolina Population Center, 1976. 301 pp. $7.50.

Seventeen anthropologists and psychologists examine the effects of diverse cultural patterns on fertility, and acceptance of contraception and family planning.

Mason, Karen Oppenheim et al. *Social and Economic Correlates of Family Fertility: A Survey of the Evidence.* Research Triangle Park, N.C.: Research Triangle Institute, 1971.

Systematic evaluation of findings from 274 sources—over half from developing countries—on social and economic variables associated with fertility.

Mason, Karen Oppenheim, assisted by Barbara S. Schulz. *Women's Labor Force Participation and Fertility.* Research Triangle Park, N.C.: Center for Population Research and Services, Research Triangle Institute, 1974. 194 pp.

Report of a study of the relationship between female employment and fertility in the U.S., based on surveys of the 1960s and an original pilot survey.

Nortman, Dorothy. "Parental Age as a Factor in Pregnancy Outcome and Child Development." *Reports on Population/Family Planning,* No. 16. New York: The Population Council, 1974. 51 pp. Free.

Quantification of major research findings on the reproduction risks associated with maternal age.

O'Hara, Donald J. *Changes in Mortality Levels and Family Decisions Regarding Children.* Report No. R-914-RF. Santa Monica, Cal.: Rand, 1972. 34 pp. $2.00.

An analysis which suggests that a decline in the level of child mortality may influence household decisions regarding family size.

Peck, Ellen. *The Baby Trap.* New York: Pinnacle Books, 1972. 245 pp. $1.50 paper.

Tips to women on how to recognize and avoid pervasive social pronatalism.

Peck, Ellen and Judith Senderowitz, eds. *Pronatalism: The Myth of Mom and Apple Pie.* New York: Crowell, 1974. $5.95.

Twenty-three articles analyze the social pressure for parenthood as it encroaches on individual needs, preferences and abilities.

Repetto, Robert C. *The Relationship of the Size Distribution of Income to Fertility, and the Implications for Development Policy* and *The Interaction of Fertility and The Size Distribution of Income.* Research Paper Series Nos. 3 and 8. Cambridge, Mass.: Harvard Center for Population Studies, March and October 1974. 15 and 20 pp.

Data from 64 countries (first paper) and application of a model (second paper) which reveal that more equitable income distribution is strongly associated with lower fertility.

Repetto, Robert. *Son-Preference and Fertility Behavior.* Washington, D.C.: World Bank, 1971. 31 pp. Free.

A critical examination of the assertion that fertility behavior is influenced by the desire to have sons to support parents in old age, negating attempts at population control.

Rich, William. *Smaller Families Through Social and Economic Programs.* Washington, D.C.: Overseas Development Council, 1973. 74 pp. $2.00.

Argues that fertility reduction programs can succeed only where the benefits of development are shared equitably, particularly rising national incomes, health services and education.

Ridker, Ronald G., ed. *Population and Development: The Search for Selective Interventions.* Baltimore: Johns Hopkins University Press, 1976. 464 pp. $22.50.

A major project of Resources for the Future, this volume reviews selected socioeconomic variables that could be manipulated to effect more rapid fertility decline in countries where current rapid population growth now thwarts the general development which encourages small family desires.

Ruprecht, Theodore K. and Frank I. Jewett. *The Micro-Economics of Demographic Change: Family Planning and Economic Well-being.* New York: Praeger, 1975. 186 pp. $16.50.

A study of economic wellbeing from the perspective of the family (micro) unit rather than the national (macro) level finds that marriage delay yields larger gains than all but the most severe cuts in family size.

Schultz, T. Paul. *Fertility Determinants: A Theory, Evidence and an Application to Policy Evaluation.* Report No. R-1016-RF/AID. Santa Monica, Cal.: Rand, 1974. 541 pp. $10.00.

An economic and methodological analysis. Contains an extensive bibliography.

Schultz, Theodore W., ed. *Economics of the Family: Marriage, Children, and Human Capital.* Chicago: University of Chicago Press, 1975. 584 pp. $12.95.

Description and empirical testing of economic principles to explain marriage and fertility by scholars subscribing to the "new home economics" developed at the University of Chicago.

Silvermann, Anna and Arnold Silvermann. *The Case Against Having Children.* New York: David McKay, 1971. 212 pp. $5.95 paper.

Explores the myth that large families are happier.

Simon, Julian L. *The Effects of Income on Fertility.* Carolina Population Center Monograph No. 19. Chapel Hill, N.C.: Carolina Population Center, 1974. 210 pp. $5.00.

Explores the short and long-run effects of income changes on fertility in less and more developed societies.

Spillane, William H. and Paul E. Ryser. *Fertility Knowledge, Attitudes and Practices of Married Men.* Cambridge, Mass.: Ballinger, 1975. 208 pp. $13.50.

Discusses both methodological issues and research findings from a survey of 424 married men in Pittsburgh.

Terhune, Kenneth W. *A Review of the Actual and Expected Consequences of Family Size.* NIH 75-779. Washington, D.C.: Department of Health, Education, and Welfare, 1974. 244 pp. $2.90.

Critical review of research literature on the "actual" consequences of family size for parents, children, and family relations, and consequences "expected" by parents and prospective parents.

Turchi, Boone A. *The Demand for Children: The Economics of Fertility in the United States.* Cambridge, Mass.: Ballinger, 1975. 238 pp. $15.00.

An attempt to formulate and statistically test a unified socioeconomic model of fertility in the U.S.

United Nations. Economic and Social Commission for Asia and the Pacific (ESCAP). *Report and Papers of the Expert Group Meeting on Social and Psychological Aspects of Fertility Behavior, Bangkok, June 10-19, 1974.* Asian Population Studies Series No. 26. Bangkok: ESCAP, 1975. 90 pp. Free.

Discussion by experts from Asia and elsewhere of past and potential psychosocial research which could provide guidelines for increasing the acceptability of contraception and family planning programs.

Welch, Finis. *Sex of Children: Prior Uncertainty and Subsequent Fertility Behavior.* Report No. R-1510-RF. Santa Monica, Cal.: Rand, 1974. 48 pp. $3.00.

The impact of the boy/girl ratio among children already born on subsequent fertility behavior and child survival, with special reference to Bangladesh.

Whelan, Elizabeth M. *A Baby?—Maybe.* Indianapolis, Ind.: Bobbs-Merrill, 1975. 237 pp. $5.95 paper.

The pros and cons of parenthood, from a demographer in a quandary over whether or not to have children; includes discussion of genetic counseling, sex predetermination and adoption.

Williams, Anne. *Effects of Economic Development on Fertility: Review and Evaluation of the Literature.* Paper No. GE74TMP-32. Santa Barbara, Cal.: TEMPO Center for Advanced Studies, 1974. 57 pp. Free.

Overview of theory and research findings on individual household determinants of fertility, especially in developing countries, listing over 200 selected references.

Wynn, Margaret. *Family Policy: A Study of the Economic Costs of Rearing Children and their Social and Political Consequences.* Harmondsworth, U.K.: Penguin Books, 1972. 384 pp.

Public and private costs of childrearing in the United Kingdom.

V. Marriage, Family, and Non-Familial Roles of Women

A. CROSS-CULTURAL AND NATIONAL STUDIES OF MARRIAGE AND THE FAMILY

Ainsworth, Charles H., Winnie T. Ainsworth, and Fern C. Ainsworth. *Selected Readings for Marriage and the Family.* New York: MSS Information Corporation, 655 Madison Ave., New York, N.Y. 10021, 1973. 249 pp. $12.00.

Thirty articles on historical and cross-cultural patterns of courtship, marriage and family.

Carter, Hugh and Paul C. Glick. *Marriage and Divorce: A Social and Economic Study.* Rev. ed. Cambridge, Mass.: Harvard University Press, 1976. 508 pp. $17.50.

Update of the authors' classic 1970 analysis of recent demographic and socioeconomic data on marriage, divorce, remarriage and living arrangements in the U.S.

Duncan, Greg J. and James N. Morgan, eds. *Five Thousand American Families—Patterns of Economic Progress.* Vol. IV. *Family Composition and Change and Other Analyses of the First Seven Years of the Panel Study of Income Dynamics.* Ann Arbor, Mich.: Institute for Social Research, University of Michigan, 1976. 527 pp. $7.50 paper.

This fourth volume of findings from a pioneering panel study of a large, nationally representative household sample, sponsored by the U.S. Department of Health, Education, and Welfare, focuses on the economic causes and effects of changes in family composition.

Fogarty International Center. *The Family in Transition.* Proceedings No. 3. Washington, D.C.: Government Printing Office, 1971. 342 pp. $3.00.

Papers from a 1969 conference at the National Institutes of Health, Bethesda, Md., plus two additional, dealing with the relationship between family and population from different perspectives.

Fox, Robin. *Kinship and Marriage: An Anthropological Perspective.* Baltimore: Penguin Books, 1970. 271 pp. $6.00.

Kinship patterns as they control marriage and inheritance and interpret "incest-taboos" in primitive and modern cultures.

Glick, Paul C. "Some Recent Changes in American Families." *Current Population Reports,* Series P-23, No. 52. Washington, D.C.: Government Printing Office, 1975, 17 pp. $.55.

A leading authority reviews demographic changes in U.S. families over the past 35 years. First in a new series of in-depth analytical reports by staff members of the Population Division, U.S. Bureau of the Census.

Gordon, Michael, ed. *The American Family in Social-Historical Perspective.* New York: St. Martin Press, 1973. 428 pp. $5.50 paper.

An anthology of readings on social and demographic aspects of the American family from colonial times to the present with some European material for comparison.

International Bibliography of Research in Marriage and the Family. Vol. 2, 1965-1972, edited by Joan Aldous and Nancy S. Dahl. Minneapolis, Minn.: University of Minnesota Press, 1974. 1,530 pp. $35.00. Vol. 3, 1972-1974, edited by David H. L. Olson and Nancy S. Dahl. St. Paul, Minn.: IMFL Project, Department of Family Social Sciences, University of Minnesota, 1975. 376 pp. $6.95 paper.

Two exhaustive indexed listings of the international literature on marriage and the family.

Meyer, M. G. *Marriage Law and Policy in the Chinese People's Republic.* 2 parts. Hongkong: Hongkong University Press, 1971. 369 pp. $16.75.

Discussion of law and traditional family patterns under the Ching dynasty (1644-1911), and the application of the 1950 Marriage Law and other marriage legislation of the Communist regime.

Prothro, Edwin T. and Najib Diab Lutfi. *Changing Family Patterns in the Arab East.* Syracuse, N.Y.: Syracuse University Press, 1974. 240 pp. $10.00.

A study of Sunni Muslim marriage customs and family patterns among some 2,000 women in villages of Lebanon, Syria and Jordan.

Queen, Stuart A. and Robert W. Habenstein. *The Family in Various Cultures.* 4th ed. Philadelphia: Lippincott, 1974. 460 pp. $4.45 paper.

Update of a standard text on cross-cultural aspects of the family, both historical and modern.

Shorter, Edward. *The Making of the Modern Family.* New York: Basic Books, 1975. 369 pp. $15.00.

A comprehensive history of the family in Western society over the last three centuries.

Staples, Robert. *The Black Woman in America: Sex, Marriage and the Family.* Chicago: Nelson-Hall, 1973. 269 pp. $8.95.

The impact of racial and sexual oppression, with special focus on sexual behavior.

United Nations. Department of Economic and Social Affairs. Population Division. *Urban-Rural Differences in the Marital-Status Composition of the Population.* Working Paper No. 51. New York: United Nations, 1973. Free on request to Population Division.

Comparisons of proportions of adults in urban and rural areas that are single, married, widowed, or divorced, for how long and at what ages, in selected countries around the world.

B. VARIANT FAMILY STYLES AND ILLEGITIMACY

Bernard, Jessie. *The Future of Marriage.* Des Plaines, Ill.: Bantam, 1973. 367 pp. $1.95 paper.

The male and female interpretations of marriage separated to reveal the psychological and physical hazards for married women.

DeLora, Jack R. and Joann S. DeLora. *Intimate Life Styles: Marriage and Its Alternatives.* Pacific Palisades, Cal.: Goodyear, 1972. 421 pp. $7.95.

Explores the multitude of intimate life styles available today, using and describing the social systems approach.

The Family Coordinator. "The Second Experience: Variant Family Norms and Life Styles." Special issue, Vol. 24, No. 4, October 1975. Minneapolis, Minn.: National Council on Family Relations. 120 pp. $3.75.

Includes articles on experimental family forms such as communes and open marriage, marriage contracts, and single-parent, no-child and three-generation families.

George, Victor and Paul Wilding. *Motherless Families.* London: Routledge & Kegan Paul, 1972. 232 pp. $4.00 paper.

A study of 600 families with only fathers present identifies financial, housing and working-time problems.

Hartley, Shirley Foster. *Illegitimacy.* Berkeley, Cal.: University of California Press, 1975. 288 pp. $10.00.

Comprehensive demographic and sociological study of illegitimacy around the world.

National Council on Illegitimacy. *Illegitimacy: Today's Realities.* New York: National Council on Illegitimacy, 1971. 77 pp. $3.25 paper.

Proceedings of a 1970 national conference on problems of declining status and services for unwed parents and their children with proposals for improvement.

Ross, Helen L. and Isabel V. Sawhill. *Time of Transition: The Growth of Families Headed by Women.* Washington, D.C.: The Urban Institute, 1975. 223 pp. $4.95 paper.

Two economists examine the recent rapid growth of fatherless families in the U.S. and the implications for society and public policy.

U.S. Bureau of the Census. "Female Family Heads." *Current Population Reports,* Series P-23, No. 50. Washington, D.C.: Government Printing Office, July 1974. 30 pp. $.75.

Detailed statistical analysis of a growing U.S. phenomenon.

C. NON-FAMILIAL ROLES OF WOMEN

Boserup, Ester. *The Role of Women in Economic Development.* 2nd ed. London: Ruskin House, 1971. 282 pp. $8.95.

A classic work describing traditional patterns of women's economic participation in different regions of the developing world which could be undermined by unthinking development policies.

Chafe, William Henry. *The American Woman: Her Changing Social, Economic and Political Roles, 1920–1970.* New York: Oxford University Press, 1972. 351 pp. $8.95.

The strong impact of World War II and the passive 1950s and stormy 1960s on sex roles.

Cook, Alice H. *The Working Mother.* Ithaca, N.Y.: Cornell University Press, 1975. 71 pp. $3.25.

A travel report on the number, motivations, and earnings of, and special services for working women in nine countries.

Cordell, Magda and John McHale. *Women in World Terms: Facts and Trends.* Binghamton, N.Y.: Center for Integrative Studies, State University of New York at Binghamton, 1975, 63 pp. $4.00 paper.

Global review of women's status with regard to population, food, education, and development trends, ancient and modern.

Ferriss, Abbott L. *Indicators of Trends in the Status of American Women.* New York: Russell Sage Foundation, 1971. 451 pp. $6.95 paper.

Extensive times-series data comparing the relative status of men and women in the U.S.

Hoffman, Lois Wladis and Ivan F. Nye. *Working Mothers: An Evaluative Review of the Consequences for Wife, Husband and Child.* San Francisco: Jossey-Bass, 1974. 272 pp. $12.50.

Non-technical analysis of research findings with suggestions for new areas of research.

Mickelwait, Donald R., Mary Ann Riegelman, and Charles F. Sweet. *Women in Rural Development: A Survey of the Roles of Women in Ghana, Lesotho, Kenya, Nigeria, Bolivia, Paraguay and Peru.* Boulder, Col.: Westview, 1976. 240 pp. $20.00.

A survey of the current and potential place of Latin American and African women in rural economies based primarily on field research in seven countries.

Organisation for Economic Co-operation and Development (OECD). *The Role of Women in the Economy.* Paris: OECD, 1975. 127 pp.

A synthesis of replies submitted by ten OECD member countries to a request for information on various aspects of women's roles, especially married women and mothers of young children.

Rosaldo, Michelle Zimbalist and Louise Lamphere, eds. *Women, Culture and Society.* Stanford, Cal.: Stanford University Press, 1974. 352 pp. $3.95 paper.

Twelve female anthropologists and four other researchers present comparisons of ideologies and women's status to explain sex status differentials in a variety of cultures.

Safilios-Rothschild, Constantina. *Women and Social Policy.* Englewood Cliffs, N.J.: Prentice-Hall, 1974. 197 pp. $3.50 paper.

Research data on sexist practices in social planning and their personal and social consequences in the Western and the Third World.

Swedish International Development Authority (SIDA). *Women in Developing Countries: Case Studies of Six Countries.* Stockholm: SIDA, 1974.

Role of the U.N. and other international agencies in improving women's lot in developing countries, and case studies in India, Kenya, Tanzania, Tunisia, Chile and South Vietnam.

Tinker, Irene and Michèle Bo Bramsen, eds. *Women in Development.* 228 pp. $3.50. *An Annotated Bibliography* by Mayra Buvinić. 162 pp. $2.50. Washington, D.C.: Overseas Development Council, 1976.

Companion volumes present an overview and background papers of a Mexico City seminar on women and development, sponsored by the American Association for the Advancement of Science prior to the June 1975 International Conference on Women, plus an extensive bibliography.

United Nations. *United Nations International Forum on the Role of Women in Population and Development, U.N. Headquarters and Airlie House, Virginia, 25 February–1 March 1974.* No. SP/ESA/SER.B/4. New York: United Nations, 1974. 55 pp. Free.

Report of a meeting of women leaders from around the world gathered to discuss an issue vital to World Population Year.

U.S. Bureau of the Census. "A Statistical Portrait of Women in the United States." *Current Population Reports,* Series P-23, No. 58. Washington, D.C.: Government Printing Office, 1976. 90 pp. $2.10.

Trend data from 1950 on all major social and demographic issues related to present-day women's roles in the U.S.

VI. Mortality and Morbidity

American Journal of Public Health. Special Supplement, September 1973. Washington, D.C.: American Public Health Association. 56 pp. $3.00.

Special issue devoted to a comprehensive examination of U.S. infant mortality by experts.

Dodge, David L. and Walter T. Martin. *Social Stress and Chronic Illness: Mortality Patterns in Industrial Society.* Notre Dame, Ind.: University of Notre Dame Press, 1970. 331 pp. $9.95.

Theory and data to explain the rise in heart disease and other chronic illnesses due to increasing stress in industrial societies.

Erhardt, Carl L. and Joyce E. Berlin, eds. *Mortality and Morbidity in the United States.* American Public Health Association. Vital and Health Statistics Monographs. Cambridge, Mass.: Harvard University Press, 1974. 289 pp. $10.00.

Presents U.S. data on mortality, infant mortality, morbidity, and longevity as well as differential care for the aged and married persons; some international comparisons.

Kitagawa, Evelyn and Philip M. Hauser. *Differential Mortality in the United States: A Study in Socioeconomic Epidemiology.* American Public Health Association, Vital and Health Statistics Monographs. Cambridge, Mass.: Harvard University Press, 1973. 255 pp. $9.00.

Education, income, occupation, race, marital status, and large families (for women) are some of the differentiating factors related to mortality data covering the period 1930-1961.

National Academy of Sciences. Institute of Medicine. *Infant Death: An Analysis by Maternal Risk and Health Care,* Vol. 1 from a series "Contrast in Health Status." Washington, D.C.: National Academy of Sciences, 1973. 203 pp. $6.00 paper.

Examines the relationship between infant death and maternal characteristics and health care in the U.S.

Population Reference Bureau. "Infant Mortality: Progress and Problems." By Leon F. Bouvier and Jean van der Tak. *Population Bulletin,* Vol. 31, No. 1, 1976. 32 pp. $1.00.

Past and current trends in infant mortality and prospects for the future in developed and developing countries, with special emphasis on the U.S.

Preston, Samuel H., Nathan Keyfitz, and Robert Schoen. *Causes of Death: Life Tables for National Populations.* New York: Academic Press, 1972. 787 pp. $25.00.

Covers 180 populations, with data by age and sex.

Puffer, Ruth Rice and Carlos V. Serrano. *Patterns of Mortality in Childhood.* Scientific Publication No. 262. Washington, D.C.: Pan American Health Organization (PAHO), 1973. 470 pp. Free to educational institutes.

Findings from a 1970-72 investigation of the causes of death among 35,000 children aged under 5 in 13 areas of Latin America and one each in California and Quebec. One of several reports based on further analysis of data from this investigation is *Birth Weight, Maternal Age and Birth Order: Three Important Dimensions in Infant Mortality* by the same authors. Scientific Publication No. 294. Washington, D.C.: PAHO, 1975. 42 pp. $0.50.

Retherford, Robert E. *The Changing Sex Differential in Mortality.* Studies in Population and Urban Demography No. 1. Westport, Conn.: Greenwood Press, 1975. 139 pp. $11.00.

Review of the literature, examination of 1910-1965 data for the U.S., England and Wales and New Zealand and evaluation of factors associated with current trends.

Shiloh, Ailon and Ida Cohen Selavan, eds. *Ethnic Groups of America: Their Morbidity, Mortality and Behavior Disorders.* Vol. 2: *The Blacks.* Springfield, Ill.: Charles C. Thomas, 1974. 296 pp. $12.95.

A collection of research articles which document the distinctive features of mortality and morbidity among the largest U.S. minority group.

United Nations. Department of Economic and Social Affairs. Population Division. *Mortality in Infancy and Childhood.* Working Paper No. 47. New York: United Nations, 1973. Free on request to Population Division.

Explanation of a method for estimating infant mortality in countries lacking accurate statistics and review of causes of infant and child mortality in the 2 percent of countries with such data. First draft report of a U.N.-World Health Organization collaborative project.

United Nations. Economic Commission for Asia and the Far East (ECAFE). *Comparative Study of Mortality Trends in ECAFE Countries.* Asian Population Studies Series No. 14. Bangkok: ECAFE, 1973. 90 pp. Free. Note: ECAFE has now been renamed Economic and Social Commission for Asia and the Pacific (ESCAP).

Documents the scarcity of reliable mortality statistics for this area.

U.S. Department of Health, Education, and Welfare. Public Health Service. *Health: United States 1975.* Washington, D.C.: Government Printing Office, 1976. 612 pp. $6.65.

First year of annual publication. Parts C and D include data on population variables including mortality for different age groups.

Vaidyanathan, K. E., ed. *Studies on Mortality in India.* Tamilnadu, India: The Gandhigram Institute of Rural Health and Family Planning, 1972. 400 pp.

Thirty papers on the measurement of historical trends, causes and demographic effects of mortality in India.

Verbrugge, Lois M. *Sex Differences in Illness and Death in the United States.* Baltimore: Johns Hopkins University Center for Metropolitan Planning and Research, June 1975. 59 pp. $2.00.

Analysis of differences in morbidity and mortality between U.S. men and women, 1958-1972.

World Health Organization (WHO). *World Health Statistics Annual.* 3 vols., issued separately under the general title. Published annually since 1962, replacing former *Annual Epidemiological and Vital Statistics.* English, French and Russian editions. Latest edition covers 1972. Geneva: WHO, 1975.

Presents international data as follows (for 1975 edition):

Vol. 1. *Vital Statistics and Causes of Death, 1972.* 559 pp. 128 Sw. francs.

Vol. 2. *Infectious Diseases: Cases, Deaths, and Vaccinations,* 1972. 219 pp. 33 Sw. francs.

Vol. 3. *Health Personnel and Hospital Establishments,* 1972. 240 pp. 33 Sw. francs.

VII. Migration and Population Distribution

A. INTERNATIONAL MIGRATION

Brody, Eugene, ed. *Behavior in New Environments: Adaptation of Migrant Populations.* Beverly Hills, Cal.: Sage Publications, 1970. 479 pp. $15.00.

> An international reader on the psychological, economic and cultural adaptation problems of immigrants, refugees and rural-urban migrants.

Castles, Stephen and Godula Kosack. *Immigrant Workers and Class Structure in Europe.* New York: Oxford University Press, 1973. 514 pp. $17.75.

> Describes characteristics, situation and problems of migrant workers in Western Europe.

Committee for International Coordination of National Research in Demography (CICRED). *International Migration: Proceedings of the Seminar on Demographic Research in Relation to International Migration, Buenos Aires, March 1974.* Edited by Georges Tapinos. Paris: CICRED, 1974. 303 pp.

> Expert papers on a wide range of issues related to current trends in international migration.

The Committee on the International Migration of Talent. *The International Migration of High-Level Manpower.* New York: Praeger, 1970. 738 pp. $22.50.

> Analyzes the causes and effects of the brain drain from Asia, the Middle East, Africa, Latin America and specific countries in those regions into Britain, Western Europe and the U.S.

The Committee on the International Migration of Talent. *Modernization and the Migration of Talent.* Available from Education and World Affairs, 522 Fifth Ave., New York, N.Y. 10036, 1970. 88 pp. Free.

> Policy recommendations to ameliorate negative effects of the brain drain on developing countries.

Handlin, Oscar. *A Pictorial History of Immigration.* New York, N.Y.: Crown Publishers, 1972. 344 pp. $12.50.

> Over 1,000 rare photographs and reproductions illustrate this record of the motivations, experiences and obstacles encountered by immigrants to the U.S. from 1600 to 1970.

Harper, Elizabeth G., ed. *Immigration Laws of the United States.* 3rd ed. Indianapolis, Ind.: Bobbs-Merrill, 1975. 756 pp. $28.50.

> Update of a textbook integrating U.S. statutes, regulations, administrative practices and leading court and administrative decisions on immigration.

Johnston, H. J. *British Emigration Policy 1815-1830: Shovelling Out Paupers.* Oxford: Clarendon Press, 1972. 197 pp. $13.75.

> Describes impact of six government experiments in state-aided emigration between 1815 and 1826 on population growth in Upper Canada and the Cape colonies.

Kennedy, Robert E. *The Irish: Emigration, Marriage and Fertility.* Berkeley, Cal.: University of California Press, 1975. 236 pp. $3.85 paper.

> Discusses demographic features which distinguish the Irish: the high incidence of postponed marriage and permanent celibacy, high fertility and incessant rural-urban migration.

Klaassen, Leo H. and Paul Drewe. *Migration Policy in Europe: A Comparative Study.* Lexington, Mass.: Lexington Books, 1973. 148 pp. $12.00.

> Analysis of migration policy in relation to regional policies in France, Great Britain, the Netherlands and Sweden.

Livi Bacci, Massimo, ed. *The Demographic and Social Pattern of Emigration from the Southern European Countries.* Florence, Italy: Department of Statistics and Mathematics, University of Florence, and Italian Commission for the Study of Population Problems, 1972. 393 pp.

> Papers and reports from the 1971 Second European Population Conference on the complex problems of intra-European migration.

Macisco, John J., Jr. and George C. Meyers. *Selective Bibliography on Migration and Fertility.* Durham, N.C.: Center for Demographic Studies, Duke University. Free.

> Some 100 citations of recent works on the relationship between migration (international and internal) and fertility.

Niland, John R. *The Asian Engineering Brain Drain.* Lexington, Mass.: Lexington Books, 1970. 198 pp. $13.00.

> The drain of high level engineering manpower from Asia implicated in students' failure to return from the U.S.

Plender, Richard. *International Migration Law.* Atlantic Highlands, N.J.: Humanities Press, 1972. 339 pp. $22.50.

> Identifies international legal restrictions on the power of individual nations to limit immigration.

Richmond, Anthony H. *Migration and Race Relations in an English City: A Study in Bristol.* London: Oxford University Press, 1973. 344 pp. $17.75.

> Nonwhite immigrants studied as "replacement" populations for residential areas losing inhabitants rather than as disreputable influences on formerly respectable neighborhoods.

Safe, Helen I. and Brian M. DuToit, eds. *Migration and Urbanization Models and Adaptive Strategies* and *Migration and Development.* Paris: Mouton, 1975. 336 pp. $16.50; 305 pp. $15.50.

> Two complementary collections of anthropological and sociological case studies of migrants in a large number of countries, focusing on the desire for cultural continuity, situational behavior and potential political power.

Samuel, T. G. *The Migration of Canadian-Born between Canada and the United States of America: 1955-1968.* Ottawa: Department of Manpower and Immigration, 1970. 46 pp. Free.

> Analyzes the declining impact of emigration to U.S. on Canada's human resources.

Shaw, Paul R. *Migration Theory and Fact: A Review and Bibliography of Current Literature.* Philadelphia: Regional Science Research Institute, 1975. 203 pp. $7.50.

> Reviews the assumptions, methodologies and empirical contributions of various approaches to determining what population groups are likely to move and why.

Thomas, Brinley. *Migration and Economic Growth.* New York: Cambridge University Press, 1972. 498 pp. $27.50.

> A study of the evolution of the Atlantic economy in which the international migration of population and capital between the U.S. and Great Britain is a central theme.

Thomas, Brinley. *Migration and Urban Development.* Scranton, Pa.: Barnes and Noble, 1972. 259 pp. $6.75 paper.

> The urban impact of various 19th century and current trends in international and internal migration in Britain and the U.S.

Tomasi, L. M. and C. B. Keeley. *Whom Have We Welcomed? The Adequacy and Quality of U.S. Immigration Data for Policy Analysis and Evaluation.* New York: Center for Migration Studies, 1975. 96 pp. $4.95 paper.

Analysis of data and policy problems ten years after the 1965 U.S. Immigration Act ended the national origin system of quota allocation.

United Nations Educational, Scientific and Cultural Organization (UNESCO). *Scientists Abroad.* Paris: UNESCO, 1971. 147 pp.

A study of the international movement of scientists and technicians.

U.S. Congress. House. Committee on the Judiciary. *Illegal Aliens. Hearings before the Subcommittee on Immigration, Citizenship, and International Law on H.R. 982 and Related Bills,* 94th Cong., 1st sess., 1975. Washington, D.C.: Government Printing Office, 1975. 450 pp. Free.

Hearings on a law to penalize U.S. employers of illegal aliens touch on most aspects of this currently sensitive U.S. issue.

Wilson, Paul R. *Immigrants and Politics.* Canberra: Australian National University Press, 1973. 175 pp. $14.75.

A study of political participation of postwar British and Italian immigrants to Australia.

B. INTERNAL MIGRATION

Barsby, Steve L. and Dennis R. Cox. *Interstate Migration of the Elderly.* Lexington, Mass.: Lexington Books, 1975. 149 pp. $14.00.

Examination of 1955-60 U.S. data in an effort to determine what special factors motivate mobility among persons aged 65 and over.

Bowles, Gladys K., A. Lloyd Bacon, and P. Neal Ritchey. *Poverty Dimensions of Rural-to-Urban Migration: A Statistical Report.* U.S. Department of Agriculture Economic Research Service. Statistical Bulletin No. 511. Washington, D.C.: Government Printing Office, 1973. 335 pp. $3.70.

Analysis of statistics from the 1967 Survey of Economic Opportunity, including family migration status and income.

Bussey, Ellen M. *The Flight from Rural Poverty—How Nations Cope.* Lexington, Mass.: Lexington Books, 1973. 132 pp. $11.50.

Describes the phenomenon and relevant policies in Mexico, Italy, and the Netherlands.

Chang, H. C. and Joe Kopachevsky. *Bibliography on Internal Migration.* Ames, Iowa: Department of Sociology, Iowa State University. Free.

Covers 400 items up to 1971.

Chudacoff, Howard P. *Mobile Americans.* New York: Oxford University Press, 1972. 195 pp. $8.95.

The relationship between residential and social mobility in Omaha, 1880-1920.

Friedland, William, and Dorothy Nelkin. *Migrant Agricultural Workers in America's Northwest.* New York: Holt, Rinehart and Winston, 1972. 281 pp. $6.95.

A narrative description of the living and work conditions of agricultural workers who are excluded from government social welfare and security programs.

Hinze, Kenneth. *Causal Factors in the Net Migration Flow to Metropolitan Areas of the United States: 1960-70.* Chicago: Community and Family Study Center, University of Chicago, 1976. 120 pp. $3.00 paper.

Analysis by age, sex, and race of economic, social, and political factors which appear to be causally related to city-ward flows in the U.S. during the 1960s.

Jackson, G. A., ed. *Migration.* Cambridge, U.K.: Cambridge University Press, 1969. 304 pp. $14.95.

A collection of ten studies on the theory of long- and short-distant migration.

Jansen, Clifford T., ed. *Readings in the Sociology of Migration.* New York: Pergamon Press, 1970. 402 pp. $6.50.

Typologies of migration and problems and characteristics of migrants in the U.S., Great Britain, France, Italy, Spain, Sweden, Japan and El Salvador.

Kosinski, Leszek A. and R. Mansell Prothero, eds. *People on the Move: Studies on Internal Migration.* London: Methuen, 1975. 393 pp. $14.50 paper.

Conceptual and theoretical aspects of internal migration with case studies in developing and developed countries.

Lansing, John B. and Eva L. Mueller. *The Geographic Mobility of Labor.* Ann Arbor, Mich.: Institute for Social Research, University of Michigan, 1973. 417 pp. $7.00 paper.

Economic determinants of geographic mobility in the U.S., especially poverty factors.

Long, Larry H. and Celia G. Boertlein. "The Geographical Mobility of Americans: An International Comparison." *Current Population Reports,* Series P-23, No. 64. Washington, D.C.: Government Printing Office, 1976. 45 pp. $1.05.

Detailed analysis of 1970 data from seven countries reveals that Americans are no more prone to internal migration than Australians and Canadians and are likely to become increasingly less so. Second in a new series of in-depth analytical reports from the Population Division, U.S. Bureau of the Census. (For first, see Glick, "Some Recent Changes in American Families," p. 17.)

Morrison, Peter A. *Migration from Distressed Areas: Its Meaning for Regional Policy.* Report No. R-1103-EDA/FF/NIH. Santa Monica, Cal.: Rand, 1973. 34 pp. $3.00.

Examines how migration restores labor market imbalance and how it affects those who leave and those who remain.

Morrison, Peter A. *Population Distribution Policy: Issues and Objectives.* Paper No. P-4793. Santa Monica, Cal.: Rand, 1972. 29 pp. $2.00.

One of a number of reports by the same author on issues and trends in the U.S. rural-urban distribution, with policy recommendations.

Packard, Vance. *A Nation of Strangers.* New York: David McKay, 1972. 368 pp. $7.95.

Best-selling analysis of the nature and implications of U.S. residential mobility and what can be done to regain a sense of community.

Price, Daniel O. and Melanie M. Sikes. *Rural-Urban Migration Research in the United States: Annotated Bibliography and Synthesis.* Bethesda, Md.: Center for Population Research, National Institute of Child Health and Human Development, 1975. 250 pp. $5.95.

Summary of research findings and annotated listing of 1,200 items covering 1950–1972.

Richmond, Anthony H. and Daniel Kubat, eds. *Internal Migration: The New World and the Third World.* Beverly Hills, Cal.: Sage Publications, 1976. 320 pp. $6.00 paper.

Selected papers on internal migration presented at the 1974 World Conference of Sociology, Toronto.

Ritchey, P. Neal. *Migration and Fertility: A Study of the Social Factors Involved.* Oak Ridge, Tenn.: Oak Ridge National Laboratory, Tenn., 1973. 53 pp. $5.00. Available from National Technical Information Service, Springfield, Va.

The impact of rural-urban migration on fertility levels in the U.S.

United Nations. Department of Economic and Social Affairs. Population Division. *The Dynamics of Rural-to-Urban Population Transfers by Sex and Age.* Working Paper No. 48. New York: United Nations, 1973. Free on request to Population Division.

Uses successive census data to analyze who migrates to cities at what ages, and extent to which urban growth is due to net in-migration, natural increase, or re-classification as "urban" of areas previously designated as "rural."

U.S. Department of Agriculture. Economic Research Service. *Net Migration of the Population, 1960–1970 by Age, Sex and Color, United States, Regions, Divisions, State and Counties.* 6 parts. By Gladys K. Bowles, Calvin L. Beale, and Everett S. Lee. Athens, Georgia: University of Georgia Printing Press, 1975. 767 pp. Free.

A cooperative venture with the Institute of Behaviorial Research of the University of Georgia and the National Science Foundation, based on published reports and tapes of the Bureau of the Census.

Walls, Dwayne E. *The Chickenbone Special.* New York: Harcourt Brace/Javanovich, 1971. 233 pp. $6.95.

A personalized account of migration by young blacks from the rural South to industrial areas in the North.

C. URBAN, SUBURBAN, RURAL DISTRIBUTION AND CHARACTERISTICS
(See also regional listings)

Baali, Fuad and Joseph S. Vandiver, eds. *Urban Sociology.* New York: Meredith Corp., 1970. 428 pp. $6.95 paper.

A reader for undergraduates on urbanization and related issues in the U.S. and developing countries.

Beale, Calvin L. *The Revival of Population Growth in Non-Metropolitan America.* Economic Research Service Series No. 605. Washington, D.C.: Economic Development Division, Economic Research Service, U.S. Dept. of Agriculture, 1975. 15 pp. Single copies free on request to Publication Services, Rm. 0054-S, ERS, U.S. Dept. of Agriculture, Washington, D.C. 20250.

Discussion of the reversal during 1970–73 of traditional U.S. rural-urban migration and its social and economic implications.

Beier, George et al. *The Task Ahead for the Cities of the Developing World.* World Bank Staff Working Paper No. 209. Washington, D.C.: World Bank, 1975. 81 pp. Free.

Readable examination of exploding urbanization in the Third World, why and where it is occurring and what can be done to cope with it. Will also be published, fall 1976, as a special issue of *World Development,* Pergamon Press, Headington Hill Hall, Oxford OX3 0BW, U.K.

Bollens, John C. and Henry J. Schmandt. *The Metropolis: Its People, Politics, and Economic Life.* 2nd ed. New York: Harper & Row, 1975. 488 pp. $7.50.

An introductory text on the demographic and social characteristics as well as the ecological and political dimensions of metropolitanization.

Brunn, Stanley D. *Urbanization in Developing Countries: An International Bibliography.* Latin American Studies Center and the Center for Urban Affairs Report No. 8. East Lansing, Mich.: Michigan State University, 1971. 693 pp. $8.00.

An international, interdisciplinary and multilingual listing of 7,000 books and articles.

Chandler, Tertius and Gerald Fox. *3,000 Years of Urban Growth.* New York: Academic Press, 1973. 431 pp. $28.00.

Estimated population of every city of the world exceeding 20,000 inhabitants (40,000 for Asia) from 1360 B.C. to 1850 A.D.

Cities: Their Origins, Growth and Human Impact. Readings from *Scientific American.* San Francisco: Freeman, 1973. 297 pp. $5.50.

These international readings describe the earliest cities, the evolution of Western industrial cities, cities in the developing world, and their environmental, social and health problems.

Davis, Kingsley. *World Urbanization 1950–1970.* Vol. 2: *Analysis of Trends, Relationships and Development.* Population Monograph Series No. 9. Berkeley, Cal.: Institute of International Studies, University of California, 1972. 319 pp. $3.00 paper.

Provocative questions and some surprising answers on world urbanization trends past, current and future.

Downs, Anthony. *Opening Up the Suburbs: An Urban Strategy for America.* New Haven, Conn.: Yale University Press, 1973. 247 pp. $7.95.

The case for low- and moderate-income housing in suburban areas for the inner-city poor and opposing views.

Dwyer, D. J. *People and Housing in Third World Cities: Perspectives on the Problem of Spontaneous Settlements.* New York: Longman, 1975. 286 pp. $18.00.

Examination of the growing squatter problem in Third World cities, particularly in Caracas, Hong Kong, India, Malaysia and the Philippines, with practical suggestions for its solution.

Edmonston, Barry. *Population Distribution in American Cities.* Lexington, Mass.: Lexington Books, 1975. 156 pp. $15.50.

Technical analysis of changes in population concentration in major U.S. metropolitan centers from 1900 to 1970.

Ford Foundation. *International Urbanization Survey Reports, 1970–72.* Average 75 pp. Free from Ford Foundation, 320 East 43rd Street, New York, N.Y. 10017.

Nineteen Ford Foundation field staff working papers for a 1970–72 survey of urbanization in developing countries.

Forman, Robert E. *Black Ghettos, White Ghettos, and Slums.* Englewood Cliffs, N.J.: Prentice-Hall, 1971. 184 pp. $2.50.

Problems of housing and residential segregation in the modern black ghetto as compared to those experienced earlier by the Irish, Italian, East European and other immigrants to the U.S.

Ginzberg, Eli, ed. *The Future of the Metropolis: People, Jobs, Income.* Salt Lake City, Utah: Olympus, 1974. 168 pp. $6.95.

Eight papers on emerging issues in metropolitan economies, such as suburban labor markets, low-wage workers, minority and racial distribution and integration patterns.

Goldstein, Sidney and David F. Sly, eds. *Basic Data Needed for the Study of Urbanization,* Working Paper 1. *The Measurement of Urbanization and Projection of Urban Population,* Working Paper 2. Published for the International Union for the Scientific Study of Population by Ordina Editions, Route de Goé 9, 4830 Dolhain, Belgium, 1975. 100 pp. $4.50; 224 pp., $8.00, respectively.

Two complementary papers reviewing data sources and measurement problems related to the study of urbanization around the world.

Halebsky, Sandor, ed. *The Sociology of the City.* New York: Scribner's, 1973. 696 pp. $10.95.

A reader for advanced students focused on urban phenonomena in advanced industrial societies and the U.S. in particular.

Hansen, Niles M. *The Future of Nonmetropolitan America.* Lexington, Mass.: Lexington Books, 1973. 256 pp. $14.00.

Looks at U.S. nonmetropolitan regions that grew during the 1960s after previous decline and examines reasons for their turnaround.

Hansen, Niles M. *Rural Poverty and the Urban Crisis.* Bloomington, Ind.: Indiana University Press, 1970. 352 pp. $12.50.

Presents an economic and policy-oriented rural development strategy.

Hawley, Amos H. *Urban Society: An Ecological Approach.* New York: Ronald Press, 1971. 348 pp. $8.50.

A textbook which includes discussion of population growth, spatial orientation, and redistribution of urban population.

Hawley, Amos H. and Vincent P. Rock, eds. *Metropolitan America in Contemporary Perspective.* New York: Halsted, 1975. 504 pp. $25.00.

Compendium and analysis of social science research of the past decade on U.S. urban society.

Hughes, James W. and Kenneth D. Bleakly, Jr. *Urban Homesteading.* New Brunswick, N.J.: Center for Urban Policy Research, Rutgers University, 1975. 296 pp. $12.95.

Evaluation of homesteading programs to combat neighborhood decline in Baltimore, Wilmington, Del., Philadelphia and Newark, N.J., with policy recommendations.

Katznelson, Ira. *Black Men, White Cities.* New York: Oxford University Press, 1973. 219 pp. $9.95.

Race, politics and migration in the U.S., 1900-1930, and Britain, 1948-68.

Mangin, William, ed. *Peasants in Cities: Readings in the Anthropology of Urbanization.* Boston, Mass.: Houghton Mifflin, 1970. 207 pp. $5.50.

Problems of cultural adaptation to new urban environments of peasants in Latin America, Africa and Indonesia.

Schwartz, Barry, ed. *The Changing Face of the Suburbs.* Chicago: University of Chicago Press, 1976. 355 pp. $16.00.

Thirteen authors analyze changing characteristics and implications of suburban population growth.

Speare, Alden, Jr., Sidney Goldstein, and William H. Frey. *Residential Mobility, Migration, and Metropolitan Change.* Cambridge, Mass.: Ballinger, 1975. 316 pp. $15.00.

Case study of U.S. metropolitan growth patterns focused on Rhode Island, including social, economic and demographic correlates of residential mobility.

Sternlieb, George and James W. Hughes, eds. *Post-Industrial America: Metropolitan Decline and Inter-Regional Job Shifts.* New Brunswick, N.J.: Center for Urban Policy Research, Rutgers University, 1975. 267 pp. $12.95.

Documentation and analysis of the decline or stagnation of America's older cities, and implications for policy.

Trewartha, Glenn T. *The Less Developed Realm: A Geography of its Population.* New York: Wiley, 1972. 449 pp. $9.00 paper.

Examines problems of population distribution, particularly in Asia, Africa, and most of Latin America.

United Nations. Department of Economic and Social Affairs. Population Division. *Trends and Prospects in the Populations of Urban Agglomerations, 1950-2000, as Assessed in 1973-1975.* Working Paper No. 58. New York: United Nations, 1975. Free on request to Population Division.

Latest U.N. population estimates and projections for all cities of at least 100,000 inhabitants, by countries, regions and the world, with special emphasis on expected increase in "million-cities."

U.S. Bureau of the Census. "Social and Economic Characteristics of the Metropolitan and Non-Metropolitan Population: 1974 and 1970." *Current Population Reports,* Series P-23, No. 55. Washington, D.C.: Government Printing Office, 1975. 120 pp. $2.55.

Data from the March 1974 Current Population Survey and the 1 in 100 samples of the 1970 Census.

Wakstein, Allen M., ed. *The Urbanization of America: An Historical Anthology.* New York: Houghton Mifflin, 1970. 502 pp. $7.50 paper.

A selection of 37 readings on the history of urban growth in the United States.

Ward, Barbara. *The Home of Man.* New York: Norton, 1976. 320 pp. $3.95 paper.

The conditions and problems of human urban settlements.

Ward, David. *Cities and Immigrants: A Geography of Change in Nineteenth Century America.* New York: Oxford University Press, 1971. 164 pp. $6.95.

This first in a series on historical geography traces the settlement pattern of rural-urban migrants as related to employment opportunities, transportation innovations, residential preference, etc.

Wilsher, Peter and Rosemary Righter. *The Exploding Cities.* New York: Quadrangle, The New York Times Book Co., 1975. 238 pp. $8.95.

Demographic causes of worldwide urban growth, the fallacious prototype of the city in the developed world, the condition of super-metropolis in the Third World and the impact of policies to control urban growth in Russia and China.

World Bank. *Urbanization: A Sector Working Paper.* Washington, D.C.: World Bank, 1972. 111 pp. Free.

Study of the dimensions and nature of the urbanization problem and the Bank's role.

VIII. Population Characteristics

A. AGE, AND POPULATION STRUCTURE

Bier, William C., ed. *Aging: Its Challenge to the Individual and Society.* Pastoral Psychology Series No. 8. New York: Fordham University Press, 1974. 292 pp. $12.50.

Proceedings of a 1973 Fordham University institute covering the full range of historic, demographic, medical, biological, sociopsychological, spiritual and policy factors associated with aging, in the U.S. and elsewhere.

Bixby, Lenore E. et al. *Demographic and Economic Characteristics of the Aged: 1968 Social Security Survey.* Washington, D.C.: Government Printing Office, 1974. 196 pp. $2.60.

Analysis of data from the most recent Social Security Administration survey of the U.S. aged.

Coale, Ansley G. *The Growth and Structure of Human Populations: A Mathematical Investigation.* Princeton, N.J.: Princeton University Press, 1972. 227 pp. $11.00.

Explanation of how fertility and mortality patterns affect the growth and age composition of populations by a pioneer in this field of demographic analysis.

National Council of Organizations for Children and Youth. *America's Children 1976: A Bicentennial Assessment.* Washington, D.C.: National Council of Organizations for Children and Youth, 1976. 87 pp. $4.00.

Well illustrated factbook on health, socioeconomic and family status and other aspects of children in the U.S.

Population Reference Bureau. "The Elderly in America." By Leon Bouvier, Elinore Atlee, and Frank McVeigh. *Population Bulletin*, Vol. 30, No. 3, 1975. 36 pp. $1.00.

Summary of demographic and socioeconomic characteristics and programs of public and self assistance.

Population Reference Bureau. "U.S. Population in 2000—Zero Growth or Not?" By Leon F. Bouvier. *Population Bulletin*, Vol. 30, No. 5, 1975. 33 pp. $1.00.

Includes a clear discussion of how age distribution of a population affects crude rates of birth, death and natural increase.

Report of the White House Conference on Youth. Washington, D.C.: Government Printing Office, 1971. 310 pp. $2.50.

Includes reports on child care, child services and institutions, changing families, etc.

United Nations. Department of Economic and Social Affairs. *The Aging: Trends and Policies.* Sales No. E.75.IV.2. New York: United Nations, 1975. 103 pp. $6.00.

Reports on international conditions of the elderly with recommendations for action and policies.

United Nations. Department of Economic and Social Affairs. *Report on Children.* Sales No. E.71.IV.3. New York: United Nations, 1971. 58 pp. $1.00.

Impact of population growth on children's needs in health, nutrition, education, etc. and implications for policy.

U.S. Bureau of the Census. "Demographic Aspects of Aging and the Older Population in the United States." By Jacob S. Siegel et al. *Current Population Reports,* Series P-23, No. 59. Washington, D.C.: Government Printing Office, 1976. 68 pp. $1.60.

Demographic study of the U.S. elderly population in the 20th century.

U.S. Bureau of the Census. "Social and Economic Characteristics of the Older Population, 1974." *Current Population Reports,* Series P-23, No. 57. Washington, D.C.: Government Printing Office, 1975. 59 pp. $1.50.

A compilation of new and already published socioeconomic data on the U.S. population aged 65 and over, primarily from the 1970 census and the Current Population Survey of March 1974.

U.S. Department of Health, Education, and Welfare. National Institute of Child Health and Human Development. *Epidemiology of Aging: Summary Report and Selected Papers from a Research Conference on Epidemiology of Aging, June 1972, Elkridge, Maryland.* Edited by Adrian M. Ostfeld and Don C. Gibson. Washington, D.C.: Government Printing Office, 1975. 286 pp. $3.40.

Papers on demographic aspects of aging in the U.S.

B. LABOR FORCE PARTICIPATION AND SOCIOECONOMIC STATUS

Bulletin of Labour Statistics. "Labour Force and World Population Growth." Special World Population Year edition. English/French/Spanish, with summaries in other languages. Geneva: International Labour Office, 1974. 86 pp. 10 Sw. francs.

Demographic aspects of global labor force participation, past, present, and projected to 2000, with numerous clear charts and tables.

Ferman, Louis A., Joyce L. Kornbluh, and Alan Haber, eds. *Poverty in America: A Book of Readings.* Ann Arbor, Mich.: University of Michigan Press, 1972. 669 pp. $6.95.

Articles on the measurement, socio-demographic characteristics, problems and value systems of the U.S. poor and the impact of public programs.

International Labour Organization. *Yearbook of Labour Statistics*. English/French/Spanish. Geneva: International Labour Office, 1975. 865 pp. 95 Sw. francs.

Thirty-fifth edition of a compilation of statistical data on labor and working conditions; covers some 190 countries and territories.

International Labour Review. "Population, Labour and Social Policy." Special issue, Vol. 109, Nos. 5-6, May-June 1974. Geneva: International Labour Office. 200 pp. $1.50.

Eleven experts discuss worldwide labor force trends, problems and policies and their interrelationships with population variables.

Kreps, Juanita and Robert Clark. *Sex, Age, and Work: The Changing Composition of the Labor Force.* Baltimore: Johns Hopkins University Press, 1975. 97 pp. $7.50.

Implications of recent changes in the U.S. in the allocation of labor market activity, home work and leisure time between the sexes and between age groups.

Lloyd, Cynthia B., ed. *Sex Discrimination and the Division of Labor.* New York: Columbia University Press, 1975. 431 pp. $6.00 paper.

Sixteen studies of female labor force participation, unemployment and wage differentials, discrimination and occupational segregation as well as economic aspects of women's non-market activities.

Masters, Stanley H. *Black-White Income Differentials: Empirical Studies and Policy Implications.* University of Wisconsin, Institute for Research on Poverty, Monograph Series. New York: Academic Press, 1975. 204 pp. $12.50.

Investigates why urban blacks have lower incomes than whites in similar occupational positions.

Sobin, Dennis P. *The Working Poor: Minority Workers in Low-Wage, Low-Skill Jobs.* Port Washington, N.Y.: Kennikat Press, 1973. 194 pp. $8.50.

Discusses how experiences of low-income black workers affect their social attitudes and leisure activities.

Seear, B. N. *Re-Entry of Women in the Labor Market after an Interruption in Employment.* Paris: Organisation for Economic Co-operation and Development, 1971. 135 pp. $3.00.

The significance and process of re-entry, opportunities and obstacles in European countries.

Sweet, James A. *Women in the Labor Force.* New York: Seminar Press, 1973. 211 pp. $11.95.

A technical analysis based on 1960 census data of employment patterns and earnings of working wives in the U.S. as related to age, education, family size, and race.

The Twentieth Century Fund Task Force on Employment Problems of Youth. *The Job Crisis for Black Youth.* New York: Praeger, 1971. 135 pp. $3.95.

Documents the declining job market for black boys since 1969 largely due to recession and military cutbacks, and for black girls for a variety of other reasons.

United Nations Educational, Scientific and Cultural Organization (UNESCO). *Statistical Yearbook.* Published annually since 1963. Latest edition covers 1974. Paris: UNESCO, 1975. 894 pp. $65.00.

Data from 212 countries on education (enrollment, attainment, and expenditures), science and technology, culture (including religion), communications, as well as basic population measures.

United Nations. Department of Economic and Social Affairs. Population Division. *Agriculture, Industry and Services in the Urban and Rural Labour Force.* Working Paper No. 57. New York: United Nations, 1975. Free on request to Population Division.

Uses available census data to document shifts from agricultural to service to industrial activities and back to services in both rural and urban labor forces as nations develop.

U.S. Bureau of Labor Statistics. *Employment and Earnings: United States, 1909–1971.* Washington, D.C.: Government Printing Office, 1971. 688 pp. $5.00.

Cumulative U.S. data.

U.S. Bureau of Labor Statistics. *Handbook of Labor Statistics 1975—Reference Edition.* Bulletin No. 1865. Washington, D.C.: Government Printing Office, 1975. 473 pp. $5.35.

Makes available in one volume the major data series produced over time by the Bureau of Labor Statistics.

C. ETHNICITY AND RELIGION

Barton, Joseph J. *Peasants and Strangers: Italians, Rumanians and Slovaks in an American City, 1890–1950.* Cambridge, Mass.: Harvard University Press, 1975. 217 pp. $12.00.

Pressures for rural-urban chain-migration of peasants and their determination to preserve their ethnic identity in Cleveland, Ohio.

Burma, John H., ed. *Mexican-Americans in the United States: A Reader.* Cambridge, Mass.: Schenkman; distributed by Canfield Press, San Francisco, 1970. 487 pp.

Authors from a variety of disciplines present a comprehensive view of Mexican-Americans today.

Engel, Madeleine H. *Inequality in America.* New York: Crowell, 1971. 329 pp. $3.95 paper.

Sociological analysis of U.S. inequality illustrated by the history of Puerto Rican immigrants and religious inequality of Jews.

Farley, Reynolds. *The Growth of the Black Population.* Chicago: Markham Publishers, 1970. 286 pp. $8.95.

History of U.S. black population trends since the American Revolution, emphasizing the impact of changes in marital status, birth control practices and health conditions.

Feinstein, Otto. *Ethnic Groups in the City: Culture, Institutions and Power.* Lexington, Mass.: Lexington Books, 1971. 382 pp. $15.00.

The influence of ethnicity on behavior, community life and power in the U.S. social structure.

Fitzpatrick, Joseph P. *Puerto Rican Americans: The Meaning of Migration to the Mainland.* Englewood Cliffs, N.J.: Prentice-Hall, 1971. 192 pp. $3.95 paper.

Identity problems, family structure, racial, religious, health and schooling conditions.

Glazer, Nathan and Daniel Patrick Moynihan, eds. *Ethnicity: Theory and Experience.* Cambridge, Mass.: Harvard University Press, 1975. 531 pp. $15.00.

> Ten authors, including the editors, explain why ethnic identity has become more salient in the U.S., self-assertion stronger and ethnic conflict more intense.

Gordon, Milton. *Assimilation in American Life: The Role of Race, Religion and National Origin.* New York: Oxford University Press, 1973. 276 pp. $2.95.

> Introduces the concept of structural pluralism to describe the complex social organization of racial, religious and nationality groups in the acculturation process of U.S. society.

Greeley, Andrew M. *Ethnicity in the United States: A Preliminary Reconnaissance.* Wiley Series in Urban Research. New York: Wiley, 1974. 347 pp. $14.95.

> Describes demographic and socioeconomic differences among religious-ethnic groups in the U.S.

Greer, Colin, ed. *Divided Society: The Ethnic Experience in America.* New York: Basic Books, 1974. 405 pp. $12.50.

> An anthology on the difficulties of immigrants in the U.S. which challenges the melting pot image.

Gordon, Milton M., ed. *Ethnic Groups in American Life Series.* Englewood Cliffs, N.J.: Prentice-Hall. Each $3.95 paper.

> A series documenting America's ethnic heritage and problems by social scientists experienced in intergroup relations of the group about which each writes.
>
> *Black Americans,* 2nd ed., by Alphonso Pinkney (1975). 242 pp.
>
> *Indian Americans,* by Murray L. Wax (1971). 232 pp.
>
> *Japanese Americans,* 2nd ed., by Harry H. L. Kitano (1976). 186 pp.
>
> *Jewish Americans,* by Sidney Goldstein and Calvin Goldscheider (1968). 274 pp.
>
> *Mexican Americans,* 2nd ed., by Joan W. Moore (1975). 172 pp.
>
> *Polish Americans,* by Helena Z. Lopota (1976). 240 pp. ($5.50).
>
> *Puerto Rican Americans,* by Joseph P. Fitzpatrick (1971). 192 pp.
>
> *White Protestant Americans,* by Charles H. Anderson (1970). 188 pp.

Groh, George. *Black Migration: The Journey to Urban America.* New York: Weybright and Talley, 1972. 301 pp. $12.00.

> Explores black migration from the rural South to Northern cities beginning with Reconstruction, with emphasis on the more recent period.

Johnson, Helen W. *American Indians in Transition.* Agricultural Economic Report No. 283. Washington, D.C.: Economic Research Service, Economic Development Division, U.S. Department of Agriculture, 1975. 37 pp. Free.

> Discussion of trends in residence, income, education, employment, health, family size and age distribution based on 1970 census data.

Lincoln, Eric C. *The Black Muslims in America.* Rev. ed. Boston: Beacon Press, 1973. 302 pp. $12.50.

> A classic study on the dynamics of black nationalism and the rise of the Black Muslim movement.

Moquin, Wayne and Charles Van Doren, eds. *Documentary History of the Mexican Americans.* New York: Praeger, 1972. 399 pp. $4.95 paper.

> Sixty-seven documents, most of them participant or contemporary observer accounts, provide a record from early conquests to recent times.

Pino, Frank. *Mexican Americans: A Research Bibliography.* 2 vols. East Lansing, Mich.: Latin American Studies Center, Michigan State University, 1974. 631 and 728 pp. $10.00.

> An extensive interdisciplinary bibliography of published and unpublished works.

Rogg, Eleanor M. *The Assimilation of Cuban Exiles: The Role of Community and Class.* New York: Aberdeen Press, 1974. 241 pp. $5.95 paper.

> Analyzes whether middle-class background and a strong sense of community facilitate initial adjustment and long-term acculturation. Evaluates effectiveness of government refugee programs.

Rose, Peter I., ed. *Ethnic Groups in Comparative Perspective.* Random House Series. Brattleboro, Vt.: The Book Press. Each $3.95 paper.

> Sociological examination of ethnic group origins and experiences in the U.S., cultural patterns and intergroup relations.
>
> *American Jews,* by Marshall Klare (1971). 252 pp.
>
> *Italian Americans,* by Joseph Lopreator (1970). 224 pp.
>
> *Japanese Americans,* by William Petersen (1971). 320 pp.
>
> *Mexican Americans,* by Ellwyn R. Storold (1973). 225 pp.
>
> *White Southerners,* by Lewis N. Kilian (1972). 168 pp.

Schmelz, U. O., P. Glikson, and S. J. Gould, eds. *Studies in Jewish Demography: Survey for 1969–1971.* London: Institute of Jewish Affairs, 1975. 354 pp. $7.50.

> A survey of worldwide research in Jewish demography, issued jointly with the Institute of Contemporary Jewry in Jerusalem.

U.S. Bureau of Labor Statistics. *Directory of Data Sources on Racial and Ethnic Minorities, 1975.* Bulletin No. 9. Washington, D.C.: Government Printing Office, 1975. 83 pp. $1.50.

> Includes recent federal government publications presenting social and economic characteristics of minority groups for the U.S. as a whole and selected areas.

Vivo, Paquita, ed. *The Puerto Ricans: An Annotated Bibliography.* New York: Bowker, 1973. 299 pp. $15.50.

> Includes sections on migration and demographic characteristics.

Wagenheim, Kal. *A Survey of Puerto Ricans on the U.S. Mainland in the 1970s.* New York: Praeger, 1975. 133 pp. $13.50.

> Documents the growth of the Puerto Rican community, education, language, literacy, employment and income.

Willie, Charles V., ed. *Family Life of Black People.* Columbus, Ohio: Merrill, 1970. 341 pp. $5.95 paper.

> Analysis of age, sex, marital status and instability, family patterns, and class structure.

IX. Causes and Consequences of Population Growth

A. GENERAL WORKS ON CURRENT POPULATION PROBLEMS

Allison, Anthony, ed. *Population Control.* Baltimore: Penguin Books, 1970. 240 pp. $1.65 paper.

Twelve articles on the socioeconomic implications of plant, animal, but in particular human population growth, and population control in primitive and modern societies.

Appleman, Philip, ed. *An Essay on the Principle of Population by Thomas Robert Malthus.* New York: Norton, 1976. 260 pp. $2.95 paper.

A collection of key articles and documents from Malthus himself to the present day which demonstrate the ever-increasing validity of his early warnings on the dangers of unchecked population growth.

Bahr, Howard M. et al, eds. *Population, Resources and the Future: Non-Malthusian Perspectives.* Provo, Utah: Brigham Young University Press, 1972. 352 pp. $4.95 paper.

The other side of the Malthusian debate.

Berelson, Bernard, with staff of The Population Council. "World Population: Status Report 1974." *Reports on Population/Family Planning,* No. 15. New York: The Population Council, January 1974. 47 pp. Free.

Comprehensive, well documented "inventory" of the world's population situation in 1974 and steps being taken to deal with it. A basic document for World Population Year discussions, with input from numerous authorities in the field.

Bird, Caroline. *The Crowding Syndrome: Learning to Live with Too Much and Too Many.* New York: McKay, 1972. 337 pp. $7.95.

A popular writer suggests restructuring our social and economic systems to meet the population overload.

Boot, John C. G. *Common Globe or Global Commons: Population Regulation and Income Distribution.* New York: Dekker, 1974. 139 pp. $10.75.

An economist lucidly reviews the threats posed by unregulated global population growth and offers a reasoned, novel solution, based on buying and selling of childbearing certificates.

Borrie, W. D. *The Growth and Control of World Population.* London: Weidenfeld & Nicholson, 1970. 340 pp. $10.00.

Comprehensive review of world population trends, problems and policies, past, present, and future, by a noted Australian demographer.

Borrie, W. D. *Population, Environment. and Society.* Auckland, N.Z.: Oxford University Press, 1973. 106 pp. $4.50 paper.

Four lectures on the above theme by the same author, which end with a call for "realistic action, not morbid despair or unreal panaceas of hope."

Brown, Harrison and Edward Hutchings, Jr., eds. *Are Our Descendants Doomed? Technological Change and Population Growth.* New York: Viking, 1972. 376 pp. $3.45 paper.

Proceedings of a conference on the world's current demographic dilemma discuss recent contraceptive technology, role of the United Nations, and close relation of GNP to population growth and environmental damage.

Brown, Lester R. *In the Human Interest: A Strategy to Stabilize World Population.* New York: Norton, 1974. 190 pp. $2.95 paper.

Urges a strategy to stabilize world population at under 6 billion to cope with accelerating ecological stresses and resource scarcities.

Brown, Lester R. *World Without Borders.* New York: Random House, 1973. 395 pp. $2.95 paper.

Discusses worldwide problems of environment, uneven income distribution, poverty, hunger and urbanization and growing international economic interdependence. Proposes education, population stabilization and a global infrastructure as solutions.

Brown, Lester R., Patricia McGrath, and Bruce Stokes. *Twenty-Two Dimensions of the Population Problem.* Worldwatch Paper Series No. 5. Washington, D.C.: Worldwatch Institute, 1976. 83 pp. $2.00.

Series of 800-word essays on the relationship between population growth and 22 ecological, social and economic issues. One of a series from an institute formed to give "early warning" on particular threats to humanity and encourage global problem-solving.

Caltech Population Program and the American Universities Field Staff. *Population: Perspective Series.* Harrison Brown and Alan Sweezy, general editors.

Three collections of articles stemming from a program combining the demographic expertise of Caltech faculty members and area knowledge of Field Staff Associates in a penetrating study of social and political factors affecting and affected by population problems.

Population: Perspective 1971.
San Francisco: Freeman, Cooper, 1972. 307 pp. $6.25.

Analyzes population problems in Afghanistan, Belgium, Bolivia, Brazil, Hong Kong, Indonesia, Ivory Coast, Japan, Kenya, Malawi, the Philippines, and Yugoslavia.

Population: Perspective 1972.
San Francisco: Freeman, Cooper, 1972. 239 pp. $5.95.

Considers the effect of population growth, economic development, and migration in the United Kingdom, China, Zaire, Malaysia, Ecuador, Singapore, Venezuela, South America, Ivory Coast, Europe, Yugoslavia, and Japan.

Population: Perspective 1973.
San Francisco: Freeman, Cooper, 1973. 284 pp. $5.95.

Focuses on population pressures, perceptions, and policy in China, Singapore, Japan, the Northeast Atlantic, Slovenia, Costa Rica, Venezuela, Egypt, Bali, Bangladesh, and Rwanda.

The Caltech Population Program has also produced an *Occasional Papers* series. Most recent issues include:

No. 5. *Demographic Trends in the Republic of Zaire,* by Joseph Boute.

No. 6. *Labor Shortage and Population Policy,* by Alan Sweezy.

No. 7. *Food Production, Population Growth, and Environmental Quality,* by Edward Groth III.

No. 8. *The Daya of Egypt: Survival in a Modernizing Society,* by Laila El-Hamamsy.

No. 9. *Population Growth and Affluence: The Fissioning of Human Society,* by Harrison Brown.

These papers are available, free, from the Caltech Population Program, California Institute of Technology, Pasadena, Cal. 91109.

Chamberlain, N. W. *Beyond Malthus: Population and Power.* New York: Basic Books, 1970. 214 pp. $7.95.

Argues that population problems are due not to population growth outstripping available resources but to the shifting political and economic power of different societal groups.

Choucri, Nazli and Robert C. North. *Nations in Conflict: National Growth and International Violence.* San Francisco: Freeman, 1974. 356 pp. $12.95.

Documents the central role of national population growth from 1870 to 1914 among the primary causes of World War I.

Cole, H. S. D. et al, eds. *Models of Doom: A Critique of the Limits of Growth.* New York: Universe Books, 1973. 244 pp. $2.95 paper.

Thirteen essayists critically analyze Forrester's "World Dynamics" systems approach and the future forecasts of the Meadows' computer model.

Committee for International Coordination of National Research in Demography (CICRED). *Seminar on Demographic Research in Relation to Population Growth Targets, April 1973, University of the West Indies.* Paris: CICRED, 1973. 102 pp.

Papers by 14 leading demographers on issues related to the setting of explicit population size or growth targets.

The Ecologist. "A Blueprint for Survival." Special issue, Vol. 2, No. 1, January 1972. Redhill, Surrey, U.K. 44 pp.

Much-publicized call for global action to meet the population-environmental crisis from 33 eminent British scientists.

Ehrlich, Paul R. and Anne H. Ehrlich. *The End of Affluence: A Blueprint for Your Future.* New York: Ballantine Books, 1974. 307 pp. $1.95 paper.

Argues that a fundamental shift in international economic relationships will end the era of abundance for the developed world and force adoption of energy saving devices.

Endres, Michael E. *On Defusing the Population Bomb.* New York: Halsted Press, 1975. 191 pp. $5.00 paper.

A critical examination of the present approach to the population problem with alternative suggestions; includes a section on genetic control and biological engineering.

Falk, Richard A. *This Endangered Planet.* New York: Random House, 1972. 495 pp. $2.95 paper.

Cites the war system, overpopulation, depletion of natural resources and environmental deterioration as primary threats to world order and suggests remedies.

Fraser, Dean. *The People Problem: What You Should Know About Growing Population and Vanishing Resources.* Bloomington, Ind.: Indiana University Press, 1971. 256 pp. $6.95.

A layman's guide to biological and mathematical aspects of population growth and its impact on environment and resources.

Hart, Harold, ed. *Population Control: For and Against.* New York: Hart, 1973. 239 pp. $2.45 paper.

Collection of essays by Mead, Etzioni, Lerner and others presenting the pros and cons of population control.

Johnson, Stanley. *The Population Problem.* New York: Halsted Press, 1974. 231 pp. $9.95.

General information about the problem; describes several U.N. agencies and their activities relative to population control.

Joyce, James A., ed. *World Population: Basic Documents.* Vol. 1: *What is the Problem?* Dobbs Ferry, N.Y.: Oceana, 1976. 432 pp. $40.00.

First of four projected volumes of basic documents, mainly from the U.N., providing an exhaustive reference source on all aspects of current population issues.

Kahn, Herman, William Brown, and Leon Martel. *The Next 200 Years: A Scenario for America and the World.* New York: Morrow, 1976. 241 pp. $2.95 paper.

Scholars of the Hudson Institute criticize the doomsayers and predict a rosy future for mankind, providing the real problems are recognized and tackled with vigor.

McCormack, Arthur. *The Population Problem.* New York: Crowell, 1970. 264 pp. $8.95.

Population pressures as they intensify poverty, hunger and similar problems of the developing world.

Meadows, Donella H., Dennis L. Meadows, Jorgen Randers, and William W. Behrens, III. *The Limits to Growth: A Report of the Club of Rome's Project on the Predicament of Mankind.* New York: Universe Books, 1972. 205 pp. $2.75 paper.

First, highly publicized report of a Massachusetts Institute of Technology group who fed data on population increase, agricultural production, nonrenewable resource depletion, industrial output, and pollution generation into a global computer model and tested the model's behavior under several sets of assumptions.

Meadows, Dennis L. et al. *Dynamics of Growth in a Finite World.* Cambridge, Mass.: Wright-Allen Press, 1974. 637 pp. $28.50.

Third Club of Rome report gives more details on data and assumptions used in the *Limits to Growth* computations.

Mesavoric, Mihajlo and Edward Pestel. *Mankind at the Turning Point.* New York: Reader's Digest Press, 1976. 208 pp. $1.95 paper.

The second report of the Club of Rome introduces the need for worldwide distribution of global resources to achieve "organic growth" and presents different scenarios to reach that goal.

Miles, Rufus E., Jr. *Awakening from the American Dream.* New York: Universe Books, 1976. 246 pp. $12.50.

Suggestions on how the U.S. might ward off some of the outcomes predicted in the *Limits to Growth* model.

Moraes, Dom. *A Matter of People.* New York: Praeger, 1974. 226 pp. $3.95 paper.

An Indian journalist's impressions of population problems and programs in 12 countries, mainly in the Third World. Commissioned by the United Nations Fund for Population Activities for World Population Year.

Oltmans, Willem L., ed. *On Growth.* New York: Capricorn Books, 1974. 493 pp. $9.95.

The opinions of 70 of the world's leading scientists and thinkers on the *Limits to Growth*.

Oppenheimer, Valerie K. *Population.* Headline Series No. 206. New York: Foreign Policy Association, 1971. 95 pp. $1.00.

Concise, balanced discussion of world population growth problems and their possible solutions in developing and industrialized nations.

Parry, H. B., ed. *Population and Its Problems.* Wolfson College Lectures. New York: Oxford University Press, 1974. 409 pp. $21.75.

Papers analyzing the magnitude and complexity of population problems from animal populations and their biological constraints to human populations and their constraints, biological and otherwise.

Reid, Sue Titus and David L. Lyon, eds. *Population Crisis: An Interdisciplinary Perspective.* Glenview, Ill.: Scott Foresman, 1972. 211 pp. $2.95 paper.

Thirty-three essays with opposing views on the population problem, its control, and its impact on man and his environment.

Revelle, Roger, ed. *Rapid Population Growth: Consequences and Policy Implications.* 2 vols. Baltimore: Published for the National Academy of Sciences by Johns Hopkins University Press, 1971. 795 pp. $2.45 and $6.50 paper.

Research reports on the social, economic, political, and educational consequences of rising birth rates, falling mortality rates, changing age patterns, and policymakers' responses to these phenomena.

Sauvy, Alfred. *Zero Growth?* New York: Praeger, 1976. 266 pp. $10.00.

A leading and literate French demographer attempts to soothe alarms roused in the U.S. in the wake of the *Limits to Growth*.

Singer, S. F., ed. *Is There an Optimum Level of Population?* A Population Council Book. New York: McGraw-Hill, 1971. 440 pp. $12.50.

Numerous scientists of many disciplines consider natural resources, environmental factors, social services, life styles and human values in relation to the concept of optimum population.

Spengler, Joseph J. *Population and America's Future.* San Francisco: Freeman, 1975. 260 pp. $3.95 paper.

The demographic and historical determinants of U.S. population growth and consequences for the environment, population age composition and distribution, and public policy.

Spengler, Joseph J., ed. *Zero Population Growth: Implications.* Chapel Hill, N.C.: Carolina Population Center, 1975. 157 pp. $5.00.

Several experts consider the implications of stationary population for the economy, society and the individual.

Thomlinson, Ralph. *Demographic Problems: Controversy Over Population Control.* 2nd ed. Encino, Cal.: Dickenson, 1975. 244 pp. $4.95.

Updated and expanded second edition of a classic sociological review of current population trends, problems and policies.

Weinsten, Jay A. *Demographic Transition and Social Change.* Morristown, N.J.: General Learning Press, 1976. 136 pp.

A critical appraisal of classical demographic transition theory and its ability to explain historical and current population trends.

Willing, Martha K. *Beyond Conception: Our Children's Children.* Boston: Gambit, 1971. 241 pp. $6.95.

Brings together the biology, ecology and demography of population to create awareness of personal responsibility.

Wilson, Thomas W., Jr. *World Population and a Global Emergency.* Washington, D.C.: Aspen Institute of Humanistic Studies, 1973. 61 pp. Out of print.

Summarizes views of 50 generalists and specialists expressed in a summer-long Aspen workshop on the world emergency created by the interlocking problems of environment, energy, food and resource shortages, and population growth in particular.

B. POPULATION, NUTRITION, AND FOOD SUPPLY

Aykrod, W. R. *The Conquest of Famine.* New York: Reader's Digest Press, 1975. 216 pp. $7.95.

A description of causes and incidence of major famines in ancient and modern times sets the stage for analysis of family planning programs to cope with food-population imbalances not attributable to natural catastrophes.

Berg, Alan. *The Nutrition Factor: Its Role in National Development.* Washington, D.C.: The Brookings Institute, 1973. 290 pp. $3.95 paper.

A leading nutrition expert discusses malnutrition as a cause and consequence of underdevelopment, and suggests strategies for improvement. Excerpts from the book were published by the Population Reference Bureau in "Nutrition, Development, and Population Growth," *Population Bulletin*, Vol. 29, No. 1, 1973. 36 pp. $1.00.

Bickel, Leonard. *Facing Starvation: A Biography of Dr. Norman E. Borlaug.* New York: Dutton, 1974. 376 pp. $8.95.

Father of the Green Revolution and Nobel Peace Prize winner.

Borgstrom, Georg. *Focal Points: A Global Food Strategy.* New York: Macmillan, 1973. 320 pp. $8.95 paper.

Identifies Mexico, Java, Egypt, the Caribbean, Pakistan and Bangladesh as high-pressure regions in the global food-population crisis. Third volume of a trilogy including the author's *The Hungry Planet* (1965, revised 1972) and *Too Many* (1969).

Borgstrom, Georg. *The Food and People Dilemma.* Belmont, Cal.: Duxburg Press, 1974. 140 pp. $3.95 paper.

The expanding food-population gap documented with data on determinants of food supply and population growth.

Brown, Lester R. *Politics and Responsibility of the North American Breadbasket.* Worldwatch Paper Series No. 2. Washington, D.C.: Worldwatch Institute, 1975. 44 pp. $2.00.

Identifies new causes of global food insecurity, and problem countries.

Brown, Lester R., with Erik P. E. Eckholm. *By Bread Alone.* New York: Praeger, 1974. 272 pp. $3.95 paper.

Analyzes rise in food demands along with affluence and population and recommends improved agricultural production, reduced protein consumption, and population control.

Clark, Colin. *Starvation or Plenty?* New York: Taplinger, 1970. 180 pp. $4.95.

An optimistic analysis of actual and potential world food production, given absence of political and administrative problems.

Correa, Hector. *Population, Health, Nutrition and Development: Theory and Planning.* Lexington, Mass.: Lexington Books, 1975. 226 pp. $21.50.

Presents mathematical techniques and economic models for measuring and planning for population growth, nutrition and socioeconomic development.

Eckholm, Eric P. *Losing Ground.* New York: Norton, 1976. 223 pp. $3.95.

Describes how food systems are being ecologically unbalanced through deforestation, overgrazing, soil erosion, flooding, and calls for agricultural reforms and population slowdown.

Food and Agriculture Organization of the United Nations (FAO). *Population, Food Supply and Agricultural Development.* Rome: FAO, 1975. 62 pp.

Base paper for FAO's report and recommendations to the 1974 World Conferences on Population and Food.

Halacy, D. S., Jr. *Geometry of Hunger.* New York: Harper & Row, 1972. 280 pp. $8.95.

Population problems, the ecological food chain and limits to agricultural development illustrate that it is a humane mechanism to establish an optimum population for the world.

Johnson, Gale D. *World Food Problems and Prospects.* Washington, D.C.: American Enterprise Institute for Public Policy Research, June 1975. 83 pp. $3.00 paper.

Argues that with sufficient political will to give food and birth control policies continued priority, there are no technological or resource constraints great enough to prevent adequate feeding of the world's population a decade hence.

Kumar, Joginder. *Population and Land in World Agriculture: Recent Trends and Relationships.* Population Monograph Series No. 12. Berkeley, Cal.: Institute of International Studies, University of California, 1973. 318 pp. $3.95 paper.

Describes historical and current international disparities between farm population density and land utilization.

Lerza, Catherine and Michael Jacobson, eds. *Food for People, Not for Profit: A Source Book on the Food Crisis.* New York: Ballantine, 1975. 466 pp. $1.95 paper.

An extensive collection of short articles on the production and cost of food, and worldwide food problems as related to poverty and government's role in the food industry.

Manocha, Sohan L. *Nutrition and Our Overpopulated Planet.* Springfield, Ill.: Thomas, 1975. 472 pp. $16.75 paper.

Analyzes the close relationship between nutritional requirements of various age groups, population size, and the task of feeding the masses.

National Academy of Sciences. Committee on World Food, Health and Population. *Population and Food: Crucial Issues.* Washington, D.C.: National Academy of Sciences, 1975. 50 pp. $4.50.

Report of an expert committee suggests short-term global food needs are manageable but without population reduction the future outlook is alarming.

National Academy of Sciences. Subcommittee on Nutrition and Fertility. *Nutrition and Fertility Interrelationships: Implications for Policy and Action.* Washington, D.C.: National Academy of Sciences, 1975. 64 pp. $4.00.

The effects of nutrition on fertility as operating through conception and gestation variables and vice versa. Focus is on policies rather than research.

National Research Council. Commission on International Relations. World Food and Nutrition Study Steering Committee. *World Food and Nutrition Study: Interim Report.* Washington, D.C.: National Academy of Sciences, 1975. 55 pp.

Describes critical determinants of world food problem, identifies priority areas for research and steps to make such research efforts more effective. This volume is bound with *Recommended Actions on Nutrition Research and Development,* by the Food and Nutrition Board, Assembly of Life Sciences, National Research Council. 27 pp. Total price: $5.50.

New York Times Company. *Food and Population: The World in Crisis.* New York: Arno Press, 1976. 387 pp. $35.00.

A collection of *New York Times* articles from 1915 to 1975 chronicling key events and issues in the global food-population crisis.

Paddock, William and Paul Paddock. *Time of Famines: America and the World Food Crisis.* Boston: Little, Brown, 1976. 286 pp. $3.95 paper.

Famine-1975! with a new introduction and postscript. Discusses the problem of overpopulation and the capacity of agricultural production.

Penchef, Esther, ed. *Four Horsemen: Pollution, Poverty, Famine and Violence.* San Francisco: Canfield Press, 1971. 411 pp. $4.95.

A reader for courses on social problems and introductory sociology; includes articles on the population-food balance and hunger in the U.S.

Poleman, Thomas T. and Donald K. Freebairn, eds. *Food, Population and Employment: The Impact of the Green Revolution.* New York: Praeger, 1973. 273 pp. $16.50.

Papers from a 1971 Cornell workshop on the technical and social potential of increased food production in developing countries.

Population Reference Bureau. "Population and Affluence: Growing Pressures on World Food Resources." By Lester R. Brown. *Population Bulletin,* Vol. 29, No. 2, 1973. 32 pp. $1.00.

Views on the present world crisis and how it might be eased by an early promoter of the Green Revolution.

Simon, Paul and Arthur Simon. *The Politics of World Hunger: Grass-Roots Politics and World Poverty.* New York: Harpers Magazine Press, 1973. 249 pp. $16.00.

A critical review of development and economic assistance policies aimed at forming a political constituency to increase U.S. participation in global economic development.

Vicker, Ray. *This Hungry World.* New York: Scribner's Sons, 1975. 270 pp. $9.95.

Ranges from an eye-witness account of famine in Africa to discussion of how political motives play a part in the imbalance between population growth and food distribution.

Willett, Joseph W., ed. *The World Food Situation: Problems and Prospects to 1985.* 2 vols. Dobbs Ferry, N.Y.: Oceana, 1976. 1,136 pp. $70.00.

A compilation of basic documents, reports and articles from the U.N., U.S. Department of Agriculture, *Science* and two original analyses on the problems and issues related to the world food situation during the next decade.

C. POPULATION, RESOURCES, AND THE ENVIRONMENT

Anderson, Walt, ed. *Politics and Environment: A Reader in Ecological Crisis.* Pacific Palisades, Cal.: Goodyear, 1970. 362 pp. $8.95.

Articles on population, politics, pollution, the urban environment, and formulation of environmental policy.

Block, Donna. *Environmental Aspects of Economic Growth in Less Developed Countries: An Annotated Bibliography.* Paris: Development Centre of the Organisation for Economic Co-operation and Development, 1973. 111 pp.

Annotated listing of 430 books, articles and reports to mid-1973 chosen to reflect the fact that less-developed countries do not uniformly accept the richer countries' definitions of their problems.

Commoner, Barry. *The Closing Circle: Nature, Man and Technology.* New York: Bantam Books, 1972. 343 pp. $1.95.

A pioneer on environmental concerns addresses himself to the environmental equilibrium as manipulated by man and his social structure.

Cox, Peter C. and John Peel, eds. *Population and Pollution.* New York: Academic Press, 1972. 163 pp. $7.50.

A review of the current world situation, including anthropological studies of pollution in ancient and less developed societies.

Ehrlich, Paul R., Anne H. Ehrlich, and John P. Holdren. *Human Ecology: Problems and Solutions.* San Francisco: Freeman, 1973. 304 pp. $4.75.

A comprehensive introduction to human ecology, less detailed then *Population, Resources, Environment: Issues in Human Ecology* by same authors (next listing).

Ehrlich, Paul H. and Anne H. Ehrlich. *Population, Resources, Environment: Issues in Human Ecology.* 2nd ed. San Francisco: Freeman, 1972. 509 pp. $9.50.

Broad discussion of the causes and possible solutions for the present world population-resources-environment "crisis."

Hardin, Garrett, ed. *Exploring New Ethics for Survival.* New York: Viking, 1972. 273 pp. $7.95.

Poses the basic dilemma of the system of the commons, i.e. individual use of pasture lands held in common by the community operating in a world with an overtaxed carrying capacity. Population control through "mutual coercion, mutually agreed upon" and other provocative solutions are required for survival.

Hayes, Denis. *Energy: The Case for Conservation.* Worldwatch Paper Series No. 4. Washington, D.C.: Worldwatch Institute, 1976. 77 pp. $2.00.

More fuel than consumed by two-thirds the world's population could be saved through conservation in the U.S.

Holdren, John P. and Paul R. Ehrlich, eds. *Global Ecology: Readings Toward a Rational Strategy for Man.* New York: Harcourt Brace/Javanovich, 1971. 295 pp. $6.40 paper.

Articles cover resource realities, environmental problems, population policies.

Huddle, Norie and Michael Reich. *Island of Dreams: Environmental Crisis in Japan.* New York: Autumn Press, 1975. 351 pp. $4.95 paper.

Environmental effects of Japan's miraculous economic growth and their impact on social values.

Jackson, Wesley, S., ed. *Man and the Environment.* Dubuque, Iowa: Brown Publishers, 1973. 329 pp. $4.95 paper.

A collection of 97 articles on the biological and historical roots of the ecological crisis, pollution, conservation, population growth, birth control policies and methods, and future shortages of food and natural resources.

Loo, Chalsa. *Crowding and Behavior.* New York: MSS Information Corp., 1974. 245 pp. $6.25 paper.

Series of articles on the demographic causes and effects of population density, and theoretical approaches to analyzing the effect of crowding on human behavior.

Macmillan Information Division. *Environmental Pollution: A Guide to Current Research.* New York: Macmillan Information, 1971. 851 pp. $29.95.

Produced from data gathered by the Smithsonian Institution in 1969 and 1970. Annotated bibliography divided into three broad subject areas: Ecological Systems, Physical Sciences Applied to Pollution, and Effects of Air and Water Pollution.

Maddox, John. *The Doomsday Syndrome.* New York: McGraw-Hill, 1972. 280 pp. $6.95.

A critique of environmentalists' concerns and doomsday theories of overpopulation.

Marden, Parker G. and Dennis Hodgson, eds. *Population, Environment and the Quality of Life.* New York: Halsted Press, 1975. 328 pp. $4.95 paper.

An introduction by the editors and an anthology of controversial articles on population growth as a crisis and its environmental, ecological, and economic impact, especially in the U.S.

Micklin, Michael, ed. *Population, Environment and Social Organization: Current Issues in Human Ecology.* Hinsdale, Ill.: Dryden Press, 1973. 509 pp. $5.95 paper.

An anthology of articles and a framework for the analysis of organizational aspects of ecological adaptation, focusing on ways to create equilibrium between population and environment.

Miller, Tyler G. *Replenish the Earth: A Primer in Human Ecology.* Belmont, Cal.: Wadsworth, 1972. 199 pp. $3.95 paper.

Introduction to population dynamics and the problems of pollution and consumption as part of a concern about the global life-support system.

Revelle, Roger, Ashok Khosla, and Maris Vinovskis. *The Survival Equation: Man, Resources and His Environment.* Boston, Mass.: Houghton Mifflin, 1971. 508 pp. $6.95 paper.

A collection of 38 articles on determinants and consequences of population growth, programs and views of fertility control, resource depletion, food production, environmental deterioration and ways for improvement.

Treshow, Michael. *The Human Environment.* New York: McGraw-Hill, 1976. 396 pp. $7.95 paper.

Discusses the past correlates of population growth, the environmental problems associated with current population and industrial growth, and future considerations for survival.

U.S. Council on Environmental Quality. *Environmental Quality—1975: Sixth Annual Report.* Washington, D.C.: Government Printing Office, 1975. 763 pp. $6.00.

Wide-ranging review of growing threats to the environment and international efforts to deal with them.

U.S. Environmental Protection Agency. Office of Research and Development. Environmental Studies Division. *Alternative Futures and Environmental Quality.* Washington, D.C.: Government Printing Office, 1973. 242 pp. Out of print.

Collection of reports on the nature of the environmental crisis, implications of zero population growth, the ecosystem capacity, and international and behavioral implications of alternative growth policies.

Waldron Ingrid and R. E. Ricklefs. *Environment and Population: Problems and Solutions.* New York: Holt, Rinehart, and Winston, 1973. 240 pp. $4.00 paper.

Integrated analysis of environment and population problems.

Ward, Barbara and Rene Dubos. *Only One Earth: The Care and Maintenance of a Small Planet.* New York: Norton, 1972. 225 pp. $6.95.

An unofficial report commissioned by the Secretary-General of the 1972 U.N. Conference on the Human Environment with assistance from consultants in 58 countries. Examines environmental problems in international perspective; discusses development, imbalance, worldwide problems of urbanization and pollution, misuse of resources and the impact of technology.

D. CULTURE, ETHICS, EDUCATION, AND POPULATION CHANGE

Callahan, Daniel. *Ethics and Population Limitation.* New York: The Population Council; distributed by Key Book Service, Bridgeport, Conn., 1971. 45 pp. $3.95 paper.

Discussion of the moral rights of individuals versus obligations of government and society in confronting problems of excessive population growth.

Educational Facilities Laboratories. *Fewer Pupils—Surplus Space.* New York: Educational Facilities Laboratories, 1974. 55 pp.

The implications of shrinking school enrollment in the U.S. since 1969 due to the "baby bust".

Hastings Center. *Bibliography of Society, Ethics and the Life Sciences.* Compiled by Sharmon Sollitto and Robert M. Veatch, and revised by Diane Fenner. Hastings-on-Hudson, N.Y.: Institute of Society, Ethics and the Life Sciences, 1975. 56 pp. $4.00.

Latest partially annotated bibliography from this Center of published materials on medical ethical issues involved in a range of population processes, e.g. death and dying, birth, genetics, birth and behavior control.

Janssen, L. H. *Population Problems and Catholic Responsibility.* Tilburg, The Netherlands: Tilburg University Press, 1975. 196 pp. $18.50.

Proceedings of an international symposium, includes reports on Asia, Africa, Latin America, and theological views of birth control, both Catholic and Protestant.

Jones, Gavin. *Population Growth and Educational Planning in Developing Nations.* A Population Council Book. New York: Halsted Press, 1975. 238 pp. $14.95.

Relationship between fertility rates and educational enrollment, attainment, and planning, with Thailand, Singapore, and Sri Lanka as case studies.

McCormack, Arthur. *The Population Explosion: A Christian Concern.* New York: Harper & Row, 1973. 78 pp. $1.95.

The attitude and future role of the Catholic Church reconsidered in view of population growth and its consequences.

McLeod, Betty, ed. *Demography and Educational Planning.* Toronto: The Ontario Institute for Studies in Education, 1970. 272 pp.

Reports on the impact of migration and fertility patterns and implications for educational planning.

Moerman, Joseph and Michael Ingram, eds. *The Population Problem: A Challenge to the People of our Time.* London: Search Press, 1975. 148 pp. £1.95.

Vatican-disapproved report of church experts, based on work of the loosely organized Conference of International Catholic Organizations, which "presents what responsible Catholics from many countries really think about contraception and related sociological and psychological questions in a world-demographic setting."

Muhsam, Helmut V., ed. *Education and Population: Mutual Impacts.* Published for the International Union for the Scientific Study of Population (IUSSP) by Ordina Editions, 9 route de Goé, 4830 Dolhain, Belgium, 1975. 337 pp. $13.75.

Systematic review of the interrelations between education and population factors and trends by a dozen experts from around the world; sponsored by the IUSSP Scientific Committee on Education and Demography established at the second World Population Conference, Belgrade, 1965.

Population Reference Bureau. "Catholic Perspectives on Population Issues." By Francis X. Murphy and Joseph F. Erhart. *Population Bulletin,* Vol. 30, No. 6, 1975. 31 pp. $1.00.

Two experts present a clear, concise background for understanding the controversy aroused within (and outside) the Roman Catholic Church by the 1968 Encyclical *Humanae Vitae* which reaffirmed traditional papal condemnation of all "artificial" means of contraception.

Population Reference Bureau. "Literacy and World Population." By the staff of World Education, Inc. *Population Bulletin,* Vol. 30, No. 2, 1975. 29 pp. $1.00.

Summarizes world literacy situation in 1970 and shows important role of literacy in socioeconomic progress. Also describes a successful functional education program in Thailand.

Smithsonian Institution. The Center for the Study of Man. *Cultural Consequences of Population Change.* Washington, D.C.: Smithsonian Institution, 1975. 402 pp.

Report of a seminar concurrent with the 1974 World Population Conference, and papers covering Bangladesh, Ghana, Indonesia, Kenya, Malawi, Nigeria, Philippines, Sri Lanka.

Subbiah, B. V. *The Tragedy of a Papal Decree (In a Crowded World).* New York: Vantage Press, 1971. 144 pp. $3.95.

The author, himself a Hindu, reviews the troubling consequences of the encyclical *Humanae Vitae* in an almost entirely demographic approach.

Ta Ngoc Châu. *Population Growth and Costs of Education in Developing Countries.* Paris: International Institute for Educational Planning, UNESCO, 1972. 313 pp. $7.00.

Tries to isolate the factors behind increasing pressures on educational systems (e.g. enrollment increases, need for qualitative improvement, long-term trends of unit costs) in order to highlight the effect of population growth on educational costs; includes four country case studies.

Tinker, Irene B. et al, eds. *Culture and Population Change.* Rev. ed. Washington, D.C.: American Association for the Advancement of Science, 1976. 80 pp. $3.50.

Examines cultural factors in population processes and the need for governments to integrate such factors into population policies.

U.S. Department of Health, Education, and Welfare. National Center for Education Statistics. *Projections of Educational Statistics to 1983-1984.* Washington, D.C.: Government Printing Office, 1975. 171 pp. $2.50.

Projections for enrollment in elementary, high school and higher educational institutions, earned degrees, demand for teachers, and expenditures.

Walters, LeRoy, ed. *Bibliography of Bioethics.* Vol. 1. Detroit: Gale Research Co., 1975. 225 pp. $24.00.

Major bibliographic work being compiled by the Center for Bioethics, Kennedy Institute, Georgetown University, on all areas of medical ethics, most related to population issues, e.g. population policies, right to reproduce, determination of death, availability of contraceptives to minors. Vol. 1 covers articles published in 1973; new volumes to be produced annually. In addition, a computerized search service of the Center's data base will be available to the public by 1977 for a minimal fee.

World Bank. *Education: Sector Working Paper.* Washington, D.C.: World Bank, 1974. 73 pp. Free.

Presents development strategies, and information on international educational trends, including comparative educational indicators in relation to population factors.

Wogaman, Philip, ed. *The Population Crisis and Moral Responsibility.* Washington, D.C.: Public Affairs Press, 1973. 339 pp. $7.50.

The views of 34 ethicists, theologians and population experts from Protestant, Catholic and Jewish religious traditions.

X. Population and Economic Development

A. DEVELOPED COUNTRIES

Daedalus. "The No-Growth Society." Special issue, Vol. 102, No. 4, Fall 1973. Boston: The American Academy of Arts and Sciences. 253 pp. $2.95.

Fourteen articles on the problems, desirability, and implications of both zero population and zero economic growth.

Denton, Frank T. and Byron G. Spencer. *Population and the Economy.* Lexington, Mass.: Lexington Books, 1975. 180 pp. $16.50.

A series of macromodels to investigate interaction of economic and demographic phenomena.

Habbakuk, H. J. *Population Growth and Economic Development since 1750.* New York: Humanities Press, 1971. 110 pp. $3.25.

Collection of lectures on historical and contemporary relationship between economic and population trends in England and Europe and the implications for the developing world.

Koeltzer, Victor et al, eds. *Population and Development: Alternative Futures in the West.* Fort Collins, Col.: Colorado State University, 1974. 365 pp.

Presents seven scenarios for alternative futures, taking environmental and growth aspects into account.

Mishan, E. J. *Technology and Growth: The Price We Pay.* New York: Praeger, 1970. 193 pp. $2.95 paper.

Discusses the consequences of the growth mystique in an affluent society in terms of city and transport congestion, the false belief in consumer sovereignty, and technological solutions.

Westoff, Charles F. et al. *Toward the End of Growth: Population in America.* Englewood Cliffs, N.J.: Prentice-Hall, 1973. 177 pp. $2.45 paper.

Current status of U.S. population growth, future prospects, and their ramifications.

B. LESS DEVELOPED COUNTRIES

Bairuch, Paul. *Urban Employment in Developing Countries.* Geneva: International Labour Office, 1973. 100 pp.

Urbanization in advance of economic growth and industrialization as causes of unemployment with suggestions for remedies.

Baldwin, Robert E. *Economic Development and Growth.* 2nd ed. New York: Wiley, 1972. 160 pp. $4.75 paper.

Covers the nature of growth problems in less developed countries and theories concerning key relationships. Includes population issues.

Brown, Lester R. *Seeds of Change: The Green Revolution and Development in the 1970's.* New York: Praeger, 1970. 205 pp. $6.95.

Discusses the technological breakthrough, the business of transferring technology, and second generation problems such as sharing the benefits, marketing, and rural-urban migration.

Coale, Ansley, J., ed. *Economic Factors in Population Growth.* New York: Wiley, 1976. 600 pp. $42.50.

Proceedings of a 1973 International Economic Association Conference. Nineteen leading economists and demographers discuss optimum population size, micro and macro factors affecting fertility, employment and other issues in different countries.

Enke, Stephen and Richard A. Brown. *Old Age Insurance with Fewer Children.* Paper No. 72TMP-6. Santa Barbara, Cal.: Center for Advanced Studies, General Electric TEMPO, 1972. 22 pp.

Five models demonstrate that prompting judicious birth spacing in less developed countries could slow population growth while not reducing the chances of each couple's having a surviving son when the father reaches age 65.

Erb, Guy F. and Valeriana Kallab, eds. *Beyond Dependency: The Development World Speaks Out.* Washington, D.C.: Overseas Development Council, 1975. 238 pp. $3.95 paper.

A collection of essays by Third World spokesmen on the economic demands of the poorer nations of the South.

Ford Foundation. *Social Science Research on Population and Development.* New York: Ford Foundation, 1975. 354 pp. Free.

Papers presented at a 1974 Ford Foundation conference by leading researchers in the field, resource persons from the developing world and representatives of donor agencies.

Grant, James P. *Growth from Below: A People Oriented Development Strategy.* Washington, D.C.: Overseas Development Council, 1973. 32 pp. $0.50.

Calls for social services and public programs to improve the quality of life for the world's poorest people.

Gray, H. Peter and Shanti S. Tangri, eds. *Economic Development and Population Growth: A Conflict?* Lexington, Mass.: D.C. Heath, 1970. 162 pp. Out of print.

A collection of articles by historical and modern authorities on the pressures of population growth and experiences with birth control programs.

Hansen, Roger D. et al. *The U.S. and World Development: Agenda for Action 1976.* Washington, D.C.: Overseas Development Council, 1976. 240 pp. $4.25.

The Council's fourth annual assessment of current U.S. economic policies towards the Third World.

Jones, Gavin W. and S. Selvaratnam. *Population Growth and Economic Development in Ceylon.* Colombo: Hansa Publishers, 1972. 249 pp. $3.00.

Relationship between rapid population growth and economic development with Ceylon (Sri Lanka) as a case study.

Keeley, Michael C., ed. *Population, Public Policy, and Economic Development.* New York, N.Y.: Praeger, 1976. 259 pp. $17.50.

Policy-oriented technical analysis of the economic benefits of slowing population growth, based on findings by population researchers at General Electrics TEMPO Center for Advanced Study under Stephen Enke.

King, Timothy, ed. *Population Policies and Economic Development: A World Bank Staff Report.* Baltimore: Johns Hopkins University Press, 1974. 214 pp. $3.50 paper.

Examines current evidence and theory on the relationship between population growth and economic development and the rationale for and administrative concerns of family planning programs.

McNamara, Robert S. *One Hundred Countries, Two Billion People.* New York: Praeger, 1973. 140 pp. $1.95 paper.

Public statements of the President of the World Bank emphasizing the need for development strategies which meet the needs of the poorest 40 percent of the population in the developing world.

Perlman, Mark et al, eds. *Spatial, Regional and Population Economics: Essays.* New York: Gordon and Breach, 1973. 392 pp. $30.00.

Writings of well-known demographers describing the relationships between economics and factors of demographic change in developing and developed countries.

Pitchford, J. D. *Population in Economic Growth.* New York: American Elsevier, 1974. 280 pp. $21.20.

Technical analysis of approaches to long-run optimum population size under different economic assumptions concerning resource usage, returns to scale, and international trade.

Pitchford, J. D. *The Economics of Population: An Introduction.* Canberra: Australian National University Press, 1974. 100 pp. $8.65.

Less technical, more concise version of the above, written for the undergraduate.

Plant, Robert. *Population and Labour.* English, French and Spanish editions. Geneva: International Labour Office, 1973. 163 pp. $6.95.

Discusses international effect of high rates of population growth on the labor force.

Robinson, Warren C., ed. *Population and Development Planning.* New York: The Population Council, 1975. 263 pp. $3.95 paper.

Ten specialists examine interaction between demographic processes and sectors of prime importance to development planning, e.g. education, employment, health, income distribution, resources, and the environment.

Robinson, Warren C. and David E. Horlacher. "Population Growth and Economic Welfare." *Reports on Population/Family Planning,* No. 6. New York: The Population Council, February 1971. 39 pp. Free.

Critical review of literature on cost-benefit analysis of population growth, discussion of the emerging economic theory of family formation, and examination of population programs in light of theoretical welfare economics.

Ruprecht, Theodore K. and Carl Wahren. *Population Programmes and Economic and Social Development.* Paris: Development Centre of the Organisation for Economic Co-operation and Development, 1970. 141 pp. $2.75.

Analyzes the population variable in economic development and the demographic impact of birth control programs in developing countries.

Smith, Robert S., Frank T. DeVyver, and William R. Allen, compilers. *Population Economics: Selected Essays of Joseph J. Spengler.* Durham, N.C.: Duke University Press, 1972. 536 pp. $19.75.

Seventeen essays by this noted Duke University economist, discussing historical and current economic theories of population, the present problem, and the economic climate of developing nations.

Spengler, Joseph J. *Population Change, Modernization, and Welfare.* Englewood Cliffs, N.J.: Prentice-Hall, 1974. 182 pp. $3.95 paper.

An economic analysis of the implications of changing population size, distribution and age composition for socioeconomic planning and population policy.

Tabah, Leon, ed. *Population Growth and Economic Development in the Third World.* 2 vols. Published for the International Union for the Scientific Study of Population by Ordina Editions, 9, route de Goé, 4830 Dolhain, Belgium, 1976. 820 pp. $35.00.

Twenty-one authorities review the manifold impact of population pressures on the functioning of society and lay out a broad corrective strategy for development.

TEMPO. Center for Advanced Studies. *The Economics of Slowing Population Growth.* Paper No. 71TMP-42. By David N. Holmes, Jr. Santa Barbara, Cal.: Center for Advanced Studies, General Electric TEMPO, 1971. 60 pp.

Well organized general review of the economic benefits of slowing population growth, intended as basis for an illustrated lecture; one of a TEMPO series based on the pioneering work of Stephen Enke.

United Nations. Department of Economic and Social Affairs. *World Economic Survey. Part 1: Population and Development.* Sales No. 74.II.C.Part 1. New York: United Nations, 1974. 148 pp. $7.00.

A statistical analysis of population and economic development in developing, developed and socialist countries.

World Bank. *Population Planning: Sector Working Paper.* Washington, D.C. World Bank, 1972. 84 pp. Free.

Reviews the economic effect of present population growth rates in developing countries, progress in funding and potential of family planning programs, and world demographic data.

XI. Population Policies and Laws

Bachrach, Peter and Elihu Bergman. *Power and Choice: The Formulation of American Population Policy.* Lexington, Mass.: Lexington Books, 1973. 130 pp. $10.50.

Comprehensive review of how U.S. population-relevant policy has been formulated and developed.

Back, Kurt and James Fawcett, eds. "Population Policy and the Person: Congruence or Conflict?" Special issue of *Journal of Social Issues,* Vol. 30, No. 4, 1974. Ann Arbor, Mich.: Society for the Psychological Study of Social Issues. 324 pp. $3.00.

Seventeen leading psychologists and sociologists discuss current knowledge and theories in psychology which could provide practical guidance to population policymakers.

Berelson, Bernard. *The Great Debate on Population Policy: An Instructive Entertainment.* New York: The Population Council, 1975. 40 pp. $2.00 paper.

Actual quotes from the literature throw into sharp focus current conflicting views on population policy of the developer ("Dev-Dev"), family planner ("FamPlan") and academic critic ("AcCrit").

Berelson, Bernard, ed. *Population Policy in Developed Countries.* A Population Council Book. New York: McGraw-Hill, 1974. 793 pp. $17.50.

National specialists report on the demographic situation and policy response in 24 developed countries with an analytical summary by the editor.

Bergman, Elihu et al, eds. *Population Policymaking in the American States.* Lexington, Mass.: Lexington Books, 1974. 336 pp. $17.50.

Seventeen articles on the formulation, substance and process of population policymaking at the state level in the U.S.

Chen, Kan et al. *Growth Policy: Population, Environment, and Beyond.* Ann Arbor, Mich.: University of Michigan Press, 1974. 237 pp. $2.95 paper.

Describes a total system or "synoptic" approach to population-environmental policymaking.

Clinton, Richard L., William Flash, and R. Kenneth Godwin, eds. *Political Science in Population Studies.* Lexington, Mass.: Lexington Books, 1972. 195 pp. $12.00.

The political context of population programs and processes.

Clinton, Richard L. and R. Kenneth Godwin, eds. *Research in the Politics of Population.* Lexington, Mass.: Lexington Books, 1972. 196 pp. $11.00.

Nine studies investigate U.S. population policies and compare them with those of other countries with recommendations for alternative government programs.

Dienes, C. Thomas. *Law, Politics and Birth Control.* Chicago: University of Illinois Press, 1972. 374 pp. $15.00.

Political context of the U.S. birth control movement from its 19th century beginnings.

Driver, Edwin D. *Essays on Population Policy.* Lexington, Mass.: Lexington Books, 1972. 222 pp. $13.50.

Discussion of the impact of U.S. government policies and Third World family planning programs on fertility and need for expanded social science and legal research on population policy.

Driver, Edwin D. *World Population Policies: An Annotated Bibliography.* Lexington, Mass.: Lexington Books, 1972. 1,308 pp. $35.00.

Includes over 3,500 items covering the whole range of demographic variables.

The Fletcher School of Law and Diplomacy. *Law and Population Monograph Series.* Medford, Mass.: Law and Population Programme, The Fletcher School of Law and Diplomacy, Tufts University. Pages vary from 55-130 approximately. $1.00 per monograph; free to developing countries.

A continuing series of monographs written by country experts, presenting findings of the Law and Population Programme, executed by the United Nations Fund for Population Activities through the Fletcher School of Law and Diplomacy of Tufts University, under direction of an International Advisory Committee on Population and Law. Reviews legal statutes and their direct and indirect effect on fertility-regulating practice and programs, government population policies and current demographic trends.

Following is a partial listing of titles available as of mid-1976:

1. *Law and Family Planning,* by Luke T. Lee (1971).

2. *Brief Survey of U.S. Population Law,* by Harriet F. Pilpel (1971).

3. *Law and Population Growth in Eastern Europe,* by Peter B. Maggs (1972).

4. *Legal Aspects of Family Planning in Indonesia,* by the Committee on Legal Aspects of the Indonesian Planned Parenthood Association (1972).

8. *The World's Laws on Voluntary Sterilization for Family Planning Purposes,* by Jan Stepan and Edmund H. Kellogg (1973).

9. *Law and Population Growth in Singapore,* by Peter Hall (1973).

10. *Law and Population Growth in Jamaica,* by Robert C. Rosen (1973).

11. *Law and Population Growth in the United Kingdom,* by Diana M. Kloss and Bertram L. Raisbeck (1973).

12. *Law and Population Growth in France,* by Jacques Doublet and Hubert de Villedary (1973).

14. *Brief Survey of Abortion Laws of Five Largest Countries,* by Luke T. Lee (1973).

15. *Anti-Contraception Laws in Sub-Saharan Francophone Africa: Sources and Ramifactions,* by Bernard Wolf (1973).

18. *Population and the Role of Law in the Americas.* Proceedings of a Seminar of the Human Rights Committee at the 18th Conference of the Inter-American Bar Association (1974).

19. *Legal Aspects of Menstrual Regulation,* by Luke T. Lee and John M. Paxman (1974).

21. *Law and Population Growth in Iran,* by Parviz Saney (1974).

22. *Law and Population Growth in Kenya,* by U. U. Uche (1974).

23. *Law and Population Growth in Mexico,* by Gerardo Cornejo, Alan Keller, Susana Lerner, and Leandro Azuara (1975).

24. *The Impact of Law on Family Planning in Australia,* by H. A. Finlay (1975).

25. *The World's Laws and Practices on Population and Sexuality Education,* by Edmund H. Kellogg, David K. Kline, and Jan Stepan (1975).

26. *Pregnancy and Abortion in Adolescence: Legal Aspects,* by Luke T. Lee and John M. Paxman (1975).

29. *Law and Population in Lebanon,* by George M. Dib (1975).

30. *Annual Review of Population Law, 1974, International Advisory Committee on Population and Law* (1975).

31. *Law and Population Growth in Chile,* by José Sulbrandt and Maria Alicia Ferrera (1975).

32. *Law and the Status of Colombian Women,* by Josefina Amezquita de Almeyda (1975).

33. *Law and Population Growth in Ghana,* by Richard B. Turkson (1975).

34. *Law and Population in Brazil,* by Walter Rodrigues et al (1975).

Godwin, R. Kenneth, ed. *Comparative Policy Analysis: The Study of Population Policy Determinants in Developing Countries.* Lexington, Mass.: Lexington Books, 1975. 333 pp. $17.00.

Thirteen experts discuss alternative frameworks for analysis of population policy in developing countries.

Gray, Virginia and Elihu Bergman. *Political Issues in U.S. Population Policy.* Lexington, Mass.: Lexington Books, 1974. 240 pp. $14.50.

Eleven political scientists discuss such topics as the policy implications of urban growth, the reaction of blacks and women to population policies, and ethical questions.

Ilchman, Warren F. et al, eds. *Policy Sciences and Population.* Lexington, Mass.: Lexington Books, 1975. 320 pp. $17.00.

Papers from a Harvard Center for Population Studies seminar on the application of policy sciences to problems of population policy with case studies from Kenya, Nigeria, Sudan, Indonesia, Brazil, India, Malaysia and the U.S.

Kirk, Maurice, Massimo Livi Bacci, and Egon Szabady, eds. *Law and Fertility in Europe: A Study of Legislation Directly or Indirectly Affecting Fertility in Europe.* 2 vols. Published for the International Union of the Scientific Study of Population by Ordina Editions, 9 route de Goé, 4830 Dolhain, Belgium, 1975. 336 and 698 pp. $30.00.

Demographers, sociologists and jurists from 21 European countries describe the national framework of law and statutory regulations within which the norms of family life are set and which in turn affect fertility behavior.

Lee, Luke T. and Arthur Larson, eds. *Population and Law.* Durham, N.C.: Rule of Law Press, 1971. 452 pp.

Reviews the population situation and relevant laws for 13 Asian, European, and Middle East countries, with articles on Islamic countries in general and the United Nations.

National Academy of Sciences. *In Search of Population Policy: Views from the Developing World.* Washington, D.C., 1974. 109 pp. Free.

A report on five 1973 seminars conducted in South Asia, the Middle East, Latin America-Caribbean, Africa, and Southeast Asia, presenting the views of policymakers and scholars of the region on the policy aspects of population issues in their area.

National Urban League. *Population Policy and the Black Community.* Washington, D.C.: Research Department, National Urban League, 1974. 95 pp. plus appendices.

Thorough review of how U.S. blacks view and are affected by official population (primarily family planning) policy.

Organisation for Economic Co-operation and Development (OECD). *Population: A Progress Report.* Paris: OECD, 1974. 43 pp. $2.00.

Short overview of trends in world population growth, policies, programs and foreign assistance in 1974.

Paxman, John N., ed. *The World Population Crisis: Policy Implications and the Role of Law.* Charlottesville, Va.: John Bassett Moore Society, 1971. 173 pp.

Papers and proceedings of a conference on international law and population.

Piotrow, Phyllis T. *World Population Crisis: The United States Response.* New York: Praeger, 1973. 276 pp. $17.50.

Recounts and analyzes the events which mobilized the U.S. government to subsidize birth control services in the U.S. and overseas.

Population Information Program. George Washington University Medical Center. "Recent Law and Policy Changes in Fertility Control." By Brenda J. Vumbaco. *Population Reports,* Series E, No. 4, March 1976. 12 pp. Free.

Review of 1974–75 changes in the laws and policies of some 40 countries which affect family planning.

Population Reference Bureau. "Policies on Population Around the World." Prepared by Richard Schroeder. *Population Bulletin,* Vol. 29, No. 6, 1973. 36 pp. $1.00.

Discusses the concept, history, and varying types of population policy, and surveys current policies in selected countries.

Simmons, Ozzie G. and Lyle Saunders. *The Present and Prospective State of Policy Approaches to Fertility.* Papers of the East-West Population Institute No. 33. Honolulu: East-West Center, 1975. 26 pp. Free.

Urges that population policy research focus only on policy explicitly intended to induce fertility reduction and suggests use of policy analysts to improve interaction between researchers and policymakers.

Smith, T. E., ed. *The Politics of Family Planning in the Third World:* Allen & Unwin, 1973. 352 pp. $7.50.

Population policymaking processes in English-speaking developing countries with case studies of Kenya, Mauritius, Fiji, Singapore, Malaysia, Sri Lanka, and sub-Saharan Africa.

Smithsonian Institution. *Comparative Study of World Law on Contraceptives: Revised and Updated.* By Jan Stepan and Edmund H. Kellogg. Occasional Monograph Series No. 1. Washington, D.C.: Interdisciplinary Communications Program, Smithsonian Institution, 1974. 102 pp. Free.

A review and analysis of laws, regulations, and judicial decisions affecting contraception in 67 countries.

Smithsonian Institution. *The Policy Relevance of Recent Social Science Research on Fertility.* By William P. McGreevey and Nancy Birdsall. Occasional Monograph Series

No. 2. Washington, D.C.: Interdisciplinary Communication Program, Smithsonian Institution, 1974. 109 pp. Free.

Evaluation of recent research on determinants of fertility and impact of family planning programs with a view to identifying policy-manipulable approaches to fertility reduction.

Sundquist, James L. *Dispersing Population: What America can Learn From Europe.* Washington, D.C.: Brookings Institute, 1975. 288 pp. $3.95 paper.

Reviews policies in Britain, France, Italy, The Netherlands and Sweden designed to check growth in overcongested areas and develop lagging regions.

Thompson, Vaida D., Mark I. Applebaum, and James E. Allen. *Population Policy Acceptance: Psychological Determinants.* Chapel Hill, N.C.: Carolina Population Center, 1974. 110 pp. $5.00.

A report on psychological theories of population policies and the development of instruments with which to test them.

United Nations. Department of Economic and Social Affairs. *Measures, Policies and Programmes Affecting Fertility, with Particular Reference to National Family Planning Programmes.* Population Studies No. 51. English/French/Russian/Spanish. Sales No. E.72.XIII.2. New York: United Nations, 1972. 162 pp. $3.00.

Discusses social, economic and other measures which affect fertility, current population policies, and many aspects of family planning programs around the world.

United Nations Fund for Population Activities (UNFPA). *Law and Population.* Population Profiles No. 2. New York: UNFPA, 1976. 42 pp. $1.50.

Background and compilation of findings from 25 country projects in the UNFPA/Fletcher School of Law and Diplomacy worldwide study of laws affecting population trends.

United Nations Fund for Population Activities (UNFPA). *The Symposium on Law and Population: Proceedings, Background Papers and Recommendations.* New York: UNFPA, 1975. 309 pp. $5.00.

Full documentation from a June 1974 symposium in Tunis which together with ongoing Law and Population Projects around the world and subsequent regional seminars forms part of an international effort to relate law and human rights to population.

XII. Fertility Control

A. FAMILY PLANNING

Abel-Smith, Brian. *People without Choice: Report of the 21st Anniversary Conference of the International Planned Parenthood Federation (IPPF).* London: IPPF, 1974. 68 pp. £1.50.

Broad review of the worldwide status of family planning as of end 1973, and role of the IPPF.

Alan Guttmacher Institute. *Data and Analyses for 1976 Revision of DHEW Five Year Plan for Family Planning Services.* New York: Alan Guttmacher Institute, Planned Parenthood Federation of America, 1976. $4.00.

Fourth in an annual series prepared by the Alan Guttmacher Institute which uses data generated by the National Reporting System for Family Planning Services of the U.S. Department of Health, Education, and Welfare and census data to monitor trends in U.S. women needing such services, patients served and their characteristics.

Bloch, Lucille Stephenson, ed. *Population Change: A Strategy for Physicians.* Washington, D.C.: Association of American Medical Colleges, 1976. 255 pp. $3.00.

Emphasizes the important role of the physician as practitioner, family counselor, teacher, educator and research scientist in the field of fertility.

Bogue, Donald, ed. *Further Sociological Contributions to Family Planning Research.* Chicago: University of Chicago Press, 1970. 455 pp. $6.95.

National case studies on attitudes and behavior towards family planning as determined by traditionalism, religious and psychological factors and the program impact itself.

Cartwright, Ann. *Parents and Family Planning Services.* Chicago: Aldine Press, 1970. 293 pp. $11.95.

Findings from a 1967-68 survey of parents and family planning professionals reveal the obstacles to effective contraception in England and Wales at that time.

Cernada, George P., ed. *Taiwan Family Planning Reader: How a Program Works.* Taichung, Taiwan: The Chinese Center for International Training in Family Planning, 1970. 381 pp.

Description of one of the first, successful countrywide efforts to reduce fertility in a developing nation.

Cernada, George and T. H. Sun. *Knowledge into Action: The Use of Research in Taiwan's Family Planning Program.* Papers of the East-West Communication Institute No. 10. Honolulu: East-West Center, 1974. 44 pp. Free.

Practical guide to research utilization in population planning programs illustrated by five case studies from Taiwan.

Chandrasekaran, C. and Albert I. Hermalin, eds. *Measuring the Effect of Family Planning Programs on Fertility.* Published for the International Union for the Scientific Study of Population by Ordina Editions, 9 route de Goé, 4830 Dolhain, Belgium, 1976. 570 pp. $23.75.

Description and analysis of the most important family planning evaluation techniques by authors from the fields of demography, statistics, program administration, medicine and public health.

Chasteen, Edgar R. *The Case for Compulsory Birth Control.* Englewood Cliffs, N.J.: Prentice-Hall, 1972. 230 pp. $1.95 paper.

    Argues that overpopulation in the U.S. should be seen as a national health problem and compulsory birth control as preventive medicine.

Columbia University. International Institute for the Study of Human Reproduction. *Manuals for Evaluation of Family Planning and Population Programs.* List and individual manuals available free from the Division of Social and Administrative Sciences, International Institute for the Study of Human Reproduction, Columbia University, 78 Haven Ave., New York, N.Y. 10032.

    Manuals presenting frameworks for evaluating family planning programs, checklists for evaluative overviews, methods of estimating future caseloads, etc.

Cuca, Roberto and Catherine S. Pierce. *Experimentation in Family Planning Delivery Systems.* A World Bank Report. Forthcoming, 1977.

    The first comprehensive review to evaluate 96 innovative family planning delivery schemes in terms of their usefulness in providing guidelines for improving regular programs and for further potentially fruitful experimentation.

Cutright, Philip and Frederick S. Jaffe. *Determinants and Demographic Impact of Organized Family Planning Programs in the United States: 1969-1970.* New York: Alan Guttmacher Institute, Planned Parenthood Federation of America. Forthcoming November 1976.

    Final report of an Alan Guttmacher Institute study which systematically evaluates the impact on fertility of the U.S. family planning clinic program, independent of other social, economic and cultural factors, utilizing county-level data on clinic enrollment in 1969 and 1970 county-level census data on women of reproductive age and their children. A monograph based on the study, *Do Family Planning Programs Reduce Fertility? The United States Experience,* will be published by Praeger in 1976.

Duncan, G. W. et al, eds. *Fertility Control Methods: Strategies for Introduction.* New York: Academic Press, 1972. 230 pp. $7.50.

    Based on a workshop convened by the Batelle Population Study Center, identifies promising procedures and research needed to upgrade family planning program efforts in culturally diverse settings.

Freedman, Ronald and Bernard Berelson. "The Record of Family Planning Programs." *Studies in Family Planning,* Vol. 7, No. 1. New York: The Population Council, January 1976. 40 pp. Free.

    With empirical data and objective, perceptive analysis, two leading authorities attempt to resolve the crucial current controversy over the relative importance of family planning programs and "modernization" in effecting fertility reduction in developing countries, concluding that both are necessary and suggesting next steps for study and action.

George Washington University Medical Center. Department of Medical and Public Affairs. Population Information Program. *Population Reports.* 2001 S. St. N.W., Washington, D.C. 20009. Free.

    Bimonthly, compact, comprehensive reports on technological developments in fertility control and related issues, issued under the following eleven general series titles. For listing of individual report titles and to be placed on the mailing list write the above address.

Series
A. Oral Contraceptives
B. Intrauterine Devices
C. Sterilization, Female
D. Sterilization, Male
E. Law and Policy
F. Pregnancy Termination
G. Prostaglandins
H. Barrier Methods
I. Periodic Abstinence
J. Family Planning Programs
K. Injectables and Implants

Green, Lawrence W. et al. *The Dacca Family Planning Experiment.* Pacific Health Education Reports No. 3. Berkeley, Cal.: School of Public Health, University of California, 1972. 169 pp. Out of print.

    Comparison of family planning educational programs aimed at groups of husbands only, wives only, and both concurrently. Findings suggest the latter as the most fruitful approach for developing countries.

Guttmacher, Alan. *Pregnancy, Birth and Family Planning.* New York: Viking, 1973. 365 pp. $10.00.

    Updated and expanded edition of a family planning pioneer's classic guide for expectant parents.

International Planned Parenthood Federation (IPPF). *Family Planning in Five Continents.* London: IPPF. Published annually since 1967. Latest issued November 1975. 28 pp. $1.45, plus postage.

    Concise summary of family planning policy, practice, programs and funding, plus basic demographic data, for the world, regions and individual countries.

International Planned Parenthood Federation (IPPF). *Islam and Family Planning.* 2 vols. Beirut: IPPF, Middle East and North Africa Region, 1974. 346 and 558 pp. $25.00.

    Proceedings of a 1971 conference of scholars and specialists to discuss the Muslim outlook on family planning, plus relevant laws and religious references.

International Planned Parenthood Federation (IPPF). *Survey of World Needs in Family Planning.* London: IPPF, 1974. 114 pp. Free.

    Findings of an IPPF survey covering family planning services and practice, international financial resources, total cost of fertility control and demographic data for the year 1971 in 209 countries.

International Project of the Association for Voluntary Sterilization. *A Comprehensive Set of Bibliographies on Voluntary Sterilization.* New York 10017: 708 Third Avenue, January 1974. 85 pp.

    Topics include attitudes, audio-visual materials, biomedical effects, male and female methods, psychological effects, and programs.

Johnson, W. Bert, Frank Wilder, and Donald J. Bogue, eds. *Information, Education and Communication for Population and Family Planning.* Chicago: Community and Family Study Center, University of Chicago, 1973. 207 pp. $6.00.

    Articles on the organization, operation and scope of information, education and communication (IEC) programs for family planning. Includes inventory of resources and activities.

Jongmans, D. G. and H. J. M. Claessen, eds. *The Neglected Factor in Family Planning: Perception and Reaction at the Base.* Assen, Netherlands: Van Gorcum, 1975. $14.50.

    Proceedings of a 1974 symposium held in Amsterdam describe findings from attitude, sociocultural, psychological and anthropological studies on people's views towards family planning with case studies in several developing countries.

Keeny, S. M. *East Asia Shares Experience in Family Planning.* Taichung, Taiwan: The Chinese Center for International Training in Family Planning, 1975. 108 pp.

    The reminiscences of a pioneer in Asian family planning provide a practical handbook on how to organize and conduct national programs in developing countries.

Kennedy, David M. *Birth Control in America: The Career of Margaret Sanger.* New Haven, Conn.: Yale University Press, 1970. 320 pp. $3.95 paper.

Explores the relation between Margaret Sanger's character and the nature of the worldwide movement she led between 1912 and World War II.

Loebl, Suzanne. *Conception, Contraception: A New Look.* New York: McGraw-Hill, 1974. 147 pp. $6.95.

The anatomy of human reproduction, current methods of family planning, and a look at the relationship of fertility to national prosperity.

Moghissi, Kamran S. and Tommy N. Evans, eds. *Regulation of Human Fertility.* Detroit: Wayne State University Press, 1976. 318 pp. $22.00.

The newest developments in contraception and evaluation of existing techniques and procedures.

Nortman, Dorothy. "Population and Family Planning Programs: A Factbook." *Reports on Population/Fa.ily Planning.* New York: The Population Council. Published annually since 1969, latest is 7th ed., October 1975. 88 pp. Free.

Annually updated empirical data, by regions and countries, on family planning programs and related variables in the developing world, presented in concise tables with explanatory commentary.

Organisation for Economic Co-operation and Development (OECD). *An Assessment of Family Planning Programmes.* Paris: Development Centre, OECD, 1972. 193 pp.

Proceedings of OECD's fourth annual population conference, 1971.

Planned Parenthood/World Population. Center for Family Planning Program Development. *Need for Subsidized Family Planning Services: United States, Each State and County, 1971.* New York: Planned Parenthood/World Population, 1973. 238 pp. Free.

A survey covering Fiscal Year 1971 which assesses the number of low-income U.S. women at risk of unintended pregnancy and hence in need of subsidized family planning services.

Pohlman, Edward. *Incentives and Compensations in Birth Planning.* Chapel Hill, N.C.: Carolina Population Center, University of North Carolina, 1971. 117 pp. $1.50.

General principles, research and record of experience, particularly in India, but also in the U.S.

The Population Council, 245 Park Ave., New York, N.Y. 10017. Rigorous reviews on what empirical research has so far revealed about the nature and effectiveness of various approaches to fertility control (including abortion) appear in the following three issues of *Reports on Population/Family Planning,* each with extensive bibliographies. Free.

"Postpartum Services in Family Planning: Findings to Date," by Jacqueline E. Forrest, No. 8, July 1971. 15 pp.

"Findings from Family Planning Research," by John A. Ross et al, No. 12, October 1972. 47 pp.

"Findings from Family Planning Research: Latin American Supplement," by Albert M. Marckwardt, No. 12 supplement, June 1974. 8 pp.

Potts, Malcolm and Clive Woods, eds. *New Concepts in Contraception.* Baltimore: University Park Press, 1972. 231 pp. $17.50.

Present and future family planning methods and the technical, social, political and physiological obstacles they face.

Presser, Harriet B. "Voluntary Sterilization: A World View." *Reports on Population/Family Planning,* No. 5. New York: The Population Council, July 1970. 36 pp. Free.

Overview of worldwide study findings of the 1960s on various aspects of voluntary sterilization.

Rawson-Jones, Daphne and Geoffrey Salkeld, eds. *Communicating Family Planning.* New York: International Publishers Service, 1972. 195 pp. $7.50 paper.

A practical handbook for family planning educators, communicators and field workers, particularly in the developing world.

Roberto, Eduardo L. *Strategic Decision-Making in a Social Program: The Case of Family-Planning Diffusion.* Lexington, Mass.: Lexington Books, 1975. 182 pp. $15.00.

Technical discussion about client segmentation, selection of program objectives, mass communication and evaluation objectives and their implementation.

Rogers, Everett M. *Communication Strategies for Family Planning.* New York: Free Press, 1973. 451 pp. $12.95.

Summarizes scientific knowledge about communication which can be used to influence family planning and indicates areas in need of future research.

Segal, Sheldon and Christopher Tietze. "Contraceptive Technology: Current and Prospective Methods." *Reports on Population/Family Planning,* No. 1. 2nd ed. New York: The Population Council, July 1971. 24 pp. Free.

Concise evaluation of available contraceptive methods, methods currently in the pipeline, and present fertility-related laboratory research and the future methods that could result.

Sivin, Irving. *Contraception and Fertility Change in the International Postpartum Program.* New York: The Population Council; distributed by Key Book Service, Bridgeport, Conn., 1974. 98 pp. $3.95.

Analysis of findings from a 1970 survey of 4,700 women in 11 countries, designed to evaluate results of a 21-country, 8-year program initiated by The Population Council in 1966 to demonstrate the feasibility of providing contraceptive services as part of hospital obstetrical care. A full review of the program and its wide influence on family planning approaches in other areas appears in "The International Postpartum Family Planning Program: Eight Years of Experience," by Robert G. Castadot et al. *Reports on Population/Family Planning,* No. 18. New York: The Population Council, 1975. 53 pp. Free.

Stycos, J. Mayone. *Clinics, Contraception, and Communications: Evaluation Studies of Family Planning Programs in Four Latin American Countries.* New York: Appleton-Century-Crofts, 1973. 207 pp. $18.95.

Field studies in Colombia, the Dominican Republic, Honduras, and Mexico demonstrate that public information programs (radio recommended) could boost waning clinic attendance.

Suitters, Beryl. *Be Brave and Angry: Chronicles of the International Planned Parenthood Federation.* London: International Planned Parenthood Federation, 1973. 424 pp. $4.00.

A history of the origins of the International Planned Parenthood Federation and first two decades of activity following its founding in 1952.

Udry, Richard J. and Earl E. Huyck, eds. *The Demographic Evaluation of Domestic Family Planning Programs.* Cambridge, Mass.: Ballinger, 1975. 119 pp. $12.00.

Workshop papers and panel reports on issues and problems in demographic evaluation of U.S. family planning programs and description of current studies in the field.

United Nations. Economic and Social Commission for Asia and the Pacific (ESCAP). *Some Techniques for Measuring the Impact of Contraception.* By Robert G. Potter and S. L. N. Rao. Asian Population Studies Series No. 18. Bangkok: ESCAP, 1974. 136 pp. Free.

Technical description and analysis of computer programs to be used in determining the number of family planning acceptors needed to achieve specific birth rate declines.

University of Chicago. Community and Family Study Center. *Rapid Feedback for Family Planning Improvement Manuals.* Price list and copies available from Community and Family Study Center, University of Chicago, 1411 East 60th St., Chicago, Ill. 60637.

A series of practical, easily understandable manuals by Donald J. Bogue and other experts aid family planning workers in collecting and analyzing data to evaluate program effectiveness.

U.S. Bureau of the Census. International Statistical Programs Center. *Family Planning Statistics, 1965-1973; Africa, Asia, Latin America.* Washington, D.C.: Government Printing Office, 1975, 74 pp. $1.80.

Latest in an annual series of data on family planning programs and clients in some 50 countries.

Watson, Walter B. and Robert J. Lapham, eds. "Family Planning Programs: World Review 1974." *Studies in Family Planning,* Vol. 6, No. 8. New York: The Population Council, August 1975. Free.

Detailed and comprehensive review of the 1974 status, recent progress, and current problems of family planning programs in Third World countries.

Weisbord, Robert G. *Genocide? Birth Control and the Black American.* Westport, Conn.: Greenwood, Press; and New York: The Two Continents Publishing Group, 1975. 219 pp. $7.95.

Positions of black leaders and black movements on birth control and the cultural and political backgrounds that have influenced current thought. An adaptation of this book, with data on contraceptive use and likely trends in family size among blacks, was published by the Population Reference Bureau in "Family Size and the Black American," *Population Bulletin,* Vol. 30, No. 4, 1975. 29 pp. $1.00.

World Health Organization (WHO). *Evaluation of Family Planning in Health Services: Report of a WHO Expert Committee.* Technical Report Series No. 569. Geneva: WHO, 1975. 67 pp. 7 Sw. francs (or equivalent in U.S. dollars).

Report of a 1974 expert meeting which provides practical guidelines on evaluating family planning programs.

Zaidan, George C. *Costs and Benefits of Family Planning Programs.* Baltimore: Johns Hopkins University Press, 1971. 51 pp. $3.00 paper.

A technique for measuring the economic returns from investing in population control as applied to the United Arab Republic.

B. ABORTION

af Geijerstam, Gunner K. *An Annotated Bibliography of Induced Abortion.* Ann Arbor, Mich.: Center for Population Planning, University of Michigan, 1969. 359 pp. $3.00.

Annotated bibliography of 1,175 references for 1960-67 covering world literature on all aspects of abortion. Two non-annotated listings, built on this bibliography, have been published by the Transnational Family Research Institute, 8307 Whitman Drive, Bethesda, Md. 20034: *Guide to the 1968-1972 International Abortion Research Literature* and *Abortion Research Literature 1973-1974.* Free.

Alan Guttmacher Institute. *Provisional Estimates of Abortion Need and Services in the Year Following the 1973 Supreme Court Decisions: United States, Each State and Metropolitan Area.* New York: Alan Guttmacher Institute, Planned Parenthood Federation of America, 1975. 88 pp. $6.50.

Findings of a nationwide survey of over 3,000 medical facilities indicate that up to 1 million women in need of abortion were unable to obtain it in the year following liberalization of all U.S. abortion laws. Findings of a repeat survey a year later will be published by the Institute in fall 1976 as *1975 Abortions,* $7.00.

American Friends Service Committee. *Who Shall Live? Man's Control over Birth and Death.* New York: Hill and Wang, 1970. 144 pp. $2.25 paper.

A Quaker report on the ethics of abortion in the context of concern for the quality of life and current contraceptive practices.

Callahan, Daniel. *Abortion: Law, Choice and Morality.* New York: Collier-Macmillan, 1970. 524 pp. $4.95 paper.

Analyzes historic and current (late 1960s) abortion legal policies of varying types around the world in light of their effects on abortion incidence, secular and particularly moral issues.

Chandrasekhar, S. *Abortion in a Crowded World: The Problem of Abortion with Special Reference to India.* Seattle, Wash.: University of Washington Press, 1974. 184 pp. $6.95.

General review of the worldwide abortion problem and the events which led to India's liberalized abortion law of 1971.

David, Henry P., ed. *Abortion Research: International Experience.* Lexington, Mass.: Lexington Books, 1974. 272 pp. $14.00.

Thirty-one articles on abortion services, techniques, psychosocial aspects and relationship with contraception in selected countries and areas; includes summary of legal and de facto status of abortion as of mid-1974 for over 100 counties.

Devereux, George. *A Study of Abortion in Primitive Societies.* Rev. ed. New York: International Universities Press, 1975. 414 pp. $4.95.

Revised edition of a classic compilation and analysis of materials on abortion practices in over 400 preindustrial societies.

Family Planning Association of Nepal and Transnational Family Research Institute (TFRI). *Psychosocial Aspects of Abortion in Asia: Proceedings of the Asian Regional Research Seminar on Psychosocial Aspects of Abortion. Kathmandu, 26–29 November 1974.* Available from TFRI, 8307 Whitman Drive, Bethesda, Md. 20034, 1974. 119 pp. Free.

Discussion of abortion research and methodology and reports by country experts on India, Iran, Indonesia, Israel, Korea, Malaysia, Nepal, Philippines, Singapore, and Thailand.

Great Britain. Committee on the Working of the Abortion Act. *Report of the Committee on the Working of the Abortion Act.* 3 vols. London: Her Majesty's Stationery Office, 1974. 288, 271, and 109 pp. £1.75.

Findings and recommendations of the committee chaired by the Hon. Mrs. Justice Lane, which was appointed in 1971 to review implementation of the liberal British abortion act of 1967.

Hall, Robert E., ed. *Abortion in a Changing World.* 2 vols. New York: Columbia University Press, 1970. 377 and 220 pp. $12.50 each volume.

Papers and proceedings of a 1968 conference of experts in Hot Springs, Va. covering a wide range of abortion-related issues with several country and regional status reports.

Hardin, Garrett. *Mandatory Motherhood: The True Meaning of "Right to Life."* Boston: Beacon Press, 1974. 136 pp. $1.95 paper.

Discussion of controversial issues on abortion designed to refute Right-to-Life arguments.

Hordern, Anthony. *Legal Abortion: The English Experience.* New York: Pergamon Press, 1971. 322 pp. $14.00.

The British situation prior to the 1967 Abortion Act and the Church, public and medical profession's reaction towards the new law.

Institute of Medicine. *Legalized Abortion and the Public Health: Report of a Study by a Committee of the Institute of Medicine.* Washington, D.C.: National Academy of Sciences, 1974. 168 pp. Free.

Extensive review of the effect of legal, and particularly early versus late, abortion with respect to mortality, morbidity, psychological effects, birth defects and contraception, primarily in the U.S.

International Planned Parenthood Federation (IPPF). *Induced Abortion and Family Health: A European View.* London: IPPF, Europe Region, 1974. 75 pp. £1.00.

Report on a 1973 meeting in Brussels. Recommends liberalized abortion and improved services to preserve women's health and freedom of choice.

Lader, Lawrence. *Abortion II: Making the Revolution.* Boston: Beacon Press, 1973. 255 pp. $7.95.

Story of the U.S. movement to repeal restrictive abortion laws from 1965 to the Supreme Court decisions of January 1973.

Moore-Cavar, Emily. *International Inventory of Induced Abortion.* New York: International Institute for the Study of Human Reproduction, Columbia University, 1974. 655 pp. $5.00.

Exhaustive synthesis and analysis of all issues of abortion, documented by copious references from the international literature and tabulations of data available as of 1973 from some 134 countries.

Newman, S. H., M. B. Beck, and S. Lewit, eds. *Abortion, Obtained and Denied: Research Approaches.* New York: The Population Council, 1971. 208 pp. $4.50.

Papers from a 1970 workshop on abortion obtained and denied and associated mortality, morbidity, mental health, family planning and fertility, and socioeconomic aspects.

Omran, Abdel R., ed. *Liberalization of Abortion Laws: Implications.* Chapel Hill, N.C.: Carolina Population Center, 1976. 305 pp. $5.00 paper.

A multidisciplinary study group considers what is now known and what might be expected under varying degrees of liberalized abortion. Chapters on incidence, laws, psychosocial and anthropological aspects, administrative problems and impact on fertility. Bibliography of 1973–74 abortion literature.

Osofsky, Howard J. and Joy D. Osofsky, eds. *The Abortion Experience: Psychological and Medical Impact.* Hagerstown, Md.: Harper & Row, 1973. 668 pp. $29.95.

Detailed reviews of services and medical, psychosocial and legal aspects of abortion in the U.S. with summaries of international developments in the same areas.

Population Information Program. George Washington University Medical Center. "Abortion Law and Practice—A Status Report." By Margot Zimmerman. *Population Reports,* Series E, No. 3, March 1976. 15 pp. Free.

Global review and implications of the current trend toward liberalization of abortion laws.

Tietze, Christopher and Marjorie Cooper Murstein. "Induced Abortion: 1975 Factbook." *Reports on Population/Family Planning,* No. 14. New York: The Population Council, December 1975. 76 pp. Free.

Update of *1973 Factbook.* Comprehensive compilation of currently available international data on abortion, primarily from the demographic and health points of view; also discusses terminology, measurement, and legal status and practice by regions.

U.S. Center for Disease Control. *Abortion Surveillance: Annual Summary.* Atlanta, Ga.: Public Health Service, U.S. Department of Health, Education, and Welfare. Published annually since 1969. Latest edition covers 1974. 49 pp. Free.

Demographic and epidemiological data on legal abortion, including abortion-related mortality and morbidity, from all reporting areas of the U.S.; reviews of special abortion studies.

van der Tak, Jean. *Abortion, Fertility and Changing Legislation: An International Review.* Lexington, Mass.: Lexington Books, 1974. 141 pp. $12.00.

Summary of available evidence which suggests that significant fertility decline is unlikely without freely available abortion (legal or illegal) as an adjunct to contraception.

Walbert, David and J. Douglas Butler, eds. *Abortion, Society and the Law.* Cleveland, Ohio: The Press of Case Western Reserve University, 1973. 394 pp. $9.95.

An anthology of articles on issues such as the evolution of abortion laws, Jewish and Catholic views, the U.S. experience and its implications for the rights of minors.

XIII. International, Regional, and National Studies

A. INTERNATIONAL

American Universities Field Staff. *Fieldstaff Reports.* Published by American Universities Field Staff, 3 Lebanon St., Hanover, N.H. 03755. 8-15 pp. on average. $1.00 each. $60.00 for annual set of 60 reports, or $15.00 for all reports on (1) Europe and Southeast Asia (including India and Bangladesh), (2) Europe and the Mediterranean (including North Africa), (3) Africa and Latin America, or (4) Population Problems of the World.

Brief readable, analytical reports by on-spot Fieldstaff specialists in politically significant developments. Includes many dealing with population issues in different regions and individual countries. For individual titles write the Field Staff Office for *List of Publications.* (Latest covers 1973.)

Committee for International Coordination of National Research in Demography (CICRED). *Country Series.* Series of comprehensive country population studies prepared by national experts to mark World Population Year. Each approximately 100 pp., in one language only. Available for 9 French francs postage each, payable in advance, from Editions-Diffusions OPHRYS, 10 rue de Nesle, 75006 Paris, France, or Avenue d'Embrun, 05002 Gap, France. The following were available as of summer 1976.

Algeria (French)
Argentina (Spanish)
Austria (English)
Belgium (French)
Brazil (French)
Bulgaria (French)
Canada (English)
Chile (Spanish)
Colombia (Spanish)
Costa Rica (Spanish)
Cuba (Spanish)
Czechoslovakia (French)
Denmark (English)
Egypt (English)
Finland (English)
France (French)
Ghana (English)
Greece (English)
Guatemala (Spanish)
Hong Kong (English)
Hungary (English)
India (English)
Indonesia (English)
Iran (French)
Israel (English)
Italy (French)
Jamaica (English)
Kenya-Uganda-Tanzania (English)
Korea (English)
Lebanon (French)
Liberia (English)
Luxembourg (French)
Malaysia (English)
Mexico (Spanish)
Morocco (French)
New Zealand (English)
Pakistan (English)
Panama (Spanish)
Paraguay (Spanish)
Peru (Spanish)
Philippines (English)
Poland (English)
Portugal (French)
Romania (French)
Spain (Spanish)
Switzerland (French)
Thailand (English)
Trinidad and Tobago (English)
Tunisia (French)
Turkey (English)
United States (English)
Venezuela (Spanish)
Yugoslavia (English)
Zambia (English)

Partan, Daniel G. *Population in the United Nations System: Developing the Legal Capacity and Programs of U.N. Agencies.* Durham, N.C.: Rule of Law Press, 1973. 219 pp. $12.50.

Analysis of the legal basis for U.N. action on population questions.

The Population Council. *Country Profiles.* New York: The Population Council. 8–56 pp. Free.

Occasional selected country reports by national experts, describing population trends, characteristics, policies and programs. Latest is for *India*, by Pravin Visaria and Anrudh K. Jain, May 1976. 56 pp.

Population Reference Bureau. *World Population Growth and Response 1965–1975: A Decade of Global Action.* Washington, D.C.: Population Reference Bureau, 1976. 271 pp. $4.00 paper.

Comprehensive review of population trends, policies and programs, worldwide, regionally, and in over 200 individual countries, during the decade which marked the beginning of global concern with population growth. Includes extensive information on U.S., multilateral and national organizations which support or conduct population programs.

Salas, Rafael M. *People: An International Choice.* Elmsford, N.Y.: Pergamon Press, 1976. 154 pp. $6.00 paper.

Story of the United Nations Fund for Population Activities by its Executive Director.

Symonds, Richard and Michael Carder. *The United Nations and the Population Question 1945–1970.* A Population Council Book. New York: McGraw-Hill, 1973. 236 pp. $8.95.

A historical review of efforts to organize the population control movement on an international basis.

United Nations. *Report of the United Nations World Population Conference, 1974, Bucharest, 19-30 August 1974.* Sales No. E.75.XIII.3. New York: United Nations, 1975. 147 pp. $7.00.

Includes World Population Plan of Action as well as resolutions, recommendations, proceedings and reports of special committees.

United Nations. Department of Economic and Social Affairs. *Concise Report on the World Population Situation in 1970–1975 and Its Long-Range Implications.* Population Studies No. 56. Sales No. E.74.XIII.4. New York: United Nations, 1975. 70 pp. $3.00.

Nontechnical comparison of the current situation in developed and developing regions in terms of demographic and socioeconomic characteristics and the outlook for the future.

United Nations. Department of Economic and Social Affairs. *The World Population Situation in 1970.* Population Studies No. 49. Sales No. E.71.XIII.4. New York: United Nations, 1971. 78 pp. $2.00.

A concise, authoritative report on the world population situation, prospects, problems and policies as of 1970.

United Nations. Economic and Social Council. *Report on the World Social Situation, 1974.* Part 2: *Population.* Sales No. E.75.IV.6. 280 pp. $11.00.

To be issued every four years beginning in 1974 covering, in alternate editions, social conditions and social programs. This 1974 issue is a combined publication.

United Nations Fund for Population Activities. *United Nations and Population: Major Resolutions and Instruments.* Dobbs Ferry, N.Y.: Oceana Publications, 1974. 212 pp. $12.50.

A compendium of documents which have served as a basis for deliberations on population questions in the U.N. family of agencies for the past 30 years.

U.S. Agency for International Development. Bureau for Population and Humanitarian Assistance. Office of Population. *Population Program Assistance.* Washington, D.C.: Government Printing Office. Published annually since fiscal year 1965. 200–250 pp. on average. Prices $2.00 to $3.50.

Annual comprehensive compendium of information on population and family planning programs in developing countries; includes extensive demographic data.

U.S. Bureau of the Census. International Statistical Programs Center. Three series of brief demographic country or international research reports. Available from U.S. Government Printing Office, at prices indicated; free to developing countries and organizations. Washington, D.C. 20402.

Demographic Reports for Foreign Countries. Series P-96. English, some in Spanish and French. $0.55–$1.25 per report.

Analysis based on most recent census data and projections based on varying fertility assumptions for Chile, Panama, Tunisia, and Peru.

Country Demographic Profiles. Series ISP-30. English, French, Spanish editions. $0.25 each.

Contain adjusted and unadjusted data on individual countries. Completed by mid-1976: Costa Rica, Ghana, Taiwan; others in progress.

International Research Documents. Series ISP-RD. Completed by mid-1976:

1. *Population and Economic Planning: A Macro-analysis,* by Eduardo Arriaga. $0.35.
2. *Levels and Trends of Mortality in Indonesia, 1961-1971,* by Larry Heligman. $0.45.
3. *Projections of the Rural and Urban Population of Colombia, 1965-2000,* by Sylvia Quick and Eduardo Arriaga. $1.20.

U.S. Bureau of Economic Analysis. Foreign Demographic Analysis Division. Washington, D.C. 20230. Publishes reports on demographic data and analysis for the Communist countries in several series. For complete listing write the above address. Most recent publications still available include the following.

Series P-90. Available from U.S. Government Printing Office, Washington, D.C. 20402. Prices vary.

24. *Manpower Trends in Czechoslovakia: 1950 to 1990,* by Andrew Elias (1972). 80 pp.

25. *The Provinces of the People's Republic of China: A Political and Economic Bibliography,* by John Philip Emerson et al (forthcoming, fall 1976). 700-800 pp. Annotated bibliography and guide to location of such materials in libraries around the world outside the People's Republic of China.

Series P-91. Available from U.S. Government Printing Office, Washington, D.C. 20402. Prices vary.

23. *Estimates and Projections of the Population of the U.S.S.R., by Age and Sex: 1950 to 2000,* by Godfrey S. Baldwin (1973). 29 pp.

25. *Projections of the Population of the Communist Countries of Eastern Europe, by Age and Sex: 1975 to 2000,* by Godfrey S. Baldwin (1976). 51 pp.

Series P-95. Free: limited distribution.

69. *Comparison of U.S. and U.S.S.R. Civilian Employment in Government: 1950–1969,* by Stephen Rapawy (1972). 37 pp.

70. *Structure and Accounting of Working Capital in the U.S.S.R.* (1972). 82 pp.

71. *Estimates of Educational Attainment of the Population and Labor Force in Hungary: 1949-1971,* by Marjory E. Searing (1972). 40 pp.

72. *Administrative and Technical Manpower in the People's Republic of China,* by John Philip Emerson (1973). 137 pp.

73. *Population Estimates for the Provinces of the People's Republic of China: 1953 to 1974,* by John S. Aird (1974). 27 pp.

B. AFRICA

Acsádi, G. T., A. A. Igun, and G. Z. Johnson. *Surveys of Fertility, Family and Family Planning in Nigeria.* Institution of Population and Manpower Studies (IPMS) Publication No. 2. Ile-Ife, Nigeria: IPMS, University of Ife, 1972. 306 pp.

A review of methods and findings of three pilot studies and Nigeria's first national fertility survey carried out 1970-72.

Akingha, J. B. *The Problem of Unwanted Pregnancies in Nigeria Today.* Lagos: University of Lagos Press, 1971. 126 pp.

To cope with this important Nigerian problem, the gynecologist author advocates sex education, birth control, and change in the popular philosophy of getting a woman pregnant before marriage to ensure that she can bear children.

Caldwell, John C., ed. *Population Growth and Socio-Economic Change in West Africa.* New York: Columbia University Press for The Population Council, 1975. 763 pp. $30.00.

Forty-three specialists from Africa and elsewhere collaborated in this voluminous study of West African fertility and fertility control, migration, urbanization, and the socioeconomic implications thereof.

Cantrelle, P. et al, eds. *Population in African Development.* 2 vols. Published for the International Union for the Scientific Study of Population by Ordina Editions, 9 route de Goé, 4830 Dolhain, Belgium, 1974. 550 and 349 pp. $35.00.

Seventy-four papers from the 1971 African Regional Population Conference held in Accra, Ghana, dealing with a broad range of the area's demographic and population issues.

Condé, Julien. *The Demographic Transition as Applied to Tropical Africa with Particular Reference to Health, Education and Economic Factors.* Paris: Organisation for Economic Co-operation and Development (OECD), 1971. 207 pp. $2.00.

Study prepared as a basis for discussion for an OECD meeting of African experts in 1970.

Ergero, Bertil and Roushdi A. Henin, eds. *The Population of Tanzania: An Analysis of the 1967 Population Census.* Dar es Salaam: BRALUP and Bureau of Statistics, 1973. 292 pp.

Detailed evaluation of data and findings by 13 social scientists, geographers and statisticians.

Hance, William A. *Population, Migration, and Urbanization in Africa.* New York: Columbia University Press, 1970. 450 pp. $15.00.
> A geographer's analysis of the socioeconomic and political problems presented by migration, population density and growth and urbanization throughout Africa, illustrated by sketches of major African cities.

Igun, Adenola and G. T. Acsádi, eds. *Demographic Statistics in Nigeria.* Ile-Ife, Nigeria: University of Ife, 1972. 272 pp.
> Fifteen papers and summary discussions of a 1970 symposium on the "Technical and Practical Problems in the Collection of Demographic Statistics for Reconstruction and Development in Nigeria."

Little, Kenneth. *Urbanization as a Social Process: An Essay on Movement and Change in Contemporary Africa.* Boston: Routledge & Kegan Paul, 1974. 153 pp.
> An attempt to summarize and evaluate writings on postwar urbanization in sub-Saharan Africa, mainly in the still colonial era of the 1950s and 1960s.

Molnos, Angela. *Cultural Source Materials for Population Planning in East Africa.* 4 vols. Institute of African Studies, University of Nairobi. Nairobi: East African Publishing House, 1972–74. Vols. 1–3, $41.00; Vol. 4, $9.00.
> Unique collection of anthropological findings on sociocultural aspects of fertility among tribes of East Africa. Vol. 4 is a 3,500-item bibliography on ethnic groups, population and family planning in the region.

Morrison, Donald George et al. *Black Africa: A Comparative Handbook.* New York: The Free Press, 1972. 483 pp. $29.95.
> Comparative data on urban, ethnic, language and political patterns for 32 independent black African nations.

Moss, R. P. and R. J. A. R. Rathbone, eds. *The Population Factor in African Studies.* New York: Holmes & Meier, 1975. 240 pp. $12.50.
> Papers from a 1972 conference on past and present population trends in sub-Saharan Africa and their impact on society, the economy and the environment.

Mott, Frank L. and Olanrewaju J. Fapohunda. *The Population of Nigeria.* Mimeographed monograph No. 3. Lagos, Nigeria: Human Resources Unit, University of Lagos, 1975. 100 pp.
> Compilation and analysis of all available evidence on current population trends and policies in Africa's most populous country.

Okediji, Francis Olu, ed. *Population Dynamics Research in Africa: Proceedings of a Workshop/Seminar, 1974.* Washington, D.C.: Interdisciplinary Communications Program, Smithsonian Institution, 1974. 295 pp. Free.
> Twenty papers on a wide range of population trends, issues, research and findings mainly in sub-Saharan Africa.

Ominde, S. H. and C. N. Ejiogu, eds. *Population Growth and Economic Development in Africa.* London: Heinemann Educational Books, 1972. 421 pp. £8.00.
> Fifty-three papers from a 1969 Nairobi conference, the first ever to gather scholars from French and English-speaking Africa and elsewhere to discuss the region's demographic situation.

Organisation for Economic Co-operation and Development (OECD). *The Demographic Transition in Tropical Africa.* Paris: OECD, 1971. 348 pp.
> Papers from a 1970 OECD meeting on various aspects of African fertility, population growth and development, education, migration and population policy.

Population Reference Bureau. "Africa and its Population Growth." By Leon F. Bouvier. *Population Bulletin,* Vol. 30, No. 1, 1975. 28 pp. $1.00.
> Background data, economic and population growth issues and current population policies and family planning programs.

Pradervand, P. *Family Planning Programmes in Africa.* Paris: Development Centre, Organisation for Economic Co-operation and Development (OECD), 1970. 76 pp.
> Analysis of obstacles to family planning in Francophone Africa, particularly continuing high mortality, low literacy and lack of health services.

Radel, D. *Population in Sub-Saharan Africa, 1965–1971.* Chapel Hill, N.C.: Carolina Population Center, 1973. 48 pp. $5.50.
> Bibliography of 736 items covering an extensive range of books, articles and papers.

Radel, David, guest ed. "Population and Family Planning in Rural Africa." *Rural Africana,* No. 14, Spring 1971. East Lansing, Mich.: African Studies Center, Michigan State University. 185 pp. $1.50.
> Special issue on population, policy formulation, and family planning in sub-Saharan Africa. Lists 64 current population and family planning research projects and 600 published items of 1965–71.

C. ASIA

Intra-regional Studies

Cho, Lee-Jay, ed. *Introduction to Censuses of Asia and the Pacific: 1970–74.* Honolulu: University Press of Hawaii, 1976. 212 pp. $6.00.
> Comprehensive coverage of contents and methodology of the 1970 round of censuses in Australia, Bangladesh, Burma, Hong Kong, India, Indonesia, Japan, Korea, Malaysia, Pakistan, Philippines, Singapore, Sri Lanka, Taiwan and Thailand.

David, Henry P. and Sung Jin Lee, eds. *Social and Psychological Aspects of Fertility in Asia: Proceedings of the Technical Seminar in Choonchun, Korea: November 7–9, 1973.* Available from Transnational Family Research Institute, 8307 Whitman Drive, Bethesda, Md. 20034, 1974. 128 pp. Free.
> Includes reports on research in Korea, Taiwan, Hong Kong, Thailand, the Philippines, Singapore, Indonesia, Australia, the U.S. and Europe with extensive reference lists.

East-Asian Pastoral Institute. *The Church and Population in East Asia.* Quezon City, Philippines: East Asian Pastoral Institute, 1973. 127 pp.
> Reports from an East Asian Seminar on population in the context of integral human development.

Food and Agriculture Organization of the United Nations (FAO). *Report on the FAO/UNFPA Seminar on Population Problems as Related to Food and Agricultural Development in Asia and the Far East.* Rome: FAO, 1975. 81 pp.
> Discussion of many facets of the fact that the 1970–80 rate of increase in food needs projected for this area outstrip the past decade's food production growth rate, except for Japan.

International Planned Parenthood Federation. *Population, Development and Environment: Indian Ocean Region Conference, December 1972, Bombay.* Bombay: Family Planning Association of India, 1972. 207 pp.

Proceedings of conference dealing with family planning problems and programs in the area and their developmental impact.

Jakobson, Leo and Sheilah Jakobson, eds. *Urbanization and National Development.* Vol. 1. South and Southeast Asia Urban Affairs Annuals. Beverly Hills, Cal.: Sage Publications, 1971. 320 pp. $17.50.

Nine articles and a selected bibliography on processes and patterns of urbanization in Southeast Asia and the impact of development policies.

Kantner, John F. and Lee McCaffrey, eds. *Population and Development in Southeast Asia.* Lexington, Mass.: Lexington Books, 1975. 323 pp. $16.00.

Papers of three 1972 seminars of the South East Asia Development Advisory Group. Includes country population profiles and general analyses.

Tachi, Minoru and Minoru M. Muramatsu, eds. *Population Problems in the Pacific: New Dimensions in Pacific Demography.* Tokyo: Institute of Population Problems, Ministry of Health and Welfare, 1971. 510 pp.

A volume of 74 papers presented at the 11th Pacific Scientific Congress in Tokyo, 1966, covering population dynamics and control, food, resources and development.

United Nations. Economic and Social Commission for Asia and the Pacific (ESCAP). *Asian Population Studies Series and Related Publications.* Bangkok: Population Division, ESCAP. Issued regularly. Most publications are free.

Regional studies on family planning and population issues, reports from expert meetings, publications, directories, and bibliographies, plus comprehensive country demographic monographs (Hong Kong, published; Korea, Thailand, Sri Lanka forthcoming). List of titles available from ESCAP (Sala Santiham, Bangkok, Thailand), U.N. Office in New York, or in each issue of *Asian Population Program News* (see "Periodicals").

World Health Organization (WHO). Regional Office for South-East Asia. *Bibliography on Human Reproduction, Family Planning and Population Dynamics: Annotated Articles and Unpublished Work in the South-East Asia Region.* New Delhi, India: WHO, Regional Office, World Health House, Ring Road.

Irregularly published detailed bibliography of books and articles in the population field. Mainly for doctors and medical researchers.

Wriggins, W. Howard and James F. Guyot, eds. *Population, Politics, and the Future of Southern Asia.* New York: Columbia University Press, 1973. 402 pp. $2.95 paper.

Papers from a 1971 conference which conclude that population per se is not the most pressing problem but rather the uneven distribution of the area's growing populations.

People's Republic of China

Aird, John S. *Population Policy and Demographic Prospects in the People's Republic of China.* Rockville, Md.: Center for Population Research, National Institute of Child Health and Human Development, 1973. 111 pp. (numbered 220-331). Free.

Review of China's changing population policy and the three birth control campaigns since 1949.

Chen Pi-chao. *The "Planned Birth" Program of the People's Republic of China, with a Brief Analysis of its Transferability.* SEADAG Papers. Published by The Asia Society, 505 Park Avenue, New York, N.Y., 10017, 1974. 30 pp. Free.

A Wayne State University political scientist offers some pertinent observations following visits in 1972 and 1973.

Orleans, Leo A. *Every Fifth Child: The Population of China.* Stanford, Cal.: Stanford University Press, 1972. 191 pp. $8.50.

Balanced treatment of what is known and not known about the current Chinese demographic situation with a bibliography of 150 listings. Extracts from this book were published by the Population Reference Bureau in "China: Population in the People's Republic," *Population Bulletin,* Vol. 27, No. 6, 1971. 37 pp. $1.00.

Sidel, Ruth. *Women and Child Care in China.* Baltimore: Penguin Books, 1973. 207 pp. $1.95 paper.

Review based on personal observations; includes such issues as marriage law, pregnancy, child birth, and contraceptive practice.

Tien, H. Yuan. *China's Population Struggle: Demographic Decisions of the People's Republic 1949-1969.* Columbus, Ohio: Ohio State University Press, 1973. 405 pp. $15.00.

Description of official policies designed to control population distribution and growth.

India

Agarwala, S. N. *A Demographic Study of Six Urbanizing Villages.* New Delhi: Vedam's Books, 1970. 195 pp. $6.00.

The findings of a series of fertility surveys conducted during the period 1958 to 1960.

Agarwala, S. N. *India's Population Problems.* New York: McGraw-Hill, 1973. 175 pp. $8.00.

Analysis of current and future demographic situation, based on 1961 and 1971 census data; includes listing of the country's population and demographic training and research facilities.

Banerji, D. *Family Planning in India: A Critique and a Perspective.* New Delhi: Vedam's Books, 1971. 85 pp. $3.75.

A Communist view of India's family planning program through 1969 and prospects for the 1970s.

Blaikie, Piers M. *Family Planning in India: Diffusion and Policy.* New York: Holmes & Meier, 1975. 168 pp. $24.00.

A systematic review of obstacles faced by India's family planning program with practical suggestions for improvement; based on field study in rural Bihar, one of the country's poorest states.

Bose, Ashish et al, eds. *Population in India's Development, 1947-2000.* New Delhi: Vikas Publishing House for the Indian Association for the Study of Population, 1974. 444 pp.

A variety of viewpoints, addressed to the "lay reader," on the past and future relationship between India's enormous population problems and hopes for development.

Bose, Ashish, P. B. Desai, and S. P. Yain. *Studies in Demography.* Chapel Hill, N.C.: University of North Carolina Press, 1970. 579 pp. $13.95.

Emphasis on census and demographic techniques as well as on problems and methods of family planning in the developing world, particularly in India.

Chand, Gyan. *Population in Perspective: Study of Population Crisis in India in the Context of New Social Horizons.* Port Washington, N.Y.: Kennikat Press, 1973. 380 pp. $12.55.

A sequel to *India's Teeming Millions* (1972) by the same author describes how reproductive behavior is affected by modernization of such social institutions as marriage and the caste system, and discusses the demographic implications of urbanization, rural development, and socialistic policies.

Chandrasekhar, S. *Infant Mortality, Population Growth and Family Planning in India.* Chapel Hill, N.C.: University of North Carolina Press, 1972. 399 pp. $12.95.

Comprehensive review of trends and implications of Indian infant mortality since 1900 and population growth since 1871, and description of official efforts to promote family planning, by the former Minister for Health and Family Planning in charge of organizing the program.

Family Planning Foundation (Madras). *A Status Study on Population Research in India.* 2 vols. New Delhi: McGraw-Hill, 1974.

Vol. 1: *Behavioral Sciences,* by Udai Pareek and T. Venkateswara Rao. 261 pp.

Vol. 2: *Demography,* by S. P. Jain. 265 pp.

Comprehensive overview of population-related behavioral science and demographic research on India.

Franda, Marcus F., ed. *Responses to Population Growth in India: Changes in Social, Political and Economic Behavior.* New York: Praeger, 1975. 277 pp. $18.00.

Papers and discussion from a 1974 conference on a wide range of factors related to India's continuing population growth.

Mamdani, Mahmood. *The Myth of Population Control: Family, Caste and Class in an Indian Village.* New York: Monthly Review Press, 1972. 173 pp. $3.45 paper.

A critical commentary on the impact of birth control programs in India, in particular the Khanna study (see Wyon below).

Mandelbaum, D. G. *Human Fertility in India.* Berkeley, Cal.: University of California Press, 1974. 132 pp. $6.00.

Discusses sociocultural constraints, and traditional approaches to regulating fertility in India.

Operations Research Group. *Family Planning Practice in India: The First All-India Survey Report.* Baroda, India: Operations Research Group, 1973. 108 pp.

Analysis of findings from a national fertility and KAP survey carried out by this group for the Ministry of Health and Family Planning in 1970-71.

Poffenberger, Thomas et al. *Fertility and Family Life in an Indian Village.* Michigan Papers on South and Southeast Asia No. 10. Ann Arbor, Mich.: The University of Michigan Center for South and Southeast Asian Studies, 1975. 114 pp.

Findings from a pioneering 1963-67 study of social norms which affect fertility patterns in rural India.

Rao, Kamala G. *Studies in Family Planning: India.* New Delhi: Abhinav Publishers; distributed by South Asia Books, Box 502, Columbia, Missouri 65201, 1976. 863 pp. $18.50.

Summarizes the aims, samples, methods, and findings of some 550 family planning-related research studies conducted 1951-74 in India.

Simmons, George B. *The Indian Investment in Family Planning.* New York: The Population Council, 1971. 213 pp. $4.50.

Economic cost-benefit analysis of the Indian family planning program during the 1960s.

Wyon, John B. and John E. Gordon. *The Khanna Study: Population Problems in the Rural Punjab.* Cambridge, Mass.: Harvard University Press, 1971. 437 pp. $15.00.

Description of a joint Harvard-Indian field study of population dynamics in rural India between 1953 and 1959, including a trial family planning program, and findings from a 1969 followup survey.

Indonesia

Iskandar, N. *Some Monographic Studies on the Population in Indonesia.* Published by Lembaga Demografi, Facultas Ekonomi, University of Indonesia, Jakarta, Salemba 4, Indonesia, 1972. 387 pp.

Demographic data and analysis for Java, Madura, and Indonesia as a whole.

Manderson, Lenore. *Overpopulation in Java: Problems and Reactions.* Canberra: Department of Demography, Australian National University, 1974. 131 pp.

Based on a survey of 194 references. Includes historical and economic aspects of population growth as well as ongoing population policies and the family planning program.

McNicoll, Geoffrey and Si Gde Made Mamas. *The Demographic Situation in Indonesia.* Papers of the East-West Population Institute No. 28. Honolulu: East-West Center, 1973. 66 pp. Free.

Current demographic patterns are described together with some background material necessary for context.

Singarimbun, Masri. *The Population of Indonesia: A Bibliography, 1930-1972.* Yogyakarta: Population Institute, Gadjah Mada University, 1974. 176 pp.

Exhaustive listing of publications on all facets of population in Indonesia.

Universitas Indonesia. Lembaga Demografi. *Demographic Factbook of Indonesia.* Published by Fakultas Ekonomi, Universitas Indonesia, Jakarta, Salemba 4, Indonesia, 1973. 383 pp.

Analysis of 1961 census data plus estimates and discussion of fertility, mortality and mobility patterns from the beginning of the 18th century to the 1960s.

Widjojo, Nitisastro. *Population Trends in Indonesia.* Ithaca, N.Y.: Cornell University Press, 1970. 266 pp. $16.50.

A review of the demographic development of Indonesia from 1775 to 1961 with projections from data of the 1961 census through 1991, mostly on Java.

Japan

Matsumoto, Y. Scott. *Demographic Research in Japan, 1955-1970: A Survey and Selected Bibliography.* Papers of the East-West Population Institute No. 30. Honolulu: East-West Center, 1974. 78 pp. Free.

Overview of postwar Japanese demographic research and listing of 373 works by Japanese scholars.

Population Problems Research Council. *Summary of Thirteenth National Survey on Family Planning.* Tokyo: Population Problems Research Council, Mainichi Newspapers, 1975. 34 pp.

Findings from the latest (1975) in a series of biennial surveys conducted since 1950 by the Mainichi Newspapers which give a comprehensive picture of the attitudes and behavior of married Japanese women with regard to fertility, contraception and abortion.

Toshio, Kuroda. *Japan's Changing Population Structure.* Tokyo: Ministry of Foreign Affairs, 1973. 95 pp.

Surveys demographic trends since World War II and outlook for the future.

Republic of Korea (South)

Cho, Lee-Jay. *The Demographic Situation in the Republic of Korea.* Papers of the East-West Population Institute No. 29. Honolulu: East-West Center, 1973. 43 pp. Free.
> Recent demographic trends in the Republic of Korea showing a rapid demographic transition since the mid-1960s.

Kim, Taek II, John A. Ross, and George C. Worth. *The Korean National Family Planning Program: Population Control and Fertility Decline.* New York: The Population Council, 1972. 240 pp. $4.50.
> Describes the setting, experience, and results of Korea's official effort to reduce fertility from its beginning in 1962 through 1970, and future prospects.

Kwan, E. Hyock. *Ten Years of Urban Population Studies in Korea.* Seoul, Korea: College of Medicine, Seoul National University, 1974. 187 pp.
> Summarizes findings from 13 Korean family planning-related surveys from 1963–1973.

The National Population Clearing House. *Korean Population and Family Planning Bibliography.* Seoul, Korea: Korean Institute for Family Planning, 1974. 68 pp.
> Cites 430 items on Korean population and family planning from 1944 to 1974.

Population and Family Planning in the Republic of Korea. Seoul: Ministry of Health and Social Affairs, Republic of Korea, 1970. 540 pp.
> Compendium of 53 English-language articles on population and family planning in Korea.

Pakistan

Aghai, M. A. *Social, Psychological and Familial Correlates of Contraceptive Use in Pakistan.* Chicago: Community and Family Study Center, University of Chicago, 1976. 272 pp. $5.00 paper.
> Analysis of contraceptive use data collected from both husbands and wives in the 3,340 households sampled in Pakistan's 1968 national IMPACT survey (see next listing).

Pakistan Population Planning Council. *National Impact Survey Report.* Lahore: Training, Research, and Evaluation Centre, Pakistan Population Planning Council, 1974. 166 pp.
> Findings from a 1968 nationwide survey (then, both East and West Pakistan) designed to evaluate the family planning program.

Smithsonian Institution. *Prologue to Development Policy and Population Policy: The Pakistan Experience.* By Shahid J. Burki and Tine Bussink. Washington, D.C.: Interdisciplinary Communication Program, Smithsonian Institution, 1975. 78 pp. Free.
> Two articles on "Food and Fertility: Formulation of Public Policy in Pakistan," and "Major Aspects of Family Planning in Pakistan," plus annotated bibliography.

The Philippines

Ballweg, John and Sandra Ward. *Assessment of Family Planning Acceptability in the Philippines.* Blacksburg, Va.: Virginia Polytechnic Institute and State University, 1973. 224 pp.
> Data on Philippine family size and family planning KAP variables from a 1972 national survey compared with a 1968 baseline study.

Flieger, Wilhelm and Peter C. Smith, eds. *A Demographic Path to Modernity: Patterns of Early-Transition in the Philippines.* Quezon City: University of the Philippines Press, 1975. 318 pp.
> Examination of Philippine marriage and childbearing patterns based on analysis of data from the 1968 National Demographic Survey.

Kintanar, Agustin Jr. et al. *Studies in Philippine Economic-Demographic Relationships.* Manila: School of Economics, University of the Philippines, 1974. 288 pp.
> Assessment of the impact of Philippine family planning and nuptiality policies on economic development.

Madigan, Francis C. et al. *Birth and Death in Cayagan de Oro: Population Dynamics in a Medium-Sized Philippine City.* Quezon City: Ateneo University Press, 1972. 239 pp.
> A pioneering case study of demographic trends and their correlates in urban areas of the Third World, based on rigorous analysis of data from a 1963 survey of 2,074 families in this Philippine provincial capital.

Republic of the Philippines. National Census and Statistics Office. *Estimates of the Life Table Functions of the Philippines: 1970,* by Luisa T. Engracia, and *Age and Sex Population Projections for the Philippines by Province: 1970–2000.* UNFPA-NCSO Population Research Project Monographs Nos. 1 and 2. Manila: National Economic and Development Authority, National Census and Statistics Office, 1973 and 1974.
> Estimates and projections based on data from the 1970 census, 1972 Fertility and 1973 National Demographic Surveys.

Tufts University. Fletcher School of Law and Diplomacy. Law and Population Programmes. *Law and Population in the Philippines.* Law and Population Book Series No. 9, Medford, Mass.: Law and Population Programme, Tufts University, 1974. 151 pp. Free.
> Experts review the interrelationship of law and population in the Philippines; includes documentation of the recent changes in official population policy.

Singapore

Chang, Chen-Tung. *Fertility Transition in Singapore.* Singapore: Singapore University Press, 1974. Sing. $35.00.
> Well-documented account of Singapore's postwar fertility decline.

Swee-Hock, Saw. *Singapore Population in Transition.* Philadelphia: University of Pennsylvania Press, 1970. 227 pp. $12.50.
> Review of demographic trends and official strategies to overcome population pressures.

Swee-Hock, Saw and Cheng Siok-Hwa. *Bibliography of the Demography of Singapore.* Singapore: University Education Press, 1975. 120 pp.
> Non-annotated listing of 652 books, pamphlets, articles, etc. published in English.

United Nations Fund for Population Activities (UNFPA). *Singapore.* Population Profiles No. 1. New York: UNFPA, 1976. 31 pp. $1.50.
> Readable review of Singapore's many-faceted approach to threatened overpopulation. First in a new UNFPA series.

Taiwan

Chinese Center for International Training in Family Planning. *Annotated Taiwan Population Bibliography.* Taichung, Taiwan: Chinese Center for International Training in Family Planning, 1974. 155 pp.

Taiwan Committee on Family Planning. *Taiwan Population Studies Summaries.* Taichung, Taiwan: Taiwan Province Department of Health, 1973. 176 pp.

Summaries of over 100 studies conducted 1962-73 to improve Taiwan's population program with a companion annotated bibliography of more than 300 publications in English.

Thailand

Alers, J. Oscar and Suvanavejh Chaichana, eds. *Continuation of Contraceptive Practice in Thailand.* Bangkok: National Family Planning Program, Ministry of Public Health, 1974. 112 pp.

Findings from a nationwide KAP survey of family planning acceptors in 1971, three years after launching of a national program.

Chulalongkorn University. Institute of Population Studies. *Research Reports.* A series begun in 1969 by Institute staff and foreign advisors on various aspects of population in Thailand. Two other series are also published: *Papers* and *Special Reports.* For prices and full listing write the Institute in Bangkok, Thailand. Some recent *Research Reports* include:

2. *Urbanization in Thailand, 1947-1967,* by Sidney Goldstein (rev. ed., 1972).

5. *Interrelationships between Migration and Fertility in Population Redistribution in Thailand,* by Sidney Goldstein (1972).

7. *Internal Migration in Thailand,* by Visid Prachuabmoh and Penporn Tirasawat (1974).

10. *The Fertility of Thai Women,* by John Knodel and Visid Prachuabmoh (1973).

11. *Perspective on Thai Population,* by Jean Bourgeois-Pichat et al.

12. *Urban-rural Migration Differentials in Thailand,* by Sidney Goldstein, Visid Prachuabmoh, and Alice Goldstein (1974).

Fawcett, James et al. *Population Research in Thailand: A Review and Bibliography.* Honolulu: East-West Population Institute and Bangkok: Chulalonghorn University, 1973. 123 pp.

Comprehensive bibliography of population data and relevant social science research through 1972 introduced by a review essay.

Maurer, Kenneth, Rosalinda Ratajczak, and T. Paul Schultz. *Marriage, Fertility, and Labor Force Participation of Thai Women: An Econometric Study.* Report No. R-829-AID/RF. Santa Monica, Cal.: Rand, 1973. 68 pp. $5.00.

Systematic analysis of 1960 census data on these variables.

Ministry of Health and Institute of Population Studies. *Population Growth in Thailand.* 2nd ed. Bangkok: Institute of Population Studies, Chulalongkorn University, 1972. 42 pp.

A wide range of population statistics presented in 21 graphs and accompanying summaries.

Thomlinson, Ralph. *Thailand's Population: Facts, Trends, Problems and Policies.* Developing Nations Monograph Series. Winston-Salem, N.C.: Overseas Research Center, Wake Forest University, 1971. 118 pp. $2.75 plus postage.

Includes discussion of cultural factors, population characteristics, distribution, growth and policies, urbanization and immigration.

Bangladesh, Hong Kong, Malaysia

Ramachandran, K. V. and G. Shantokumar. *Fertility Differentials in West Malaysia.* Research Monograph Series No. 6. Devnar, Bombay: International Institute for Population Studies, 1974. 88 pp.

Demonstrates use of census data (1957 in this case) for estimating fertility patterns in countries lacking registration systems.

Stoeckel, John and Moqbel A. Choudhury. *Fertility, Infant Mortality and Family Planning in Rural Bangladesh.* Dacca: Oxford University Press, 1973. 154 pp. $1.25.

Analytical report of a fertility survey among 600 married women carried out in 1967-68 by the Bangladesh Academy for Rural Development in Comilla.

Swee-Hock, Saw and Cheng Siok-Hwa. *A Bibliography of the Demography of Malaysia and Brunei.* Singapore: University Education Press, 1975. 103 pp.

Non-annotated listing of 631 books, articles, etc. published in English.

United Nations. Economic and Social Commission for Asia and the Pacific (ESCAP). *The Demographic Situation in Hong Kong.* ESCAP Country Monograph Series No. 1. Bangkok: ESCAP, 1974. 170 pp. Free (priority to governments and institutions).

Comprehensive review of past, current and prospective population trends. First of a new series prepared by ESCAP Population Division and country experts as guides to government program planners.

D. EUROPE AND THE U.S.S.R

Hofsten, Erland and Hans Lundstrom. *Swedish Population History: Main Trends from 1750 to 1970.* Urval No. 8 Stockholm: 1976. 186 pp. Available from Liber distribution, S-16289 Vällingby. Sweden. Sw. Crs. 26.35.

Comprehensive description of Swedish population developments based on the world's longest series of official vital statistics data made compulsory by law in 1749; written for non-demographers.

Knodel, John E. *The Decline of Fertility in Germany, 1871-1939.* Princeton, N.J.: Princeton University Press, 1974. 306 pp. $14.50.

Second country study to emerge from a major investigation by Princeton's Office of Population Research of the circumstances associated with fertility decline since the early 19th century in each of Europe's more than 700 provinces.

Kosinski, Leszek. *The Population of Europe: A Geographical Perspective.* London: Longman Geography Paperbacks, 1970. 161 pp. £1.40.

Contains extensive demographic information, particularly on population distribution, age and sex structure, intra-European migration and out-migration from Europe.

Lewis, Robert A., Richard H. Rowland, and Ralph S. Clem. *Nationality and Population Change in Russia and the USSR: An Evaluation of Census Data, 1897-1970.* New York: Praeger, 1976. 456 pp. $27.50.

An investigation of demographic and socioeconomic trends among Soviet ethnic groups since 1897. First of a planned trilogy designed to demonstrate that the USSR is no exception to the general rule that "demographic processes are related largely to socioeconomic conditions, and not to the type of government under which they develop."

Livi Bacci, Massimo. *A Century of Portuguese Fertility.* Princeton, N.J.: Princeton University Press, 1971. 149 pp. $8.50.

First of the Princeton national studies mentioned under Knodel (above). Covers the period from 1864—date of Portugal's first modern census—to 1960, revealing a surprisingly low level of fertility before start of the modern decline and a clear north-south differential.

Moors, Hein G. *Child Spacing and Family Life in The Netherlands.* A publication of the Netherlands Interuniversity Demographic Institute. Leiden, The Netherlands: Stenfert Kroese, 1974. 193 pp.

Presents the major findings of the Netherlands National Fertility Survey of 1969 in an analysis of the fertility decline after 1964.

Moors, H. G. et al, eds. *Population and Family in the Low Countries.* Publications of the Netherlands Interuniversity Demographic Institute and the Population and Family Study Centre Vol. 1. Leiden, The Netherlands: Martinus Nijhoff Social Sciences Division, 1976. 179 pp. 37.50 Dutch guilders.

First in a planned annual series designed to give international readers and researchers access to results of the extensive population studies conducted in The Netherlands and Belgium.

Ross, C. R. et al. *Report of the Population Panel.* London: Her Majesty's Stationery Office, 1973. 135 pp.

Findings and recommendations of Britain's Population Panel, created by Parliament in 1971 to report on population growth and its consequences as a first step towards a population policy.

Sweden. Royal Ministry of Foreign Affairs. *The Biography of a People: Past and Future Population Changes in Sweden—Conditions and Consequences.* Stockholm, Sweden, 1974. 204 pp.

Compilation of data by the National Preparatory Committee for the World Population Conference on Swedish population development, past and future.

United Nations. Economic Commission for Europe. *Economic Survey of Europe in 1974.* Part 2: *Post-War Demographic Trends in Europe and the Outlook Until the Year 2000.* Sales No. 75.II.E.16. New York: United Nations, 1975. 252 pp. $11.00.

Thorough, well-documented review of trends in European mortality, nuptiality, fertility, migration and population growth and structure in the post-World War II period, with a look back to 1900 and detailed projections to 2000, prepared by the Secretariat of the Economic Commission for Europe in Geneva.

E. LATIN AMERICA AND THE CARIBBEAN

Arriaga, Eduardo E. *Mortality Decline and its Demographic Effects in Latin America.* Population Monograph Series No. 6. Berkeley, Cal.: Institute of International Studies, University of California, 1970. 232 pp. $3.25 paper.

Technical but readable and sobering account of what Latin America's unprecedentedly rapid rate of mortality decline, unaccompanied by lower fertility, signifies for future population growth; based mainly on 1930 and 1960 census data.

Balan, Jorge, Harley L. Browning, and Elizabeth Jelin. *Men in a Developing Society: Geographic and Social Mobility in Monterrey, Mexico.* Latin American Monographs No. 30. Austin, Tex.: University of Texas Press, 1973. 384 pp. $12.50.

A first case study of the effect of heavy Latin American rural-urban migration on men's careers, the cities to which they go and the villages they leave.

Beaver, Steven E. *Demographic Transition Theory Reinterpreted: An Application to Recent Natality Trends in Latin America.* Lexington, Mass.: Lexington Books, 1975. 208 pp. $15.50.

Demonstrates that, contrary to much prior research, there is no evidence that Latin America will prove to be peculiarly resistant to natality reduction.

Boyer, Richard E. and Keith A. Davies. *Urbanization in 19th Century Latin America: Statistics and Sources.* Los Angeles, Cal.: Latin American Center, University of California, 1973. $3.25 paper.

Demographic profiles of cities of 19th century Argentina, Brazil, Mexico and Peru, compiled from viceregal, national and regional censuses, estimates of travellers and residents, and data in government tracts.

Carvajal, Manuel J., ed. *Population Growth and Human Productivity.* English/Spanish. Gainesville, Fla.: Center for Latin American Studies, University of Florida, 1976. 296 pp. $7.50 paper.

Report of a 1974 symposium focused on the relationship between population growth and labor, education, and health, with cases studies of Brazil, Colombia, Mexico, and Venezuela.

Centro Latinoamericano de Demografía (CELADE) and Community and Family Study Center (CFSC). *Fertility and Family Planning in Metropolitan Latin America.* Chicago: CFSC, University of Chicago, 1972. 323 pp. $4.00 paper.

Describes CELADE's program of comparative Latin American fertility studies and analyzes findings from 1964 and 1966 surveys in nine major cities.

Chaplin, David, ed. *Population Policies and Growth in Latin America.* Lexington, Mass.: Lexington Books, 1971. 287 pp. $13.50.

Fourteen chapters on policies relating to family planning, labor, welfare and agriculture and their demographic implications.

Cornelius, Wayne A. and Felicity M. Trueblood. *Anthropological Perspectives on Latin American Urbanization.* Latin American Urban Research Vol. 4. Beverly Hills, Cal.: Sage Publications, 1974. 296 pp. $17.50.

Collection of recent research on the socioeconomic characteristics of Latin American cities and effects of rural-urban migration.

Fox, Robert W. *Urban Population Growth Trends in Latin America.* Washington, D.C.: Inter-American Development Bank, 1975. 103 pp. Free.

Urban population projections to the year 2000 for Argentina, Brazil, Chile, Mexico, Peru and Venezuela, based on recent national censuses and 1971-72 field research.

Hardoy, Jorge E., ed. *Urbanization in Latin America: Approaches and Issues.* Garden City, N.Y.: Anchor Press/Doubleday, 1975. 456 pp. $4.50 paper.

Twelve articles on the history, structure and future of Latin American cities with case studies in Argentina, Mexico and Sao Paulo.

Macisco, John J., Jr. *Migrants to Metropolitan Lima: A Case Study.* Monograph Series A, No. 133. Santiago, Chile: Centro Latinoamericano de Demografía (CELADE), 1975. 135 pp.

Analysis of findings from a 1965-66 household survey in Lima, Peru.

McCoy, Terry L., ed. *The Dynamics of Population Policy in Latin America.* Cambridge, Mass.: Ballinger, 1974. 410 pp. $17.50.

Contemporary Latin American population politics, programs and their determinants by policymakers and policy research scholars, plus case studies of Chile, Costa Rica, Colombia, the Dominican Republic, Venezuela, Peru and Mexico.

Pan American Health Organization (PAHO) and Transnational Family Research Institute. *Epidemiology of Abortion and Practices of Fertility Regulation in Latin America: Selected Reports.* PAHO Scientific Publication No. 306. Washington, D.C.: Pan American Sanitary Bureau, Regional Office of the World Health Organization, 1975. 142 pp. $7.50.

A pioneering collection of empirical findings from recent Latin American fertility and abortion research, current status of abortion legislation, and bibliography of 903 relevant materials published 1950 to 1975.

Presser, Harriet B. *Sterilization and Fertility Decline in Puerto Rico.* Population Monograph Series No. 13. Berkeley, Cal.: Institute of International Studies, University of California, 1973. 211 pp. $3.25 paper.

Analysis of the social conditions which led to the widespread use of sterilization in Puerto Rico and the impact on fertility attitudes and behavior.

Ramos, Joseph. *Labor and Development in Latin America.* New York: Columbia University Press, 1970. 281 pp. $13.50.

Examination of Latin American employment statistics as they relate to changes in population structure.

Sable, Martin H. *Latin American Urbanization: A Guide to the Literature, Organization and Personnel.* Metuchen, N.J.: Scarecrow Press, 1971. 1,077 pp. $27.50.

Non-annotated bibliographic section lists materials on practically every topic concerned with Latin American cities (in English and Spanish).

Sanchez-Albornoz, Nicolas. *The Population of Latin America: A History.* Translated by W.A.R. Richardson. Berkeley, Cal.: University of California Press, 1974. 299 pp. $17.50.

The demographic history of Latin America from pre-Columbian to modern times.

Segal, Aaron, ed. *Population Policies in the Caribbean.* Lexington, Mass.: Lexington Books, 1975. 256 pp. $15.00.

Review of current population policies in the Bahamas, Belize, Barbados, Cuba, Jamaica, Trinidad and Puerto Rico.

Smith, T. Lynn. *The Race between Population and Food Supply in Latin America.* Albuquerque, N.M.: University of New Mexico Press, 1976. 194 pp. $12.50.

Well-documented analysis of obstacles and possible solutions to achieving a population-food balance in Latin America, particularly in Brazil and Colombia.

Stycos, J. Mayone. *Ideology, Faith and Family Planning in Latin America: Studies in Public and Private Opinion on Fertility Control.* A Population Council Book. New York: McGraw-Hill, 1971. 440 pp. $15.00.

Examines the attitudes of the Latin American elite and general public towards family planning.

Taylor, Philip B., Jr. and Sam Schulman, eds. *Population and Urbanization Problems of Latin America.* Houston, Texas: Latin American Studies Department, Office of International Affairs, University of Houston, 1971. 124 pp. $3.00.

Papers from a 1971 conference by Stycos, Viel and other authorities on Latin American population issues.

Thomas, Robert N., ed. *Population Dynamics of Latin America: A Review and Bibliography.* East Lansing, Mich.: Conference of Latin American Geographers, 1973. 200 pp. $4.75.

Unique guide to a wide variety of original sources for Latin American population data and review of population trends.

United Nations. Economic Commission for Latin America. *Latin America: Demographic Situation Around 1973 and Prospects for the Year 2000.* Santiago, Chile: Centro Latinoamericano de Demografía (CELADE), 1974. 49 pp.

Statistical country data including population age structure and rates of increase.

United Nations. Economic and Social Council. Economic Commission for Latin America, 14th Session. *Population Trends and Policy Alternatives in Latin America: Conference Document, 8 February 1971.* No. E/CN.12/874. New York: United Nations, 1971. 71 pp.

Useful outline of the development dilemmas created by current Latin American demographic phenomena; extensive bibliography, particularly of U.N. documents on Latin America.

Viel, Benjamin. *The Demographic Explosion: The Latin American Experience.* New York: Halsted Press, 1975. 250 pp. $14.95.

Analysis of biological, medical, socioeconomic and political aspects of population growth in Latin America forms a background for description of how family planning services should be organized.

F. MIDDLE EAST

Asayesh, K. A. *Iran,* and *Family Planning in Iran.* Chapel Hill, N.C.: Department of Health Administration and Carolina Population Center, University of North Carolina, 1974. 133 and 46 pp.

Basic information on Iran and its national family planning program by a former assistant director-general of the program.

Cairo Demographic Centre. *Research Monographs Series.* Cairo Demographic Centre, 6 Sharia Willcocks, Zamaleck, Cairo. A continuing series presenting data and analysis of population-related trends in Arab countries. Includes the following to date:

1. *Demographic Measures and Population Growth in Arab Countries,* 1970. 352 pp. $12.00.

2. *Fertility Trends and Differentials in Arab Countries,* 1971. 398 pp. $15.00.

3. *Demographic Aspects of Manpower in Arab Countries,* 1976. $18.00.

5. *Urbanization and Migration in Some Arab and African Countries,* 1976.

Clarke, J. I. and W. B. Fisher, eds. *Populations of the Middle East and North Africa: A Geographical Approach.* New York: Holmes & Meier, 1972. 432 pp. $25.00.

Broad-ranging review of population distribution, migration, composition and growth, based on what scarce data there are for this area.

Cooper, Charles A. and Sidney S. Alexander, eds. *Economic Development and Population Growth in the Middle East.* New York: American Elsevier Publishing, 1972. 620 pp. $34.50.

Focus is mainly economic growth per se, but includes the Schultz and DaVanzo paper (see below) and a chapter by Yoram Ben-Porath on "Fertility in Israel: An Economic Interpretation: Differentials and Trends, 1950–1977."

International Labour Office (ILO). *Problems of Employment Creation in Iran.* Geneva: ILO, 1970. 86 pp. $1.50.

Despite Iran's high rates of economic growth, continued unemployment and underemployment can be anticipated in view of estimated and projected high rates of population growth.

Omran, Abdel R., ed. *Egypt: Population Problems and Prospects.* Chapel Hill, N.C.: Carolina Population Center, University of North Carolina, 1973. 448 pp. $6.50 paper.

Comprehensive discussion of all aspects of Egypt's population problems with proposed solutions.

Schultz, T. Paul and Julia DaVanzo. *Fertility Patterns and Their Determinants in the Arab Middle East.* Santa Monica, Cal.: Rand, 1970. 116 pp. $7.00.

Fertility and employment and education interrelations in the Middle East, based on analysis of 1960 census data.

Valaoras, V. G. *Population Analysis of Egypt (1935–1970): With Special Reference to Mortality.* Occasional Paper No. 1. Cairo: Cairo Demographic Centre, 1972. 63 pp.

Population growth trends of the past 35 years in Egypt based on corrected census and registration materials.

G. NORTH AMERICA

Commission on Population Growth and the American Future. *Final Report, Research Papers, Statements,* and *Index.* Washington, D.C.: Government Printing Office, 1972–1975. Priced according to volume.

This Commission was established in 1969 to examine population growth and its impact upon the American future. After an extensive inquiry, the Commission Chairman, John D. Rockefeller, 3d, submitted the final report to President Nixon on March 27, 1972. Published since that time, the specially-commissioned research reports by experts in each field constitute perhaps the most comprehensive, thoughtful review ever undertaken of one nation's population situation, past, present, and prospective. Following is a listing of individual volumes, available from the Government Printing Office:

Population and the American Future: The Report of the Commission on Population Growth and the American Future. Final Report, 1972. 186 pp. $1.75.

Themes and Highlights of the Final Report of the Commission on Population Growth and the American Future. Summary. 16 pp. Free.

Volume I: *Demographic and Social Aspects of Population Growth,* edited by Charles F. Westoff and Robert Parke, Jr., 1972. 674 pp. $5.55.

Volume II: *Economic Aspects of Population Change,* edited by Elliott R. Morse and Ritchie Reed, 1972. 379 pp. $3.70.

Volume III: *Population, Resources, and the Environment,* edited by Ronald G. Ridker, 1972. 377 pp. $4.25.

Volume IV: *Governance and Population: The Governmental Implications of Population Change,* edited by A. E. Keir Nash, 1972. 342 pp. $3.75.

Volume V: *Population Distribution and Policy,* edited by Sara Mills Mazie, 1972. 719 pp. $6.15.

Volume VI: *Aspects of Growth Policy,* edited by Robert Parke, Jr. and Charles F. Westoff, 1972. 607 pp. $5.30.

Volume VII: *Statements at Public Hearings of the Commission on Population Growth and the American Future,* 1972. 230 pp. $2.30.

Subject and Name Indexes to Publications of the Commission on Population Growth and the American Future, prepared by U.S. Congress, House Committee on Post Office and Civil Service, Subcommittee on Census and Population, 1975. 290 pp. $1.75.

Davis, Kingsley and Frederick G. Styles, eds. *California's Twenty Million.* Population Monograph Series No. 10. Berkeley, Cal.: Institute of International Studies, University of California, 1971. 349 pp. $4.25.

A discussion of population policy by Davis, plus expert research papers on migration, environmental attitudes, marriage, illegitimacy and abortion in California.

Gardner, Robert W. and Eleanor C. Nordyke. *The Demographic Situation in Hawaii.* Papers of the East-West Population Institute No. 31. Honolulu: East-West Center, 1974. 120 pp. Free.

Major demographic patterns of Hawaii since 1900 and special issues such as the ethnic composition of the state and the effects of changing military presence on the total population.

Grindstaff, Carl F. et al, eds. *Population Issues in Canada: Canadian Studies.* Toronto: Holt, Rinehart and Winston of Canada, 1971. 102 pp. $2.88.

Collection of articles designed as a concise reader for persons with a specific interest in the study of Canadian population.

Kahn, E. J., Jr. *The American People.* New York: Weybright and Talley, 1973. 340 pp. $8.95.

A noted journalist explores findings of the 1970 census including mobility, socioeconomic status, and race, without tables or graphs.

Kalbach, Warren E. and Wayne W. McVey. *The Demographic Bases of Canadian Society.* Toronto: McGraw-Hill of Canada, 1971. 354 pp. $6.75.

A basic textbook for students of Canadian demography; reviews historical developments in national and regional population growth and recent trends in education, occupation, labor force and marital status.

Kubat, Daniel and David Thornton. *A Statistical Profile of Canadian Society.* Toronto: McGraw-Hill Ryerson, 1974. 200 pp. $3.95.

A useful compendium of times series and most recent data on Canadian demographic and social characteristics.

Rosenwaike, Ira. *Population History of New York City.* Syracuse, N.Y.: Syracuse University Press, 1972. 224 pp. $12.00.

The demographic history of America's largest city.

Southern Regional Demographic Group. *Demography of the South.* 3 vols. plus Summary and Index. Oak Ridge, Tenn.: Southern Regional Demographic Group, 1973. Over 300 pp.

Papers on current demographic trends of the U.S. South, prepared for a meeting of demographers and state government officials in 1973.

Taeuber, Irene B. and Conrad Taeuber. *People of the United States in the Twentieth Century.* Washington, D.C.: Government Printing Office, 1971. 1,046 pp. $5.75.

In-depth, exhaustively documented analysis of population change during the period 1900–1960 in which the formation of metropolitan America occurred. Supported by specially processed census data.

U.S. Congress. House. Committee on the Post Office and Civil Service. *Population. Hearings before the Subcommittee on Census and Population,* 94th Cong., 2nd sess., 1975-76. Washington, D.C.: Government Printing Office, 1976. Free.

Experts evaluate implications of U.S. population trends since the 1972 Population Commission Report (see also p. 66).

U.S. Office of Management and Budget. *Social Indicators, 1973.* Washington, D.C.: Government Printing Office, 1973. 258 pp. $7.80. New edition forthcoming fall 1976.

A pioneering collection of trend data on U.S. conditions of health, public safety, education, employment, income, housing, leisure and recreation, and population.

Wattenberg, Ben G. *The Real America: A Surprising Examination of the State of the Union.* Garden City, N.Y.: Doubleday, 1974. 367 pp. $10.00.

Latest of the author's very personal interpretations of official U.S. population statistics.

H. OCEANIA

Burnley, I. M. *Urbanization in Australia: The Post-War Experience.* London: Cambridge University Press, 1973. $13.95.

A collection of 14 articles on demographic, economic and social aspects of urbanization in Australia between 1947 and 1971.

Carroll, Vern, ed. *Pacific Atoll Populations.* Association for Social Anthropology in Oceania Monograph No. 3. An East-West Center Book. Honolulu: University Press of Hawaii, 1975. 528 pp. $20.00.

First report of a 1972–73 East-West Population Institute study discusses techniques for studying small populations and includes seven case studies from the Pacific.

Hargreaves, R. P. and L. D. B. Heenan. *An Annotated Bibliography of New Zealand Population.* Dunedin, N.Z.: University of Otago Press, 1972. 230 pp.

Covers writings on New Zealand population from 1838 to 1970.

Johnston, Ruth. *Future Australians: Immigrant Children in Perth, Western Australia.* Immigrants in Australia Series No. 2. Canberra: Australian National University, 1972. 290 pp. $14.75.

Analyzes second-generation immigrants of Polish, German and British origin, aged 13 to 19 years.

McDonald, Peter F. *Marriage in Australia.* Australian Family Formation Project Monograph No. 2. Canberra: Australian National University, 1974. 311 pp.

Study of marriage patterns in Australia from 1860 to 1972.

The Parliament of the Commonwealth of Australia. *Population and Australia: A Demographic Analysis and Projection.* 2 vols. Canberra: Government Printer of Australia, 1975. 748 pp. Vol. 1, $(Aust) 7.30; Vol. 2: $(Aust.)4.90.

First exhaustive report of the three-year Australian National Population Inquiry.

Ware, Helen, ed. *Fertility and Family Formation: Australian Bibliography and Essays, 1972.* Australian Family Formation Project Monograph No. 1. Canberra: Australian National University, 1973. 349 pp. $7.45.

Primarily a bibliography plus findings from a pilot survey of fertility attitudes among urban married women.

XIV. Population Education*

Bouvier, Leon F. and Everett S. Lee. *Population Profiles.* Washington, Conn.: Center for Information on America, 1972–1975. 8 pp. each. $0.50 each.

Designed for use in high school, college, or community classes, each of 14 units in the series presents population concepts and information in traditional descriptive form. Study guides for the units are available.

Burleson, Noel-David. "Population Education: Problems and Perspectives," *Educational Documentation and Information* No. 19. Geneva: UNESCO, 1974. 100 pp. $2.75.

Deals with definitions and concepts in population education and describes different approaches according to regional needs. Includes an annotated bibliography of curriculum materials and programs for world regions.

Environment-Population Education Services. *Planning for People: Land Use Decision Making Kit.* Hamden, Conn.: Environment-Population Education Services, 21 Merritt St., 1975. $28.00 for this unit.

One of 13 self-instructional curriculum units on population growth, alternative patterns for future population growth, and the role of population data in land use decision making. The State of Connecticut is used as a model for study, but data from other states can easily be substituted.

Fletcher, Carol and Rebecca Davison. *Food for Thought: A Population Simulation Kit.* Washington, D.C.: Population Reference Bureau and Population Institute, 1976. 41 pp. $3.00.

Designed to foster understanding through role playing of the relationships, problems and consequences involved in population growth and distribution of people, food, and land area.

---

*This section was compiled by Judith Seltzer and Carol Fletcher, Director and Assistant Director, Population Education Program, Population Reference Bureau.

Horsley, Kathryn et al. *Environment and Population: A Sourcebook for Teachers.* Washington, D.C.: National Education Association, 1972. 112 pp. $3.75.

Sourcebook on population variables in relation to various social and natural pressures. Concepts are developed at junior and senior high levels for use in courses in contemporary issues, family life, history social studies, and sciences.

Horsley, Kathryn et al. *Options: A Study Guide to Population and the American Future.* Washington, D.C.: Population Reference Bureau, 1973. 75 pp. Free, except for postage.

Study guide for teachers and community group leaders to explore U.S. population issues. Designed to be used independently or in conjunction with the written and film versions of the U.S. Commission Report on *Population Growth and the American Future.*

Hughes, Helen MacGill, ed. *Population Growth and Complex Society.* Sociological Resources for the Social Studies. Boston: Allyn and Bacon, 1972. 211 pp. $1.68 paper.

Adaptations of 19 articles by demographers and other social scientists on the complex relationship between population size, distribution and composition, and our rapidly changing society.

King, Pat and John Landahl. *Teaching Population Concepts.* Olympia, Wash.: Office of the Superintendent of Public Instruction, 1973. 60 pp. Free.

The three sections of this pamphlet present some of the basic concepts of population study, a brief overview of the population issue, and some sample teaching-learning activities that illustrate the range of possibilities for incorporating population study into the school curriculum.

Kline, David and David Harman, eds. *Issues in Population Education.* Lexington, Mass.: Lexington Books, 1976. 286 pp. $10.00.

Issues discussed include context, objectives, ethics, curriculum development and research and evaluation.

Leighton, Andrew J. *A Selected Annotated Bibliography for United States Schools.* New York: The Population Council, 1976. 16 pp. Free.

This review of materials prepared for use by teachers, students, curriculum designers, and others interested in population includes four sections: (1) population background, (2) population education, (3) points of view, and (4) reports on the U.N. World Population Conference in Bucharest, August 1974.

Marden, Parker G. *Population Workbook: A Series of Learning Exercises in Population Studies for Undergraduates.* New York: Learning Resources in International Studies, 1974. 56 pp. $2.00 paper.

Thirteen exercises designed to introduce high school and undergraduate students to population dynamics and issues through active involvement in problem solving and role playing.

Marden, Parker G., ed. *Teaching Notes on Population: An Occasional Newsletter for College Teachers.* New York: Foreign Area Materials Center, State Education Department, 1973. Pp. vary. Six issues published to date. Free.

Newsletter containing evaluation of textbooks and other teaching materials including videotapes and games, teaching notes on population, modules, and articles on aspects of the systematic study of population for undergraduate students.

Murphy, Elaine. *Population and Human Development: A Course Curriculum Including Lessons Plans, Activities and Bibliography.* Washington, D.C.: The Population Institute, 1975. 41 pp. $1.00.

Multidisciplinary population course outline for teacher training, undergraduates, and advanced high school students.

National Association for Foreign Student Affairs. *The People Packet.* Washington, D.C.: National Association for Foreign Student Affairs, 1975. 55 pp. Single copies free.

Resource packet for use in awareness programs concerned with world and national population issues.

National Catholic Education Association (NCEA). *Population Education Workshop Proceedings.* Washington, D.C.: NCEA, 1975. 62 pp. $2.75.

The proceedings of the December 1974 workshop cover the following issues: population problems in building a just society, food and population, teaching about global interdependence, each individual's responsibility, and population issues in Catholic curricula.

Population Reference Bureau. *The World Population Dilemma.* Washington, D.C.: Columbia Books, 1972. 80 pp. $2.00.

Factual text for grades 10 to junior college presenting demographic trends; discusses the linkages between population growth and nuclear war, environmental pollution, racism, nationalism, and world poverty.

Population Reference Bureau. *World and U.S. Population Charts,* I. Washington, D.C., 1975. $3.50 for set of eight wall charts and 10 sets of notebook size reproductions. Series includes: World Population Growth; World Birth and Death Rates (estimated); World Urbanization, 1800–2000; The Development Gap; Age-Sex Population Pyramids, Rapid, Slow and No Growth Models; Components of U.S. Population Growth, 1900–1974; Distribution of U.S. Population 1975; U.S. Immigrants by Region of Origin, 1820–1974. Each notebook size chart includes questions and explanatory texts for student use.

The 1976 series (II) includes: World Grain Consumption, 1976; World Energy Production, Consumption and Population, 1950 and 1974; Major Causes of Death in the United States, 1900–1975; Age Structure of the U.S. Population in the 20th Century; Status of Women in the United States, 1950 and 1975 by Education and Labor Force; and U.S. School Enrollment, 1950–2000. $3.00 for set of six wall charts and 10 sets of notebook size reproductions.

Seltzer, Judith R., editor, and Carol Fletcher. *Interchange.* Washington, D.C.: Population Reference Bureau. 5 issues annually. 4 pp. Free.

A national population education newsletter for educators designed to promote understanding of current population trends and issues, provide information on training opportunities and teaching materials, and outline instructional activities useful in the classroom for illustrating population studies.

Seltzer, Judith R. and JoAnn Robinson. *Population Education: Sources and Resources.* Washington, D.C.: Population Reference Bureau, 1975. 231 pp. Single copy free; bulk $1.00 each.

A comprehensive annotated listing of population organizations and materials (including charts, films, and games) for teachers and community leaders.

Social Issues Resources Series. *Population.* Gaithersburg, Md.: Social Issues Resources Series, Inc., 1975. $40.00 for initial volume of 104 articles and annual supplements of 20 articles for $10.00.

Reprints of population-related articles from a wide variety of sources.

Sociological Resources for the Social Studies. *Episodes in Social Inquiry.* Boston: Allyn and Bacon, 1972–75. Four *Episodes* are related to population:

"Family Size & Society." 54 pp. 10 copies $6.30.

"Migration Within the U.S." 51 pp. 10 copies $6.50.

"Population Change: A Case Study of Puerto Rico." 54 pp. 10 copies $7.20.

"Roles of Modern Women." 66 pp. 10 copies $6.72.

UNESCO. Division of Equality of Educational Opportunity and Special Programs. Population Education Section. *Report of the International Study of the Conceptualization and Methodology of Population Education (ISCOMPE).* Paris: forthcoming 1976.

> This report is intended as an international consensus on the concepts and methods of population education which includes a review of population education programs throughout the world, and an attempt to answer the who, what, where, when and why of population education.

UNESCO. Regional Office for Education in Asia. *Population Education in Asia: A Sourcebook.* 5 vols. Bangkok: UNESCO, Regional Office for Education in Asia, 1975. 348 pp. $38.00 paper.

> Designed as a model for curriculum development specialists and for use in teacher training programs in Asia. Includes an orientation to population education, demographic data on growth and distribution in Asian regions, a section on quality of life themes, and references, tables, and charts.

Urban Life-Population Education Institute. *The Population-Education Teachers' Workshop Package.* Baltimore: Urban Life Population Education Institute, 1976. $20.00.

> The package includes a 13 minute, 16 millimeter, color film, "Population Education: So What? Who Cares? Big Deal," a leader's guide, copies of four curricula, evaluation forms, and samples of available materials.

U.S. Bureau of the Census. *Census Portraits.* Washington, D.C.: Government Printing Office, 1974. 52 leaflets of 4 pp. each, $10.00 per set.

> Leaflets for each of the 50 states, the District of Columbia, and Puerto Rico, each containing basic demographic data.

U.S. Bureau of the Census. *We, The Americans.* Washington, D.C.: Government Printing Office, 1972–73. 12–20 pp. $0.35 each.

> A series of well-illustrated pamphlets designed for high school use presenting 1970 census data on black Americans, American homes, women, Spanish-speaking Americans, American Indians, youth, immigrants, jobs, the elderly, schooling and income.

Viederman, Stephen. "Towards a Broader Definition of Population Education," *International Social Science Journal,* Vol. XXVI, No. 2, 1974. Pp. 315–327.

> An article discussing the need for learner based population education and the content of population education at the macro and micro levels including an exploration of values and attitudes within appropriate educational settings.

Viederman, Stephen, ed. "Population Education." *Social Education,* Vol. 36, No. 4, April 1972. Washington, D.C.: National Council for the Social Studies. 103 pp. Out of print.

> This special issue provides a theoretical basis for both content of and approach to population education as part of school curricula in the U.S. A section on sources for population education includes comprehensive annotations of written and audiovisual materials.

Zero Population Growth. *Population Education Kit.* Washington, D.C.: Zero Population Growth, Inc., 1976. 23 pp. $1.00.

> A colorful folder containing, among other items, reviews of resource materials and films for teachers, charts, games and riddles, and a teaching unit.

XV. General Bibliographies and Computerized Information Retrieval Services Located in the United States

A. GENERAL BIBLIOGRAPHIES

This section excludes library acquisitions lists, "reading lists," and bibliographies focused on specific areas pertaining to population. For the latter see the appropriate topical sections, e.g., fertility, migration, environment, abortion.

American Association for the Advancement of Science (AAAS). *Science for Society: A Bibliography.* 6th ed. Prepared by Joseph M. Dasbach. Washington, D.C.: Office of Science Education, AAAS, 1776 Massachusetts Ave., N.W. 20036, 1976. 104 pp. $3.00.

> Sixth edition of an annotated, cross-indexed bibliography focused on the "interrelationships of humankind, the environment, science, and technology." Covers recently published books and articles on aging and death, conflict, energy, environmental manipulation, ethics, values, responsibility and science, health care, natural resources, pollution, population, technology and humankind, and transportation.

Council of Planning Librarians. *Exchange Bibliographies.* Monticello, Ill.: Council of Planning Librarians, Exchange Bibliographies, P.O. Box 229, Monticello, Ill. 61856. Prices vary.

> Bibliographies on a variety of subjects, some on migration, population, family planning. Prepared by librarians or specialists in the particular field. Some are annotated. For a complete listing of titles and prices, write to above address. Recent titles pertinent to population are:
>
> No. 861. *The History of Birth Control in the United States: A Working Bibliography,* by Lenwood G. Davis, 1975. 18 pp. $2.00.
>
> No. 989. *A Selected Bibliographic Research Guide to Regional Population Studies,* by Prakash C. Sharma, 1976. 17 pp. $1.50.
>
> No. 1024. *Out-Migration in Appalachia: An Annotated Bibliography,* by Carolynne Moore, 1976. 8 pp. $1.50.

East-West Communication Institute. *Information, Education, Communication in Population: Cumulative List of Materials Available, 1971–1974.* 3rd ed. Honolulu: East-West Communication Institute, 1777 East-West Road. 31 pp. Free.

> Non-annotated worldwide listing of population/family planning IEC materials, stressing unpublished reports and documents not routinely listed in standard bibliographies. New materials are listed routinely in a supplement to the *IEC Newsletter* of the East-West Communication Institute (free). Photocopy or microfiche reproductions of materials listed can be supplied by the East-West Communication Institute at cost or on an exchange basis. For further information write above address.

European Centre for Population Studies. *European Demographic Information Bulletin.* The Hague: European Centre for Population Studies, Pauwenlaan 17. Published quarterly. Annual subscription 40 Dutch guilders plus 7.50 guilders postage. Separate issues, 12.50 guilders.

> Partially annotated listing of books, articles and reports published in English, French and German on broad range of demographic and population topics, with special focus on Europe. Includes special articles and reports on meetings, etc.

Goode, Stephen H., ed. *Population and the Population Explosion: A Bibliography for 1973.* Compiled by Charles W. Triche III and Diane Samson Triche. Troy, N.Y.: Whitston Publishing, 1975. 173 pp. $13.00.

> Fourth annual non-annotated bibliography of books, monographs, pamphlets and articles which attempts to cover the world literature on problems related to overpopulation. English with some French and German.

Interdisciplinary Communication Program (ICP). *Annotated Bibliography Series.* Washington, D.C.: International Program for Population Analysis, ICP, Smithsonian Institution, 1717 Massachusetts Ave. N.W. 20036. (Program discontinued after 1976.) Single copies free.

> Series of short, semi-annual annotated bibliographies on the social science aspects of population programs and policies. Series includes bibliographies on agricultural development and small farm families, the organization and management of family planning and population programs, "woman's place" and fertility in the developing world, and health and population.

International Planned Parenthood Federation (IPPF). *IPPF Bibliographies: New Series.* London: IPPF Central Office, 18-20 Lower Regent Street, London SW1Y 4PW, U.K. Single copies free.

> A series of 28 short annotated bibliographies compiled by the IPPF Central Library on topics such as family planning communication, organization and administration, abortion, distribution of contraceptives, sex education, illegitimacy, status of women, and law and population. Updated occasionally. Complete listing available from the librarian at above address.

Planned Parenthood Federation of America. Katharine Dexter McCormick Library. *Current Literature in Family Planning.* New York: Planned Parenthood Federation of America, 810 Seventh Avenue. Monthly. $15.00/year.

> Classified listing and review of books and articles in the field of family planning. Addresses of book publishers are provided. Reprints or copies of articles may be ordered at $0.10 per page.

The Population Council. *Current Publications in Population/Family Planning.* New York: The Population Council, 245 Park Avenue. Bimonthly from April 1969 to December 1975. Back issues available free.

> Annotated listings of books and articles on population and family planning. Now discontinued, but back issues are still useful. Literature listings and reviews now appear regularly in The Council's *Studies in Family Planning* and *Population and Development Review* (see "Periodicals").

Princeton University. Office of Population Research. *Population Index.* Published quarterly for the Population Association of America. Princeton, N.J.: Office of Population Research, 21 Prospect Ave. $20.00/year.

> The single most comprehensive, up-to-date, annotated listing of books, articles, reports, official statistical materials, etc., available in population and related fields around the world in English and European languages. Also publishes in-depth demographic articles, abstracts from papers delivered at the annual meetings of the Population Association of America, notices of meetings, etc.

Simon Population Trust. *Bibliography of Family Planning and Population.* Cambridge, U.K.: Simon Population Trust, 141 Newmarket Road, Cambridge CB5 8HA, U.K.

> Classified bimonthly list of international references. Published only from July 1972 to November 1973, but still useful.

University of North Carolina at Chapel Hill. Carolina Population Center. Technical Information Service (TIS). *Bibliography Series.* Chapel Hill: TIS, Carolina Population Center, University Square, Chapel Hill, N.C. 27514. Prices vary.

> Series of bibliographies on population and family planning topics, some annotated. For complete listing and price list write above address.
> Recent titles include:

No. 9. *Breastfeeding and Human Infertility,* by Mayling Simpson-Hebert, 1975. 47 citations, annotated. $1.00.

No. 10. *A Selected Annotated Bibliography on Population and Family Planning in Iran,* 2d ed. By Hama Ghasemi-Gonabadi (Asayesh), 1975. 199 citations, annotated. $3.50.

U.S. Department of Health, Education, and Welfare. National Institute of Child Health and Human Development. Center for Population Research. *Population Sciences: Index of Biomedical Research.* Monthly. U.S.: $21.80/year; foreign: $27.25/year.

> Available only through a subscription placed directly with Superintendent of Documents, U.S. Government Printing Office, Washington, D.C. 20402. Sample issue available on request to Center for Population Research, National Institute for Child Health and Human Development, Landow Building, Bethesda, Md. 20014. A bibliographic citation journal of biomedical research literature in the population sciences, including monographs and conference proceedings. Produced in cooperation with the National Library of Medicine.

B. COMPUTERIZED INFORMATION RETRIEVAL SERVICES LOCATED IN THE U.S.

BioSciences Information Service of Biological Abstracts. *Bioresearch Today: Population, Fertility and Birth Control.* Monthly. $40.00 year.

Monthly listing of selected citations and abstracts from *Biological Abstracts.* Scope includes studies on chemical and physical regulation of fertility and population in humans, endocrine control of fertility, demographic statistics, genetic counseling, family planning and birth control modification including improvement and control through animal research which have a direct influence on human population. Personalized searches of BIOSIS's total file are also available. For details write to above at 2100 Arch St., Philadelphia, Pa. 19103.

George Washington University Medical Center. Department of Medical and Public Affairs. Population Information Program. POPINFORM.

A comprehensive collection of computerized population and family planning information and international data assembled by the Population Information Program and made available by Informatics, Inc. for on-line access by subscribers. POPINFORM data bases include those of the Population Information Program and the Prostaglandin Information Center of George Washington University, the International Institute for the Study of Human Reproduction at Columbia University, and sample records from the Family Planning Evaluation Division of the Center for Disease Control, the International Demographic Data Directory of the U.S. Bureau of the Census, and the East-West Communication Institute. These data bases contain nearly 40,000 citations (as of mid-1976) with abstracts and/or index terms of published and unpublished research studies on all fertility control methods, family planning programs, and population law and policy. Hard copy is available from the contributing organization.

Subscription contracts for on-line services in the U.S. and Canada are available from Informatics, Inc., 6000 Executive Blvd., Rockville, Md. 20852. Searches for people from developing countries are free of charge upon request to Population Information Program, George Washington University, 2001 S St., N.W., Washington, D.C. 20009 or to Center for Population and Family Health, International Institute for the Study of Human Reproduction, Columbia University, 60 Haven Ave., New York, N.Y. 10032.

Institute for Scientific Information (ISI). ASCATOPICS. Weekly. $100.00/year for U.S., Canada, Mexico; $130.00/year for Japan; $110.00/year all other countries.

Computerized literature alerting service which checks 5,000 professional journals to locate articles pertinent to topics selected by subscriber. The weekly listing provides full bibliographic information for each citation but no annotations. Tear sheet service available. Pertinent topics which can be selected: Demography and Population (JD 12), Contraception—Family Planning (CD 30), Adverse Effects of Oral Contraceptives (DD 2), Fertility and Sterility (BD 44), and Marriage and Family (JD 26). ISI's Automatic Subject Citation Alert (ASCA) service provides personalized literature searches according to computer profile. Prices vary. For information write ISI, 325 Chestnut St., Philadelphia, Pa. 19106.

University of North Carolina at Chapel Hill. Carolina Population Center. Technical Information Service (TIS). *Popscan Bibliography Series.* Prices vary.

Subject bibliographies produced from computer searches of the TIS data base. Over 200 POPSCAN bibliographies already completed on specific subjects within the fields of population, family planning, and demography, covering books, monographs, reprints, papers, bibliographies, journal articles, conference proceedings, and book chapters. References are listed alphabetically by title with subject, author, and geographic indexes. Photocopies of listed articles available at $0.10 per page. New searches or updates may be requested at $0.05 per citation plus consultation fee of $20.00 for a new POPSCAN and $10.00 for a supplement. For a price list of already completed POPSCANS, write Reference Librarian, TIS, Carolina Population Center, University Square, Chapel Hill, N.C. 27514.

U.S. Department of Health, Education, and Welfare. National Library of Medicine. *Literature Searches.* Free copies (3 or 4 maximum for individuals, up to 50 for institutions).

Computer-generated bibliographies produced by the Library's Medical Literature Analysis and Retrieval System (MEDLARS). Entries are not annotated but include a list of descriptors under which the article was indexed. Updates are performed. Recent bibliographies of interest to the population field are:

No. 74-20. *Adverse Effects of Oral Contraceptives.* Updates No. 70-2. January 1970-June 1974. 943 citations.

No. 75-24. *Contraception in Males.* January 1973-November 1975, 142 citations.

XVI. Periodicals

The following periodicals are all either entirely devoted to population issues or frequently carry such articles. A few population-oriented newsletters of particular importance are also included.

Abortion Research Notes. Transnational Family Research Institute, 8307 Whitman Drive, Bethesda, Md. 20034. Quarterly. $25.00/year.

Worldwide coverage of abortion-related research, legislation, trends and publications.

American Journal of Public Health. American Public Health Association, 1015 18th St. N.W., Washington, D.C. 20036. Monthly. U.S.: $30.00/year; foreign: $36.00/year.

Articles on public health issues and research, including many pertinent to population and family planning trends.

American Journal of Sociology. University of Chicago Press, 5801 Ellis Ave., Chicago, Ill. 66037. Bimonthly. U.S.: $15.00/year (individuals); foreign: add $1.50.

Scholarly articles, commentary and book reviews on sociological issues.

American Sociological Review. American Sociological Association, 1722 N St., N.W., Washington, D.C. 20036. Bimonthly. U.S.: $15.00/year.

Scientific articles on topics of interest to sociologists and demographers; book reviews.

Asian and Pacific Census Newsletter. East-West Population Institute, 1777 East-West Rd., Honolulu, Hawaii 96822. Quarterly. Free.

News, analysis, and publication reviews of census materials in the Asia-Pacific region.

Asian Population Programme News. Population Division, U.N. Economic and Social Commission for Asia and the Pacific (ESCAP), Sala Santitham, Bangkok, Thailand. Irregular. Free.

Articles, news, country reports and book reviews on population developments related to the ESCAP region.

Background Notes. Office of Media Services, Bureau of Public Affairs, U.S. Department of State. Available from U.S. Government Printing Office, Washington, D.C. 20402. 70-80 issues annually. $23.10/year, $0.30 per issue.

Regularly updated brief notes on geography, population, government, history and political conditions for 165 individual countries.

Boletin Demografico. Centro Latinoamericano de Demografía (CELADE), J. M. Infante 9, Casilla 91, Santiago, Chile. English/Spanish. Semi-annual. $5.00/year.

Demographic data and analysis for Latin American countries.

Canadian Studies in Population. Population Research Laboratory, Department of Sociology, University of Alberta, Edmonton, Alberta, Canada T6G 2H4. English and French. Publishing schedule uncertain. $5.00/year (individuals).

Recently launched first Canadian professional journal of demography; book reviews.

Ceres: FAO Review on Development. UNIPUB, Inc., 650 First Ave., P.O. Box 433, New York, N.Y. 10016. English, French, Spanish editions. $6.00/year.

Articles, debate and book reviews related to social and economic development around the world.

CICRED Bulletin. Committee for International Coordination of National Research in Demography, 27 rue du Commandeur, 75675 Paris Cedex 14, France. Semi-annual. Price n.a.

Reports on demographic research centers, demographic projects in progress and meetings. Recently launched a "Review of Population Reviews" which aims to provide pre-publication summaries of the some 1,000 articles published annually around the world on population matters, to appear every three months.

Common Ground. American Universities Field Staff, Inc., 4 West Wheelock St., Hanover, N.H. 03755. Quarterly. Included in $15.00 annual membership.

Each issue presents in-depth country reports on a theme of major contemporary concern, e.g., sex roles, urban problems, food.

Daedalus. American Academy of Arts and Sciences, 165 Allandale St., Jamaica Plain Station, Boston, Mass. 02130. Quarterly. $10.00/year.

Scholarly articles on individual issue topics. Recent such issues include: "In praise of books," "Adulthood," "The Oil Crisis," "American Higher Education."

Data Asia. Press Foundation of Asia, P.O. Box 1843, Manila, Philippines. Weekly. Free.

News clippings on economic, population, and government developments in 24 Asian countries.

Demography. Population Association of America, P.O. Box 14182, Benjamin Franklin Station, Washington, D.C. 20044. Quarterly. $25.00/year.

Articles and occasional book commentaries geared to professional demographers but many are of interest to the general reader.

Draper World Population Fund Report. (Formerly *The Victor-Bostrom Fund Report.*) Population Crisis Committee, 1835 K St., N.W., Washington, D.C. 20006. Semi-annual. Free.

Articles by country experts and leaders on individual issue topics. Recent such topics include: "Mothers Too Soon," and "The Problems of Human Settlements."

The Ecologist: Journal of the Post Industrial Age. Ecosystem Ltd., registered Office, 73 Molesworth St., Wadebridge, Cornwall, U.K. Monthly. $14.50/year.

Articles on the energy crisis, resource depletion and conservation, health, social change, etc.

Ekistics: The Problems and Science of Human Settlements. Athens Center of Ekistics of the Athens Technological Organization, 25 Strat. Syndesmou, Athens 136, Greece. 12 issues per year. $24.00/year.

Scholarly articles on contemporary problems of human settlements.

The Family Coordinator. National Council for Family Relations, 1219 University Ave., Minneapolis, Minn. 55414. Quarterly. $15.00/year.

Articles directed to educators, counselors and community workers in the fields of marriage and the family.

Family Planning Perspectives. Planned Parenthood Federation of America, Alan Guttmacher Institute, 515 Madison Ave., New York, N.Y. 10022. Bimonthly. $15.00/year.

Developments in family planning, including abortion, primarily in the U.S., presented in major articles, briefer digests, and book reviews.

Family Planning/Population Reporter. Planned Parenthood Federation of America, Alan Guttmacher Institute, 515 Madison Ave., New York, N.Y. 10022. 6 issues per year. $20.00/year (individuals).

Reports by the Washington office of the Alan Guttmacher Institute on legislative, judicial and policy developments related to fertility control and population in individual states of the U.S.

Family Planning Resumé. Community and Family Study Center, University of Chicago, 1411 East 60th St., Chicago, Ill. 60637. Semi-annual. $12.00/year.

To begin publication fall 1976. Summaries of solicited reports and key articles from some 30 U.S., European and Third World periodicals on developments in family planning.

Family Planning Services. Center for Disease Control, Public Health Service, U.S. Department of Health, Education, and Welfare, Atlanta, Ga. 30333. Annual. Free.

Descriptive data on U.S. public family planning clinics and clients and reviews of specia family planning studies.

The Futurist. World Future Society, P.O. Box 30369, Bethesda Branch, Washington, D.C. 20014. Bimonthly. $15.00/year (individuals).

Articles covering a wide range of contemporary issues, including population.

ICMC Migration News. International Catholic Migration Commission, 65 rue de Lausanne, CH 1202 Geneva, Switzerland. Bimonthly. $5.00/year.

Articles, reviews and news on population movements, land settlement and refugees around the world.

Intercom. Population Reference Bureau, Inc., 1754 N St., N.W., Washington, D.C. 20036. Monthly. Included with other publications in $20.00 (individuals) annual membership.

Reports on worldwide trends and activities in population and family planning; book reviews.

International Family Planning Digest. Published for Planned Parenthood Federation of America's division of Family Planning International Assistance by the Alan Guttmacher Institute, 515 Madison Ave., New York, N.Y. 10022. Quarterly. Free on request to non-U.S. residents and institutions; U.S. distribution limited to selected organizations.

Reports of published research findings, meetings and ongoing programs related to family planning, with emphasis on developments most significant for the Third World.

International Labour Review. International Labour Office, Geneva, Switzerland. Bimonthly. $15.75/year.

Worldwide coverage of developments in labor force participation.

Initiatives in Population. Population Center Foundation, P.O. Box 2065, Makati Commercial Center, Rizal, Philippines 3117. Quarterly. Free.

Reports on population and family planning-related developments in the Philippines.

International Migration. Intergovernmental Committee for European Migration, P.O. Box 106, CH 1211 Geneva, Switzerland. Articles in English, French or Spanish with summaries in other two languages. Quarterly. $12.00/year.

Studies of international migration and problems of assimilation, with special emphasis on refugees; book reviews.

International Migration Review. Center for Migration Studies of New York, Inc., 209 Flagg Place, Staten Island, N.Y. 10304. Quarterly. U.S.: $14.50/year (individuals); foreign: add $1.00.

Articles on migration trends around the world, including internal migration; book reviews.

IPPF Medical Bulletin. International Planned Parenthood Association, 18-20 Lower Regent St., London SW1Y 4PW, U.K. Bimonthly. Free.

Reports on worldwide developments in family planning methodology and related issues.

IPPF News. International Planned Parenthood Association, 18-20 Lower Regent St., London SW1Y 4PW, U.K. Bimonthly. Free.

Covers family planning activities around the world.

IPPF/WHR News Service. International Planned Parenthood, Western Hemisphere Region, 111 Fourth Ave., New York, N.Y. 10003. Bimonthly. Free.

Brief reports and literature reviews on family planning developments in the Western Hemisphere, particularly Latin America.

Journal of Biosocial Science. The Galton Foundation, P.O. Box 32, Commerce Way, Colchester CO2 8HP, U.K. Quarterly. $37.50/year.

Papers, reviews, lectures, proceedings and major book reviews on social aspects of human biology, reproduction, demography, etc.

Journal of Family Welfare. Family Planning Association of India, 1 Jeevan Udyog, Dadabhai Naoroji Rd., Bombay 1, India. Quarterly. $2.50/year.

Scholarly papers on demographic and family planning research in India.

Journal of Marriage and the Family. National Council on Family Relations, 1219 University Ave. S.E., Minneapolis, Minn. 55414. Quarterly. $20.00/year.

Scholarly articles on theory, research and literature related to marriage, fertility and the family in the U.S. and other countries.

Migration Today. Secretariat for Migration, World Council of Churches, 150 route de Ferney, 1211 Geneva 20, Switzerland. English, French, German editions. Occasional, usually once a year. Free.

Scholarly articles focused on migration policies around the world and their influence on population size and structure.

Morbidity and Mortality Weekly Report. Center for Disease Control, Public Health Service, U.S. Department of Health, Education, and Welfare, Atlanta, Ga. 30333. Weekly. Free.

Trend reports and weekly data on mortality and morbidity in the U.S. as reported by state health officials, with notes on trends elsewhere.

Monthly Labor Review. Bureau of Labor Statistics, U.S. Department of Labor. Available from U.S. Government Printing Office, Washington, D.C. 20402. Monthly. U.S.: $20.00/year; foreign: $25.00/year.

Articles, reports, book reviews and current statistics related to U.S. labor force trends.

Notas de Poblacion. Centro Latinoamericano de Demografía (CELADE), J.M. Infante 9, Casilla 91, Santiago, Chile. Spanish with English summaries. Quarterly. $10.00/year.

Articles on demographic research, research in progress, and population activities related to Latin America.

People. International Planned Parenthood Federation, 18-20 Lower Regent St., London SW1Y 4PW, U.K. English, French, Spanish editions. Quarterly. $15.00/year.

Feature articles, news and literature reviews on population-related developments around the world.

Planned Parenthood/World Population Washington Memo. Planned Parenthood Federation of America, Alan Guttmacher Institute, 515 Madison Ave., New York, N.Y. 10022. 20 issues per year. $20.00/year (individuals).

Brief reports on latest developments in U.S. federal policies in family planning and related areas, prepared by Washington office of the Alan Guttmacher Institute.

Population. Institut National d'Etudes Démographiques, 27 rue du Commandeur, 75675 Paris Cedex 14, France. French with English summaries. Bimonthly. Fr. francs 85.00/year.

Scientific articles on all aspects of population dynamics and reports of population developments around the world; book reviews.

Population Bulletin. Population Reference Bureau, Inc., 1754 N St. N.W., Washington, D.C. 20036. 6 issues per year. Included with other publications in $20.00 (individuals) annual membership.

Each issue devoted to an in-depth report by a recognized authority on a population-related topic of national or international concern.

Population Bulletin. U.N. Economic Commission for Western Asia, P.O. Box 4656, Beirut, Lebanon. Semi-annual. Free.

Papers and reports on population developments in the Arab region; book reviews.

Population and Development Review. The Population Council, 245 Park Ave., New York, N.Y. 10017. Quarterly. Free.

Scholarly articles on relationships between population processes and socioeconomic development and related policy issues; book reviews.

Population Review. 8976 Cliffridge Ave., La Jolla, Cal. 92307. Semi-annual; occasional double-issue annual volumes. $5.00/year (individuals).

Articles on all aspects of population problems particularly in developing countries; book reviews.

Population Studies. Research Office, Population and Family Planning Board, Cairo, U.A.R. English/Arabic. Monthly. Free.

Articles on demographic research in the Middle East and North Africa.

Population Studies. Population Investigation Committee, London School of Economics, Houghton St., London WC2A 2AE, U.K. 3 issues per year. $30.00/year.

A demographic journal presenting articles by demographic professionals from around the world; book reviews.

Populi. United Nations Fund for Population Activities, 485 Lexington Ave., New York, N.Y. 10017. Quarterly. $5.00/year.

Articles by professionals on worldwide population problems; some book reviews.

Reports on Population/Family Planning. The Population Council, 245 Park Ave., New York, N.Y. 10017. Irregular. Free.

Current information and in-depth analysis on individual issue topics related to population and family planning around the world.

Reporter on Human Reproduction and the Law. Legal-Medical Studies, Inc., Box 8219, John F. Kennedy Station, Boston, Mass. 02114. $39.00/year.

Looseleaf binder with regularly up-dated documents, legislation abstracts, court decisions and publications on legal, medical, ethical, and social developments in abortion, artificial insemination, conception control, medical malpractice, the family and reproduction. Primarily U.S., with some from Canada and the U.K.

Rural Africana. African Studies Center, Michigan State University, East Lansing, Mich. 48823. 3 issues per year. $4.50/year.

Articles on current research related to socioeconomic development in rural Sub-Saharan Africa; book reviews.

Rural Sociology. Rural Sociological Society, c/o John E. Dunkelberger, Dept. of Ag. Ec. and Rur. Soc., Auburn University, Auburn, Ala. 36830. Quarterly. $12.00/year.

Reports on research relevant to the sociology and demography of rural areas around the world; book reviews.

Social Biology. Society for the Study of Social Biology, 1180 Observatory Drive, Madison, Wis. 53706. Quarterly. $25.00/year.

Articles concerning biological and sociocultural factors which affect the structure and composition of human populations; book reviews.

Statistical Bulletin. Metropolitan Life Insurance Co., One Madison Ave., New York, N.Y. 10010. Monthly. Free.

Current data and analysis of U.S. population trends with some international comparisons.

Statistical Reporter. U.S. Office of Management and Budget. Available from U.S. Government Printing Office, Washington, D.C. 20402. Monthly. $6.00/year.

Reports on U.S. government statistical and research activities, with many relevant to population issues.

Studies in Family Planning. The Population Council, 245 Park Ave., New York, N.Y. 10017. Monthly. Free.

Scholarly articles on a wide range of population and family planning research and programs around the world; literature reviews.

UNFPA Newsletter. United Nations Fund for Population Activities, 485 Lexington Ave., New York, N.Y. 10017. Monthly. Free.

News of UNFPA-sponsored population programs and related activities in the developing world; book notices.

WHO Chronicle. Distribution and Sales Service, World Health Organization, 1211 Geneva 27, Switzerland. English, French, Spanish editions. Monthly. $6.30/year.

Articles on family planning and health programs and research around the world.

Zero Population Growth National Reporter. Zero Population Growth, 1346 Connecticut Ave., N.W., Washington, D.C. 20036. Monthly. $5.50/year.

News and analysis of population-related developments in the U.S.

Population Programs and Organizations

I. Graduate Training Programs in Demography and Population Studies in the United States

This listing, compiled in summer 1976, includes graduate training programs at universities in the U.S. which offer more than a minimum number (four) of courses and seminars in demography or population studies. Training is offered either in a special population program or as an area of specialization in the Departments of Sociology, Economics, Public Health, or other relevant fields. For more information prospective students should write to the appropriate university.

Academic research centers and programs in the U.S. are not listed separately. Such centers are included in the CICRED Directory described in section V below, where guides to training sources outside the U.S. are also identified.

What the field of demography or population studies encompasses can be learned from a small guide called *Careers in Demography,* a free publication of the Population Association of America, P.O. Box 14182, Benjamin Franklin Station, Washington, D.C. 20044.

A thorough and still useful review of the status, prospects and future needs of graduate training in demography, population studies and family planning in the U.S. as of 1970 appears in *Population and Family Planning Manpower and Training* (1971; 118 pp.), by Lee L. Bean, Richmond K. Anderson, and Howard J. Tatum, available for $3.75 from The Population Council, 245 Park Ave., New York, N.Y. 10017.

Brown University. Dr. Sidney Goldstein, Director; Population Studies and Training Center, Brown University, Providence, R.I. 02912.

M.A. and Ph.D. programs in sociology with concentration in all aspects of demography. Full coverage of population theory, demographic methods; also population growth and economic development, population policy, migration, and urbanization.

University of California, Berkeley. Dr. Kingsley Davis, Director; International Population and Urban Research, University of California, 2234 Piedmont Avenue, Berkeley, Cal. 94720.

M.S. and Ph.D. programs in sociology with demography as an area of specialization. Emphasis is on population studies and the sociological aspects of demography, demographic methods and urban research.

University of California, Los Angeles. Dr. Georges Sabagh, Chairman; Department of Sociology, UCLA, Los Angeles, Cal. 90024.

M.A. and Ph.D. programs in sociology with specialization in demography. Courses and seminars in demographic and ecological analysis and population problems.

University of Chicago. Dr. Donald J. Bogue, Director: Community and Family Study Center, University of Chicago, 1411 East 60th St., Chicago, Ill. 60637.

Master's degree programs offered in Communications, Research and Evaluation, or Adult Education designed to equip students for family planning work in developing countries.

University of Chicago. Dr. Philip M. Hauser, Director; Population Research Center, University of Chicago, 1126 E. 59th St., Chicago, Ill. 60637.

Core courses and seminars in demography, fertility, migration, human ecology, population and development in the Department of Sociology leading to an M.A. or Ph.D. degree in sociology with specialization in demography. Also an intensive demographic training program leading to an M.A. degree.

Columbia University. Dr. Allen Rosenfield, Director; Center for Population and Family Health, Columbia University, 60 Haven Ave., New York, N.Y. 10032.

Interdisciplinary program in School of Public Health focusing on relationships between population and public health, and statistical and management training in population and family planning programs, leading to an M.P.H. or Dr.P.H. degree.

University of Connecticut. Dr. Thomas E. Steahr, Chairman; Department of Sociology, University of Connecticut, Storrs, Conn. 06268.

Courses in demographic analysis, seminars in fertility, mortality and migration leading to an M.A. or Ph.D. degree in sociology with area specialization in demography.

Cornell University. Dr. J. Mayone Stycos, Director; International Population Program, Cornell University, Social Science Building, Ithaca, N.Y. 14850.

Full range of courses in population studies and demographic analysis leading to a Ph.D. degree from the Department of Sociology with specialization in demography, or Master of Professional Studies in International Development with concentrations in demography, planning or nutrition.

Duke University. Dr. George C. Myers, Director; Center for Demographic Studies, Box 4732 Duke Station, Duke University, Durham, N.C. 27706.

Doctoral programs with specialized training in all aspects of demography offered in the Departments of Sociology and Economics.

Emory University. Dr. W. W. Pendleton, Director; Demographic Research and Training Center, Department of Sociology and Anthropology, Emory University, Atlanta, Ga. 30322.

Courses in demographic analysis and the sociology of human reproduction leading to an M.A. or Ph.D. degree from the Department of Sociology and Anthropology.

University of Florida. Dr. Gustavo Antonini, Director; Latin American Demographic Studies Program, Center for Latin American Studies, Grinter Hall, University of Florida, Gainesville, Fla. 32611.

Interdisciplinary program offering courses particularly related to Latin American demography leading to an M.A. or Ph.D. degree in sociology or geography. Two certificate programs also offered.

Florida State University. Dr. Charles B. Nam, Director; Center for the Study of Population, Florida State University, Tallahassee, Fla. 32206.

Full range of courses in demography and population studies leading to an M.A. or Ph.D. degree in the Departments of Sociology, Economics, Statistics, or Government. A non-degree program in demography is also offered.

Georgetown University. Dr. Murray Gendell, Director; M.A. Program, Center for Population Research, Kennedy Institute for the Study of Human Reproduction and Bioethics, Georgetown University, Washington, D.C. 20057.

Core courses in demography, theory, method and analysis, and related population studies, leading to an M.A. from the Department of Sociology.

Harvard University. Dr. George S. Masnick, Head; Department of Population Sciences, School of Public Health, Health, Harvard University, 665 Huntington Ave., Boston, Mass. 02115.

M.P.H., M.Sc. or D.Sc. degrees from the School of Public Health. Courses offered in demographic methods, human ecology and biological aspects of population as areas of specialization.

Harvard University. Dr. Elihu Bergman, Assistant Director; Center for Population Studies, Harvard University, 9 Bow St., Cambridge, Mass. 02138.

Ph.D. programs and post-doctoral study available in the Departments of Sociology, Economics, Government and Population Science with specialization in different areas of population and demography.

University of Hawaii. Dr. Alan Howard, Director; Population Studies Program, College of Arts and Sciences, University of Hawaii, Honolulu, Hawaii 96822.

Interdisciplinary program leading to a Population Studies Certificate. Courses include population theory, fertility, demographic methods and analysis.

University of Hawaii. Dr. Robert Wolff, Chairman; Population and Family Planning Studies, International Health Program, School of Public Health, University of Hawaii, 1890 East-West Rd., Honolulu, Hawaii 96822.

Courses offered in demographic techniques and population problems as specialization in programs for M.P.H. or M.S. degrees.

Iowa State University. Dr. George Beale, Chairman; Department of Sociology and Anthropology, 204 East Hall, Iowa State University, Ames, Iowa 50010.

Courses in demographic methods and population studies, with emphasis on population and human ecology, leading to an M.A. or Ph.D. degree from the Department of Sociology and Anthropology.

Johns Hopkins University. Dr. W. H. Mosley, Director; Johns Hopkins Population Center, School of Hygiene and Public Health, Department of Population Dynamics, Johns Hopkins University, 615 N. Wolfe St., Baltimore, Md. 21205.

Emphasis on social and mathematical demography, family planning administration and reproductive biology, leading to an M.S. in Public Health, Ph.D., D.P.H., or D.Sc.

Kansas State University. Dr. Cornelia B. Flora, Director; Population Research Laboratory, Kansas State University, Manhattan, Kan. 66506.

Courses in population studies, demographic analysis, migration, and fertility, leading to an M.S. or Ph.D. degree from the Department of Sociology and Anthropology.

University of Kentucky. Dr. Thomas R. Ford, Chairman; Sociology Department, University of Kentucky, Lexington, Ky. 40506.

Ph.D. program in sociology with specialization in demography, including population analysis, demographic methods, and social ecology.

University of Massachusetts. Dr. T. O. Wilkinson, Director; Population Research Institute, University of Massachusetts, Amherst, Mass. 01002.

Training in demography and population studies with emphasis on international aspects leading to an M.A. or Ph.D. degree from the Department of Sociology and Anthropology.

University of Michigan. Dr. David Goldberg, Director; Population Studies Center, University of Michigan, 1225 South University Ave., Ann Arbor, Mich. 48104.

Course offerings in all aspects of demography and population leading to an M.A. or Ph.D. degree from the Departments of Sociology or Economics.

University of Michigan. Dr. Leslie Corsa, Chairman; Department of Population Planning, School of Public Health, University of Michigan, Ann Arbor, Mich. 48109.

Specialized graduate programs in population planning leading to degrees of M.P.H., M.S., Ph.D., or D.P.H.

Michigan State University. Dr. Jay Artis, Chairman; Department of Sociology, Michigan State University, East Lansing, Mich. 48823.

Courses in population studies and demographic methods with emphasis on migration and population redistribution, leading to a Ph.D. degree from the Department of Sociology.

University of Minnesota. Dr. Harry Foreman, Director; Center for Population Studies, University of Minnesota, Box 395, Mayo, Minneapolis, Minn. 55455.

M.A. and Ph.D. programs in the Departments of Sociology, Geography and History, with a concentration in population and related topics.

University of Missouri-Columbia. Dr. Michael F. Nolan, Director of Graduate Studies; Department of Sociology and Rural Sociology, Sociology Building, University of Missouri-Columbia, Columbia, Mo. 65201.

Department of Sociology offers specialization in demography-ecology leading to M.A. or Ph.D. degree.

University of North Carolina at Chapel Hill. Dr. Thomas L. Hall, Director; Carolina Population Center, 123 West Franklin St., Chapel Hill, N.C. 27514.

Master's and doctoral degree programs with concentration in population studies are offered in the Departments of Anthropology, Biostatistics, Economics, Epidemiology, Geography, Political Science, Psychology, Sociology, Health Administration and Education, and in the Ecology Curriculum Program.

Ohio State University. Dr. William Petersen, Director; Office of Population Studies, Ohio State University, 1775 South College Rd., Columbus, Ohio 43210.

Courses in demographic analysis, fertility, migration, urbanization, race, leading to an M.A. or Ph.D. degree from the Sociology Department.

University of Pennsylvania. Dr. Etienne van de Walle, Director; Population Studies Center, Graduate Group in Demography, University of Pennsylvania, 3718 Locust Walk, Philadelphia, Pa. 19174.

Full range of core courses in demography, population and related areas leading to an M.A. or Ph.D. degree.

Pennsylvania State University. Dr. Gordon F. DeJong, Director; Population Studies Program, Population Issues Research Office, Pennsylvania State University, 22 Burrowes Building, University Park, Pa. 16802.

M.A. or Ph.D. from Departments of Sociology, Economics, Geography, or Rural Sociology with a major concentration in all aspects of demographic and population studies.

University of Pittsburgh. Dr. Richard S. Thorn, Chairman; Department of Economics, University of Pittsburgh, Pittsburgh, Pa. 15213.

Four courses leading to an M.A. or Ph.D. degree from the Department of Economics with demography as an area of specialization.

University of Pittsburgh. Dr. John C. Cutler, Director; Population Division, Graduate School of Public Health, University of Pittsburgh, 130 DeSoto St., Pittsburgh, Pa. 15261.

M.A. degree awarded in public health with demography as an area of specialization and an emphasis on family planning program administration.

Princeton University. Dr. Charles F. Westoff, Director; Office of Population Research, 21 Prospect Ave., Princeton, N.J. 08540.

Graduate Program in Demography leads to a joint Ph.D. in Demography and Economics, Sociology, or Statistics. Special one year non-degree program for foreign statisticians, economists and sociologists.

University of Southern California. Dr. Maurice D. Van Arsdol, Jr., Director; Population Research Laboratory, University of Southern California, University Park, Los Angeles, Cal. 90007.

Training program offers full range of demographic and population studies leading to Ph.D. degree in the Department of Sociology.

Stanford University. Dr. Dudley Kirk, Professor of Population Studies; Food Research Institute Stanford University, Stanford, Cal. 94305.

M.A. and Ph.D. programs in the Food Research Institute and the Department of Sociology offering courses in demographic analysis and methods and population studies with emphasis on developing countries, especially Latin America.

University of Tennessee. Dr. James A. Black, Chairman; Department of Sociology, University of Tennessee, 115 Volunteer Blvd., Knoxville, Tenn. 37976.

Courses offered in population theory and demographic techniques, seminars in migration and fertility for an M.A. or Ph.D. degree in sociology, with specialization in population studies.

University of Texas at Austin. Dr. Harley L. Browning, Director; Population Research Center, University of Texas, 200 East 26½ St., Austin, Tex. 78705.

Wide range of courses in demography and human ecology leading to an M.A. or Ph.D. degree from the Department of Sociology.

Tulane University. Dr. Carl L. Harter, Chairman; Department of Sociology, 104 Social Sciences Building, Tulane University, New Orleans, La. 70118.

M.A. and Ph.D. degrees in sociology with specialization in human ecology and demography. Courses are offered in demographic analysis and social demography with emphasis on Latin America.

Utah State University. Dr. Yun Kim, Head; Department of Sociology, Social Work and Anthropology, Utah State University, Logan, Utah 84321.

M.S. and Ph.D. programs in sociology with concentration in demography. Courses in population analysis and problems and human ecology.

University of Virginia. Dr. Jeanne C. Biggar, Associate Professor of Sociology; Department of Sociology, Cabell 542, University of Virginia, Charlottesville, Va. 22903.

Courses in demographic techniques, social demography, demography of the American South, and urban ecology offered in M.A. and Ph.D. programs in sociology.

University of Washington. Dr. Samuel H. Preston, Director; Center for Studies in Demography and Ecology, Department of Sociology, DK-40, University of Washington, Seattle, Wash. 98195.

Courses in demographic methods, demography and ecology, population policies and programs, leading to M.A. or Ph.D. in sociology with specialization in demography.

University of Wisconsin—Madison. Dr. James A. Sweet, Director; Center for Demography and Ecology, 3224 Social Science Building, University of Wisconsin, 1180 Observatory Drive, Madison, Wis. 53706.

Training leads to M.A. or Ph.D. degree in sociology with specialization in demography and ecology.

II. Major Private Organizations in the Fields of Population and Family Planning Located in the United States

Association for Voluntary Sterilization, 708 Third Ave., New York, N.Y. 10017.

International Project established in 1972 to promote voluntary sterilization as a method of fertility regulation by means of project grants to medical and health groups in developing countries, support for development of new sterilization techniques, physician training, and international conferences. International Project and the parent association issue regular newsletters. 1976 budget: $2.3 million.

East-West Communication Institute, 1777 East-West Rd., Honolulu, Hawaii 96822.

Has worked since 1970 to improve the public information, education, and communication (IEC) elements of population and family planning programs through training, research, collection of IEC materials, publication of information directories and a newsletter, international conferences, and support of internships for degree and non-degree study. 1976 budget: $620,000.

Family Planning International Assistance, 810 Seventh Ave., New York, N.Y. 10019.

International division of Planned Parenthood Federation of America, established in 1971. Develops and supports nongovernmental family planning programs in developing countries, emphasizing services, training, IEC, and provision of contraceptives. Sponsors publication of *International Family Planning Digest* (see "Periodicals"). 1976 budget: about $6 million.

Ford Foundation, 320 East 43rd St., New York, N.Y. 10017.

Population program established in 1952. Provides funding for research and training in reproductive biology, contraceptive development, family planning program management and evaluation, policy-oriented social science research in population, conferences, seminars and publications. 1976 population budget: $10.8 million.

International Fertility Research Program, Research Triangle Park, N.C. 27709.

Established in 1971 to accelerate the development, field testing and worldwide use of new and improved methods of fertility regulation through standardized collection, processing, analysis and rapid reporting of data from field studies in more than 39 nations. 1976 budget: over $3 million.

International Planned Parenthood Federation (IPPF), Western Hemisphere Region, 111 Fourth Ave., New York, N.Y. 10003.

Established shortly after founding of the worldwide parent organization in 1952. Develops, coordinates and supports activities of national family planning affiliate associations in Latin America, the Caribbean and northern America. Publishes *IPPF/WHR News Service* (See "Periodicals"). 1974 regional resources: $8.59 million in funds, $4.3 million in commodities.

National Abortion Rights Action League (NARAL), 706 7th St. S.E., Washington, D.C. 20003.

Organized in 1969 as National Association for the Repeal of Abortion Laws. Adopted its present name after legalization of abortion on request by decision of the U.S. Supreme Court in 1973, which it seeks to uphold by monitoring of legislation and providing relevant information to public officials and agencies nationally and through a coalition of state groups. Bimonthly newsletter. 1975 budget: $191,200.

National Organization for Non-Parents (N.O.N.), 806 Reisterstown Rd., Baltimore, Md. 21208.

Established in 1972 to promote the childfree lifestyle as a realistic and socially accepted and respected option through education and media programs. Publishes a bimonthly newsletter and other materials. 1976 budget: $110,000.

National Right to Life Committee, Suite 557, National Press Building, 529 14th St. N.W., Washington, D.C. 20045.

An association of individual state Right-to-Life organizations working to overturn the Supreme Court 1973 decision on abortion by means of a constitutional amendment and other measures to protect human life before birth and endorsement of such programs as Birth Right and Pregnancy Aid.

The Pathfinder Fund, 1330 Boylston St., Chestnut Hill, Mass. 02167.

Incorporated in 1957 to continue work of the late Clarence Gamble in promoting family planning services beginning 1929 in the U.S. and internationally in 1952. Initiates and supports innovative projects in developing countries to introduce family planning services, fertility control methods not currently in use, training programs and increased awareness of population problems. 1975 grants totaled $3.5 million.

Planned Parenthood Federation of America, 810 Seventh Ave., New York, N.Y. 10019.

Established in 1917; now affiliated with International Planned Parenthood Federation (IPPF). Largest national association within IPPF. Operating through a countrywide clinic network of 187 affiliates, provides low-cost contraceptive and abortion services, diagnostic tests and examinations, and counseling; also conducts training and mass communication/education in family planning. 1975 budget: about $75 million.

The Alan Guttmacher Institute (established in 1974, formerly Center for Family Planning and Program Development, established in 1968) is the Federation's research and development division. The New York office (515 Madison Ave., New York, N.Y. 10019) publishes *Family Planning Perspectives* (see "Periodicals"). The Washington office (1666 K St. N.W., Washington, D.C. 20006) monitors and analyzes laws, policies, regulations and court decisions affecting availability of family planning and publishes *Family Planning/Population Reporter* and *Planned Parenthood Washington Memo* (see "Periodicals").

Population Association of America, P.O. Box 14182, Benjamin Franklin Station, Washington, D.C. 20044.

Established in 1932. A professional society of demographers and scholars in the field of population studies. Publishes *Demography* (see "Periodicals"), *Population Index* (with the Office of Population Research, Princeton University, see "General Bibliographies"), and a quarterly newsletter *PAA Affairs*.

The Population Council, 245 Park Ave., New York, N.Y. 10017.

Established in 1952. Conducts an extensive program of in-house research in demography, reproductive biology, and new methods of fertility control and supports such research, training and development and innovative family planning information, education, delivery and evaluation programs in developing countries. Publishes *Studies in Family Planning, Reports on Population/Family Planning, Population and Development Review* (see "Periodicals") and *Country Profiles* (see p. 42). 1975 budget: $13 million.

Population Crisis Committee, Suite 200, 1835 K St. N.W., Washington, D.C. 20006.

An educational and catalytic organization devoted to raising an awareness of population issues among world leaders and the general public. Established the Draper World Population Fund in 1975 to carry on the work of the late General William H. Draper, Jr. by raising approximately $1 million annually, primarily for support of the International Planned Parenthood Federation. Publishes *Draper World Population Fund Report* (see "Periodicals"), and *Population,* a series of 4-page "briefing notes" on population issues, e.g., human settlements, population and food. 1976 budget: about $650,000.

Population Information Program, The George Washington University Medical Center, 2001 S St. N.W., Washington, D.C. 20009.

Established in 1973. Conducts two major programs: publication of *Population Reports* (see p. 38) and coordination of POPINFORM (see "Computerized Information Retrieval Services").

The Population Institute, 110 Maryland Ave. N.E., Washington, D.C. 20002.

Established in 1969. Seeks to stimulate public awareness of population issues through work with nongovernmental membership organizations and the media, internships for college students, and encouragement of population education. Publishes *Population Issues,* a bimonthly newsletter. 1976 budget: $1.2 million.

Population Reference Bureau, Inc., 1754 N St. N.W., Washington, D.C. 20036.

Established in 1929. Continues its pioneering role in providing information and education on worldwide population issues through population education workshops and materials, library and information services, and regular publication of *Intercom, Population Bulletin* (see "Periodicals"), *Interchange* (see "Population Education"), an annual *World Population Data Sheet* (see p. 12), and occasional reports and books. 1975 budget: $642,000.

Population Services International, 110 East 59th St., New York, N.Y. 10022.

Established in 1970. Utilizes mass media, consumer goods distribution networks, and local business expertise to promote and market condoms and oral contraceptives in developing countries. 1976 budget: $2.6 million.

Resources for the Future, Inc., 1755 Massachusetts Ave. N.W., Washington, D.C. 20036.

Population formally incorporated into research program in 1970. Conducts major research and publishes findings on the relationships between population growth and distribution and resources and the environment in both industrialized and developing nations, and on the socioeconomic determinants of fertility.

Rockefeller Foundation, 1133 Avenue of the Americas, New York, N.Y. 10036.

Population program established in 1954. Supports basic and applied research in social science aspects of population and development, reproductive biology, contraceptive technology, and population training and educational programs in the U.S. and developing countries. 1975 population grant commitments: $6.2 million.

World Population Society, P.O. Box 106, Eagle Station, Washington, D.C. 20016.

Established in 1973. A professional association which promotes a multi-disciplinary, international approach to population and related problems through meetings and publications. 1975 budget: about $100,000.

Worldwatch Institute, 1776 Massachusetts Ave. N.W., Washington, D.C. 20036.

Established in 1975 as an "early warning system" to identify and encourage rational timely response to world problems, including population. Research findings are issued in *Worldwatch Papers,* journal articles and books.

Zero Population Growth, 1346 Connecticut Ave. N.W., Washington, D.C. 20036.

Established in 1968 to promote the achievement of "zero population growth in the U.S. and elsewhere as soon as possible." Works with public officials and the news media, promotes adoption of population education, and publishes *Zero Population Growth National Reporter* (see "Periodicals") and other materials. 1976 budget: $374,000.

III. Population and Family Planning Programs of the U.S. Government and of Multilateral Agencies Headquartered in the United States

U.S. Government

U.S. Department of Agriculture, Economic Research Service, Washington, D.C. 20250.

Carries out an extensive program of demographic research and publishes findings related to the U.S. rural population and internal migration.

U.S. Department of Commerce, Washington, D.C. 20230. This Department incorporates the Bureau of the Census and the Bureau of Economic Analysis.

Bureau of the Census

This is the statistical agency of the U.S. government which tabulates and releases data on the U.S. population and economy gathered in decennial censuses and Current Population Surveys (see "United States") conducts basic demographic research (see "Demographic Methods"), trains foreign nationals, and provides technical assistance to developing nations in census-taking methodology. The Bureau incorporates the *International Statistical Programs Center* which collects, analyzes and publishes data on developing countries (see "International Studies") and provides assistance to such countries in developing national systems of demographic data.

Bureau of Economic Analysis.

This agency collects data on the U.S. economy. It incorporates the *Foreign Demographic Analysis Division* which researches and publishes data on the Communist countries of Eastern Europe, Soviet Russia, the People's Republic of China and Cuba (see "International Studies").

U.S. Department of Health, Education and Welfare (HEW). This umbrella department of the U.S. government incorporates a number of U.S. government agencies concerned with demographic and population programs, including the following seven.

Office of Population Affairs, 330 Independence Ave. S.W., Washington, D.C. 20201.

This Office coordinates population research and family planning service programs within HEW. Actual implementation of the programs is delegated to numerous agencies within the Department, including the following.

Health Resources Administration, National Center for Health Statistics (NCHS), 5600 Fishers Lane, Rockville, Md. 20852.

This Center is the chief agency for collection, analysis and publication of U.S. vital registration data: marriages, divorces, births and deaths, as reported from the various states (see "United States"). Also conducts basic and applied research in statistical methodology (see "Demographic Methods"). Latest of recurring surveys of the NCHS conducted to collect health and demographic data on the U.S. population is the National Survey of Family Growth, a biennial fertility survey begun in 1973, based on a representative national sample of approximately 10,000 ever-married women. First findings from this survey will appear in a series of reports beginning fall 1976 (see p. 11).

Health Services Administration, Bureau of Community Health Services, Office for Family Planning, 5600 Fishers Lane, Rockville, Md. 20852.

This Office is the major coordinator of HEW funding and support of U.S. domestic family planning services. It provides project grants for family planning services, research and distribution of information, as well as for improvement of health services for mothers and children, especially in rural areas. Fiscal 1975 HEW budget for organized family planning programs in the U.S.: $201 million.

Health Services Administration, Center for Disease Control, 1600 Clifton Rd. N.E., Atlanta, Ga. 30333.

Among its activities, this Center collects, tabulates and publishes annual data on legal abortions (see *Abortion Surveillance,* p. 41) and family planning services (see "Periodicals") and weekly reports on U.S. morbidity and mortality (see "Periodicals").

National Institutes of Health, National Institute of Child Health and Human Development, Center for Population Research, Landow Building, Bethesda, Md. 20014.

The National Institute of Child Health and Human Development and its Center for Population Research (CPR) have primary responsibility for the U.S. federal effort in population research. Through grants and contracts, the CPR supports research to develop new means of fertility regulation, to evaluate contraceptive methods currently in use, and to analyze the social and behavioral determinants and consequences of population size, composition, and distribution. The CPR also administers HEW grants to centers of population research and training.

The Director of CPR serves as Chairman of the *Interagency Committee on Population Research,* established in 1970. Comprised of representatives of U.S. federal agencies interested in research related to human population problems, this Committee works to improve the coordination, communication and utilization of such research, prepares inventories and analyses of U.S. federal and private agency population research (see p. 68), and offers recommendations concerning additional U.S. federal efforts needed in this area.

Office of Human Development, Office of Child Development, Children's Bureau, P.O. Box 1182, Washington, D.C. 20013.

Collects, analyzes and publishes data on the condition and characteristics of U.S. children; bimonthly journal, *Children Today,* available from U.S. Government Printing Office, Washington, D.C. 20402, $6.10/year.

Office of the Assistant Secretary for Education, National Center for Education Statistics, 400 Maryland Ave. S.W., Washington, D.C. 20202.

Collects and disseminates statistics and other data related to education in the U.S. and in other nations.

U.S. Department of Justice, Immigration and Naturalization Service, 425 I St. N.W., Washington, D.C. 20536.

Collects and disseminates data relating to emigration, aliens residing in the U.S., and immigration, including illegal immigration.

U.S. Department of Labor, Washington, D.C. 20212.

This Department incorporates the Bureau of Labor Statistics and the Women's Bureau.

Bureau of Labor Statistics.

Collects data and conducts research related to manpower and labor force participation, including projections. Findings are issued in monthly press releases, special publications, and the *Monthly Labor Review* (see "Periodicals").

Women's Bureau.

This agency is a source of information and analysis on all matters pertinent to working women in the U.S.

U.S. Department of State, Office of Population, Washington, D.C. 20520.

This Office advises all branches of the Department of State and its overseas officers on population questions and serves as coordinator between the State Department and the AID population program (see next listing).

U.S. Department of State, Agency for International Development (AID), Office of Population, Rosslyn Plaza East, Washington, D.C. 20523.

Largest donor of international assistance for population programs in the developing world. Provides assistance for demographic data collection and analysis, population policy development, biomedical research to improve fertility control technology and operational research to improve implementation of family planning programs, family planning supplies, services and communications, and training of family planning manpower and institutional development. Publishes the annual *Population Program Assistance* (see p. 43), comprehensive review of population aid programs of the U.S. and other governments and multilateral agencies. AID fiscal 1976 budget for population planning programs: $103 million.

U.S. House of Representatives, House Committee on the Post Office and Civil Service, Subcommittee on Census and Population, House Office Building Annex, Room 601, Washington, D.C. 20515.

This Congressional subcommittee is concerned with U.S. population data needs, implementation of recommendations of the 1972 Report of the Presidential Commission on Population Growth and The American Future, and alerting the U.S. Congress to the need for a national population policy.

Chaired by Rep. Patricia Schroeder, the subcommittee held nine hearings on these issues 1975-76, with results published in the fall of 1976 (see p. 52). The subcommittee also prepared and published in 1975 the *Subject and Names Indexes to Publications of the Commission on Population Growth and the American Future* (see p. 51).

Multilateral Agencies

Many multilateral agencies now engage in and provide support for population-related activities. The following list is limited to those headquartered in the U.S. For a comprehensive listing and full description see publications of the United Nations Fund for Population Activities and Population Reference Bureau in section V below.

Inter-American Development Bank, 808 17th St. N.W., Washington, D.C. 20577.

Population program formally announced in 1974. The Bank's Social and Economic Development Department has for some years conducted research on a variety of demographic topics, particularly urbanization in Latin America, with results published in an *Urban Population Growth* series and the 1975 volume *Urban Population Growth Trends in Latin America* by Robert W. Fox, (see p. 49). Also conducts research on the revolutionary impact of new computer software on the development and use of statistics. Annually publishes *Economic and Social Progress in Latin America,* a comprehensive review by region and individual country of social and economic trends in the area.

Inter-American Statistical Institute, 1725 I St. N.W., Washington, D.C. 20006.

A professional organization founded in 1940 and coordinated within the structure of the Organization of American States. Program related to census methodology begun in 1950 to foster and improve collection, tabulation and analysis of population censuses in the Western Hemisphere. Biennially issues *America en Cifras* (in Spanish), multi-volume publication with one volume devoted to demographic data (see "International Data").

Pan American Health Organization (PAHO), 525 23rd St. N.W., Washington, D.C. 20037.

Regional office for Latin America of the World Health Organization, PAHO provides technical assistance and support to 29 member countries in the Western Hemisphere in the areas of health and health-related programs. Within the Organization, the Division of Family Health, established in 1970, is responsible for activities in population dynamics and family planning as these relate to maternal and child health and family welfare. It prepares educational materials and publications for the use of member countries and provides such services to others upon request. 1976 budgeted assistance for population activities: $6.9 million.

United Nations, Department of Economic and Social Affairs, United Nations Plaza, New York, N.Y. 10017.

This department of the U.N. incorporates the *Population Division* and the *Statistical Office,* both established in 1946. These divisions bear the chief responsibility for coordinating the U.N. program for preparation and publication of demographic studies, reports, technical manuals and handbooks (see "Demographic Methods"); worldwide dissemination of national statistics in as comparable a form as possible (see "International Data"); advisory services mainly to developing countries on development and improvement of national systems of demographic data; convening of population conferences, seminars, and training courses; provision of fellowships; and coordination of the six U.N. regional demographic training and research centers, who also do demographic research and publish reports (Centro Latinoamericano de Demografía in Santiago, Chile, with a branch office in San José, Costa Rica; the International Institute of Population Studies, Bombay, India; Cairo Demographic Centre; Regional Institute for Population Studies, Accra, Ghana; Institut de Formation et de Recherche Démographique, Yaoundé, Cameroons; and Centre Démographique ONU-Roumanie, Bucharest).

United Nations Fund for Population Activities (UNFPA), 485 Lexington Ave., New York, N.Y. 10017.

Established in 1969, the UNFPA, under the Governing Council of the U.N. Development Program, is the primary arm of the U.N. in providing support and funding, through voluntary contributions, for population action programs in developing countries. Has published the comprehensive, two-volume directory of *Population Programmes and Assistance* (see section V below), publishes *Populi* and *UNFPA Newsletter* (see "Periodicals") and has begun a series of *Population Profiles* (see *Singapore,* and *Law and Population,* p. 37). 1976 budget: $90 million.

World Bank (International Bank for Reconstruction and Development), 1818 H St. N.W., Washington, D.C. 20433.

Population program established 1968. Conducts demographic research, publishes *Sector Policy Papers* and *Working Papers* on population planning, education, health, rural development, nutrition, urbanization, etc., and the annual *World Bank Atlas* (see "International Data"), and provides loans for population programs to developing countries. 1976 population program loan commitments: $123 million.

IV. Population Libraries and Information Sources Around the World.

For information on libraries and other resource and service centers in the population field throughout the world consult the *International Directory of Population Information and Library Resources: First Edition,* compiled and edited by Catherine Fogle, Karin Gleiter and Marilyn McIntyre, 1972. 324 pp.; *Supplement to First Edition,* compiled and edited by Karin Gleiter and Catherine Fogle, 1972, 84 pp. ($7.00 together); and *Part 2: 1975 Address List,* compiled and edited by Karin Gleiter, 1975, 321 pp., $15.00.

The Directory is published by and may be ordered from the Technical Information Service of the Carolina Population Center, University of North Carolina, University Square, Chapel Hill, N.C. 27514. It contains entries of 975 organizations ordered by country with descriptions of their resources and activities.

A specialized source of information on Asia is provided by *Sources of Information on Population/Family Planning: A Handbook for Asia,* by Sumiye Konoshima, David Radel, and Elizabeth Bentzel Buck, 1975. 263 pp. The Handbook is published by and may be ordered free of charge from the East-West Communication Institute, 1777 East-West Rd., Honolulu, Hawaii 96822.

It contains profiles of 64 national, regional, and international sources of information and six indexes which enable the user to identify information sources on different subjects, geographical areas, and in various formats.

V. Population Research and Training Programs and Sources of International Assistance Around the World

The following two companion volumes published by the United Nations Fund for Population Activities in 1976 under the overall title *Population Programmes and Projects* constitute the most comprehensive collection of data to date about agencies, organizations, programs and projects in the population field. The orientation is, however, towards programs, projects, and assistance available for or being carried out in developing countries. For relevant information on developed as well as developing countries see the listings in this section under CICRED, IPPF, Population Reference Bureau, and U.S. Department of Health, Education, and Welfare.

United Nations Fund for Population Activities (UNFPA). *Population Programmes and Projects, 1976.* 2 vols. Available at $17.50 a set or $10.00 each from UNIPUB, Box 433, Murray Hill Station, New York, N.Y. 10016.

Vol. 1. *Guide to Sources of International Population Assistance.* 319 pp.

Mandated by the World Population Plan of Action, this is a guide to international population assistance for developing countries interpreted in the broadest possible sense including advisory, training, research and information services as well as direct and indirect funding. The types of such assistance that can be provided, reporting requirements and how to apply are given along with general descriptions of organization activities for each of some 150 multilateral, regional, bilateral, nongovernmental, university, and research and training agencies, organizations and institutions throughout the world.

Vol. 2. *Inventory of Population Projects in Developing Countries Around the World 1974/75.* 418 pp.

This is an update of the UNFPA publication *Inventory of Population Projects in Developing Countries Around the World 1973/74*, and covers the period 1 January 1974 through 30 June 1975, with some overlap. UNFPA plans to make this *Inventory* an annual publication. Part 1 is organized by countries, listing for each: basic demographic data, government views on population, and full details on what projects are being assisted from which external sources. Part 2 summarizes projects funded by different agencies on a regional, interregional or global basis.

Committee for International Coordination of National Research in Demography (CICRED). *Directory of Demographic Research Centers.* Published in 1974 and updated in 1975 by CICRED, 27 rue du Commandeur, 75657 Paris Cedex 14, France.

A looseleaf publication listing by country full details for some 300 government, university and other institutions engaged in demographic research throughout the world.

International Planned Parenthood Federation (IPPF). *Catalogue of Training Opportunities in Population and Family Planning.* Revised 1975. 25 pp. Available from IPPF, Department of Education and Training, 18-20 Lower Regent Street, London SW1Y 4PW, U.K. Free.

Details on training programs in information, education, and communication; training of trainers; management of population/family planning; clinical administration; contraceptive technology; and counseling.

International Planned Parenthood Federation (IPPF). Western Hemisphere Region. *Training Facilities in Demography, Family Planning, and Physiology of Reproduction Available in Latin America, the United States and Canada.* August 1974 (New edition scheduled for 1976). 32 pp. Available from IPPF, Western Hemisphere Region, 111 Fourth Ave., New York, N.Y. 10003. Free.

A comprehensive listing of types of training programs offered, length of courses and assistance available in government, university, and other centers.

Population Reference Bureau. *World Population Growth and Response 1965-1975: A Decade of Global Action.* 1976. 271 pp. Available from Population Reference Bureau, Inc., 1754 N Street, N.W., Washington, D.C. 20036. $4.00.

A global review of population trends, programs (with emphasis on family planning), and policy during the past decade, organized by country (over 200 included), regions, major multilateral agencies, private organizations, and the U.S. Agency for International Development which has been the foremost supporter of global action to meet the crisis of runaway population growth since 1965.

United Nations. Economic and Social Commission for Asia and the Pacific (ESCAP). *Research, Teaching and Training in Demography: A Directory of Institutions in the ESCAP Region.* Asian Population Studies Series No. 8. Published 1973 with two supplements issued in 1974. Order from the United Nations Sales Department, New York, N.Y. 10017, Sales No. E/CN.11/1007/Add. 1, or from ESCAP, Population Division, Bangkok, Thailand. $3.50.

Full details for over 200 institutions in 19 countries of the ESCAP area.

U.S. Department of Health, Education, and Welfare (HEW). *Inventory of Federal Population Research.* Prepared by the Interagency Committee on Population Research. Published annually. Latest available covers fiscal year 1975. DHEW Publication No. (NIH) 75-133. 149 pp. Free.

Information on all population-related research projects and centers currently supported by U.S. federal agencies (mainly HEW and the Agency for International Development).

Inventory of Private Agency Population Research: 1974. Prepared by the Interagency Committee on Population Research. DHEW Publication No. (NIH) 76-694. 103 pp. Free.

Second compilation of information on all research projects focused primarily on population which are currently supported by the Ford Foundation, The Population Council, or the Rockefeller Foundation.

Analysis of Federal Population Research. Prepared by the Interagency Committee on Population Research. Published annually. Latest available covers fiscal year 1975. 50 pp. Free.

Discussion and recommendations for needed population research in the biological sciences and social and behavioral sciences based on analysis of projects reported in the above two publications.

These three reports, prepared by the Interagency Committee on Population Research (see p. 66), are available, free, from the Center for Population Research, National Institute of Child Health and Human Development, Landow Building, Bethesda, Md. 20014.

Author Index

Abel-Smith, Brian, 37
Acsádi, György T., 12, 13, 43, 44
af Geijerstam, Gunner K., 40
Agarwala, S. N., 45
Aghai, M. A., 47
Ainsworth, Charles H., 16
Ainsworth, Fern C., 16
Ainsworth, Winnie T., 16
Aird, John S., 43, 45
Akingha, J. B., 43
Alan Guttmacher Institute, 37, 40
Aldous, Joan, 17
Alers, J. Oscar, 48
Alexander, Sidney S., 51
Allen, James E., 37
Allen, William R., 34
Allingham, J. D., 13
Allison, Anthony, 27
American Association for the Advancement of Science, 54
American Friends Service Committee, 40
American Universities Field Staff, 27, 42
Amezquita de Almeyda, Josefina, 36
Anderson, Charles H., 26
Anderson, Walt, 31
Applebaum, Mark I., 37
Appleman, Philip, 27, 37
Arriaga, Eduardo E., 43, 49
Asayesh, K. A., 50
Askham, Janet, 14
Atlee, Elinore, 24
Aykrod, W. R., 29
Azuara, Leandro, 36
Baali, Fuad, 22
Bachrach, Peter, 35
Back, Kurt, 35
Bacon, A. Lloyd, 21
Bahr, Howard M., 27
Bairuch, Paul, 33
Baldwin, Godfrey S., 43
Baldwin, Robert E., 33
Balakrishnan, T. R., 13
Balan, Jorge, 49
Ballonoff, Paul A., 7
Ballweg, John, 47
Banerji, D., 45
Barsby, Steve L., 21
Barton, Joseph J., 25
Baum, Samuel, 13
Beale, Calvin L., 22
Beaver, Steven E., 49
Beck, M. B., 41
Behrens, William W., III., 28
Beier, George, 22
Benjamin, Bernard, 6
Ben-Porath, Yoram, 14, 51
Berelson, Bernard, 27, 35, 38
Berg, Alan, 29
Bergman, Elihu, 35, 36
Berlin, Joyce E., 19
Bernard, Jessie, 14, 17
Bernhardt, Eva, 13
Berry, Brian J. L., 6
Bickel, Leonard, 29
Bier, William C., 24
BioSciences Information Service, 56
Bird, Caroline, 27
Birdsall, Nancy, 36
Bixby, Lenore E., 24
Blaikie, Piers M., 45
Blake, Judith, 11
Bleakly, Kenneth D., Jr., 23
Bloch, Lucille Stephenson, 37
Block, Donna, 31
Bodmer, W. F., 6
Boertlein, Celia G., 21
Bogue, Donald J., 7, 13, 37, 38
Bollens, John C., 22
Boot, John C. G., 27

Borah, Woodrow, 6
Borgstrom, Georg, 29
Borrie, W. D., 27
Bose, Ashish, 45
Boserup, Ester, 18
Boughey, Arthur S., 6
Bourgeois-Pichat, Jean, 48
Boute, Julien, 27
Bouvier, Leon F., 14, 19, 24, 44, 52
Bowles, Gladys K., 21
Boyce, A. J., 7
Boyer, Richard E., 49
Bramsen, Michèle Bo., 18
Brass, William, 9
Brody, Eugene, 20
Brown, Harrison, 27
Brown, Lester R., 27, 29
Brown, Richard A., 34
Brown, William, 28
Browning, Harley L., 49
Brunn, Stanley D., 22
Buck, Elizabeth Bentzel, 67
Bumpass, Larry, 13
Burki, Shahid J., 47
Burleson, Noel-David, 52
Burma, John H., 25
Burnley, I. M., 52
Bussey, Ellen M., 21
Bussink, Tine, 47
Butler, J. Douglas, 41
Butz, William P., 14
Buvinić, Myra, 18

Cairo Demographic Centre, 50
Caldwell, John C., 13, 43
Callahan, Daniel, 5, 32, 40
Caltech Population Program, 27
Cantrell, P., 43
Carder, Michael, 42
Carr, Griselda, 13
Carrier, Norman, 7
Carroll, Vern, 52
Carter, Hugh, 16
Cartwright, Ann, 37
Carvajal, Manuel J., 49
Castles, Stephen, 20
Cavalli-Sforza, L. L., 6
Centro Latinoamericano de Demografia (CELADE), 49, 50
Cernada, George P., 37
Chaichana, Suvanavejh, 48
Chamberlain, N. W., 28
Chafe, William Henry, 18
Chambers, J. D., 5
Chand, Gyan, 45
Chandler, Tertius, 22
Chandrasekaran, C., 37
Chandrasekhar, S., 40, 46
Chang, Chen-Tung, 47
Chang, H. C., 21
Chaplin, David, 49
Chasteen, Edgar R., 38
Chen, Kan, 35
Chen, Pi-chao, 45
Chinese Center for International Training in Family Planning, 47
Cho, Lee-Jay, 13, 44, 47
Choucri, Nazli, 28
Choudhury, Moqbel A., 48
Chudacoff, Howard P., 21
Chulalongkorn University, Institute of Population Studies, 48
Chung, Bom Mo, 14
Cicourel, Aaron V., 13
Claessen, H. J. M., 38
Clark, Colin, 29
Clark, Robert, 25
Clarke, J. I., 6, 50
Clem, Ralph S., 48
Clinton, Richard L., 35

Coale, Ansley J., 24, 33
Cogswell, Seddie, 5
Cole, H. S. D., 28
Columbia University, International Institute for the Study of Human Reproduction, 38
Commission on Population Growth and the American Future, 51
Committee for International Coordination of National Research in Demography (CICRED), 14, 20, 28, 42, 68
Committee on International Migration of Talent, 20
Commoner, Barry, 31
Community and Family Study Center, 49
Condé, Julien, 43
Congressional Information Service, 9
Conkling, Edgar C., 6
Cook, Alice H., 18
Cook, Sherburne F., 6
Coombs, Lolagene C., 14, 15
Cordell, Magda, 18
Cornelius, Wayne A., 49
Cooper, Charles A., 51
Cornejo, Gerardo, 36
Correa, Hector, 29
Council of Planning Librarians, 54
Cox, Dennis R., 21
Cox, Peter R., 4, 31
Cuca, Roberto, 38
Cutright, Philip, 38
Dahl, Nancy S., 17
Dasbach, Joseph M., 54
DaVanzo, Julie, 14, 51
David, Henry P., 40, 44
Davies, Keith A., 49
Davis, Kingsley, 22, 51
Davis, Lenwood G., 54
Davis, Wayne H., 5
Davison, Rebecca, 52
DeJong, Gordon F., 5
DeLora, Jack R., 17
DeLora, Joann S., 17
Demographic Research Institute, University of Gothenburg, 7
Denton, Frank T., 33
Desai, P. B., 45
Devereux, George, 40
de Villedary, Hubert, 35
DeVyver, Frank T., 34
Dib, George M., 36
Dienes, C. Thomas, 35
Dixon, Ruth, 14
Dodge, David L., 19
Donovan, Jerry J., 11
Doublet, Jacques, 35
Downs, Anthony, 22
Drewe, Paul, 20
Driver, Edwin D., 35
Dubos, Rene, 32
Duncan, G. W., 38
Duncan, Greg J., 16
Duncan, William G., 13
Du Toit, Brian M., 20
Dwyer, D. J., 22
East-Asian Pastoral Institute, 44
East-West Communication Institute, 55, 67
East-West Population Institute, 14
Eckholm, Eric P., 29, 30
Edmonston, Barry, 22
Educational Facilities Laboratories, 32
Ehrlich, Anne H., 31
Ehrlich, Paul R., 28, 31
Ejiogu, C. N., 44
El-Hamamsy, Laila, 27
Elias, Andrew, 43
Emerson, John Philip, 43
Endres, Michael E., 28
Engel, Madeleine, H., 25
Enke, Stephen, 34

Environment-Population Education Services, 52
Erb, Guy F., 34
Ergero, Bertil, 43
Erhardt, Carl L., 19
Erhart, Joseph F., 32
Etzioni, Amitai, 7
European Centre for Population Studies, 55
Evans, Tommy N., 39
Falk, Richard A., 28
Family Planning Association of Nepal, 40
Family Planning Foundation (Madras), 46
Fapohunda, Olanrewaju J., 44
Farley, Reynolds, 25
Fawcett, James T., 14, 15, 35, 48
Feinstein, Otto, 25
Fenner, Diane, 32
Ferman, Louis A., 24
Ferrera, Maria Alicia, 36
Ferriss, Abbott L., 18
Finlay, H. A., 36
Fisher, W. B., 50
Fitzpatrick, Joseph P., 25, 26
Fletcher, Carol, 52, 53
Fletcher School of Law and Diplomacy, The, 35
Flieger, Wilhelm, 8, 47
Fogarty International Center, 17
Fogle, Catharine, 67
Food and Agriculture Organization of the United Nations, 30, 44
Ford Foundation, 22, 34
Ford, Thomas R., 5
Forman, Robert E., 23
Forrest, Jacqueline E., 39
Fox, Gerald, 22
Fox, Robert W., 49
Fox, Robin, 17
Francoeur, Robert T., 15
Franda, Marcus F., 46
Fraser, Dean, 28
Freebairn, Donald K., 30
Freedman, Deborah S., 13
Freedman, Ronald, 13, 15, 38
Friedland, William, 21
Frejka, Tomas, 7
Frey, William H., 23
Gardner, Robert W., 51
George, Victor, 17
George Washington University Medical Center, Department of Medical and Public Affairs, Population Information Program, 38, 56
Ghasemi-Gonabadi, Hama, 55
Gibson, Don C., 24
Ginzberg, Eli, 23
Glass, David V., 6
Glazer, Nathan, 26
Gleiter, Karin, 67
Glick, Paul C., 16, 17
Glikson, P., 26
Godwin, R. Kenneth, 35, 36
Goldberg, David, 13
Goldscheider, Calvin, 4, 26
Goldstein, Alice, 48
Goldstein, Sidney, 23, 26, 48
Goode, Stephen H., 55
Gordon, John E., 44
Gordon, Michael, 17
Gordon, Milton M., 26
Gould, S. J., 26
Grabill, Wilson, 13
Grant, James P., 34
Gray, H. Peter, 34
Gray, Virginia, 36
Great Britain, Committee on the Working of the Abortion Act, 41
Grebenik, E., 7
Greeley, Andrew M., 26
Green, Lawrence W., 38
Greer, Colin, 26
Greville, T. N. E., 7
Grier, George, 13
Grindstaff, Carl F., 51
Groat, H. Theodore, 15
Groh, George, 26

Groth, Edward III, 27
Gustavus, Susan O., 4
Guttmacher, Alan, 38
Guyot, James F., 45
Habbakuk, H. J., 33
Habenstein, Robert W., 17
Haber, Alan, 24
Halacy, D. S., Jr., 30
Halebsky, Sandor, 23
Hall, Peter, 35
Hall, Robert E., 40
Hance, William A., 44
Handlin, Oscar, 20
Hansen, Niles M., 23
Hansen, Roger D., 34
Hardin, Garrett, 31, 41
Hardoy, Jorge E., 49
Hargreaves, R. P., 52
Harman, David, 53
Harper, Elizabeth G., 20
Harrison, G. A., 7
Hart, Harold, 28
Hartley, Shirley Foster, 4, 17
Hastings Center, 32
Hauser, Philip M., 19
Hawley, Amos H., 23
Hayes, Denis, 31
Heenan, L. D. B., 52
Heer, David M., 4
Heligman, Larry, 43
Hellman, Hal, 4
Henin, Roushai A., 43
Henry, Louis, 7
Hermalin, Albert I., 37
Hernandez, Jose, 4
Hill, A., 7
Hinze, Kenneth, 21
Hobcraft, John, 7
Hodgson, Dennis, 31
Hoffman, Lois Wladis, 18
Hofsten, Erland, 48
Holdren, John P., 31
Holmes, David N., Jr., 34
Hordern, Anthony, 40
Horlacher, David E., 34
Horsley, Kathryn, 53
Huddle, Norie, 31
Hughes, Helen MacGill, 53
Hughes, James W., 23
Hutchings, Edward, Jr., 27
Huyck, Earl E., 39
Igun, Adenola, 43, 44
Ilchman, Warren F., 36
Ingram, Michael, 32
Institute of Medicine, 41
Institute for Scientific Information, 56
Inter-American Development Bank, 67
Inter-American Statistical Institute, 11, 67
Interdisciplinary Communication Program, 55
International Labour Office, 51
International Labour Organization, 25
International Planned Parenthood Federation, 38, 41, 45, 55, 68
International Project of the Association for Voluntary Sterilization, 38
International Statistical Institute, 13
International Union for the Scientific Study of Population (IUSSP), 5
Iskandar, N., 46
Jackson, G. A., 21
Jackson, Wesley S., 31
Jacobson, Michael, 30
Jaffe, Frederick S., 38
Jain, Anrudh, 42
Jain, S. P., 46
Jakobson, Leo, 45
Jakobson, Sheilah, 45
Jansen, Clifford T., 21
Janssen, L. H., 32
Jelin, Elizabeth, 49
Jewett, Frank I., 15
Johnson, Gale D., 30
Johnson, G. Z., 43
Johnson, Helen W., 26
Johnson, Stanley, 5, 28

Johnson, W. Bert, 38
Johnston, H. J., 20
Johnston, Ruth, 52
Jones, Elizabeth A., 7
Jones, Gavin W., 32, 34
Jones, Owen H., 7
Jongmans, D. G., 38
Joyce, James A., 28
Kahn, E. J., Jr., 51
Kahn, Herman, 28
Kalbach, Warren E., 51
Kallab, Valeriana, 34
Kammeyer, Kenneth C. W., 4, 5
Kantner, John F., 13, 45
Kaplan, Bernice A., 15
Katznelson, Ira, 23
Keeley, C. B., 21
Keeley, Michael C., 34
Keeny, S. M., 38
Keller, Alan, 36
Kellog, Edmund H., 35, 36
Kennedy, David M., 39
Kennedy, Robert E., 20
Keyfitz, Nathan, 8, 19
Khosla, Ashok, 31
Kilian, Lewis N., 26
Kim, Taek, II, 47
King, Pat, 53
King, Timothy, 34
Kintanar, Agustin, Jr., 47
Kirk, Maurice, 36
Kiser, Clyde V., 13
Kish, L., 13
Kitagawa, Evelyn, 19
Kitano, Harry A. L., 26
Klaasen, Leo H., 20
Klare, Marshall, 26
Kline, David K., 36, 53
Klinger, Andras,
Kloss, Diana M., 35
Knodel, John E., 48
Kocher, James E., 15
Koeltzer, Victor, 33
Konoshima, Sumiye, 67
Kopachevsky, Joe, 21
Kornbluh, Joyce L., 24
Kosack, Godula, 20
Kosinski, Leszek A., 21, 48
Kreps, Juanita, 25
Krótki, Karol G., 8
Kubat, Daniel, 22, 51
Kumar, Joginder, 30
Kwan, E. Hyock, 47
Lader, Lawrence, 41
Lamphere, Louise, 18
Landahl, John 53
Lansing, John B., 21
Larson, Arthur, 36
Lapham, Robert J., 40
Laslett, Peter, 6
Lee, Everett S., 52
Lee, Luke T., 35, 36
Lee, Sung Jin, 44
Leighton, Andrew J., 53
Lerner, Susana, 36
Lerza, Catherine, 30
Lewis, Robert A., 48
Lewit, S., 41
Lingner, Joan W., 49
Little, Kenneth, 44
Lincoln, Eric C., 26
Livi Bacci, Massimo, 20, 36, 49
Llewellyn-Jones, Derek, 15
Lloyd, Cynthia B., 25
Loebl, Suzanne, 39
Long, Larry H., 21
Loo, Chalsa, 31
Lopota, Helena Z., 26
Lopreator, Joseph, 26
Lunde, Anders S., 9
Lundstrom, Hans, 47
Lutfi, Najib Diab, 17
Lyon, David L., 5, 29
Macisco, John J., Jr., 20, 49
MacLeod, M. J., 6
Macmillan Information Division, 31

Maddox, John, 31
Madigan, Francis C., 47
Maggs, Peter B., 35
Mamas, Si Gde Made, 46
Mamdani, Mahmood, 46
Mandelbaum, D. G., 46
Manderson, Lenore, 46
Mangin, William, 23
Manocha, Sohan L., 30
Marckwardt, Albert M., 39
Marden, Parker G., 31, 53
Marks, Eli S., 8
Marshall, John F., 15
Martel, Leon, 28
Martin, Walter T., 19
Mason, Karen Oppenheim, 15
Masters, Stanley H., 25
Matras, Judah, 4
Matsumoto, Y. Scott, 47
Maurer, Kenneth, 48
Mazie, Sara Mills, 51
McCaffrey, Lee, 45
McCormack, Arthur, 28, 32
McCoy, Terry L., 50
McDonald, Peter F., 52
McGranahan, D. V., 8
McGrath, Patricia, 27
McGreevey, William P., 36
McHale, John, 18
McIntyre, Marilyn,, 67
McLeod, Betty, 32
McNamara, Robert S., 34
McNicoll, Geoffrey, 47
McVeigh, Frank, 24
McVey, Wayne W., 51
Meadows, Dennis L., 28
Meadows, Donella H., 28
Menken, Jane, 8
Mesavoric, Mihajlo, 28
Meyer, M. G., 17
Meyers, George C., 20
Mickelwait, Donald R., 18
Micklin, Michael, 31
Miles, Rufus E., Jr., 28
Miller, Tyler G., 31
Mishan, E. J., 33
Moerman, Joseph, 32
Moghissi, Kamran S., 39
Molnos, Angela, 44
Moore, Carolynne, 54
Moore, Joan W., 26
Moore-Cavar, Emily, 41
Moors, Hein G., 49
Moquin, Wayne, 26
Moraes, Dom, 28
Morgan, James N., 16
Morrison, Donald George, 44
Morrison, Peter A., 21
Morse, Elliott R., 51
Moss, R. P., 44
Mott, Frank L., 44
Moynihan, Daniel Patrick, 26
Mueller, Eva L., 13, 21
Muhsam, Helmut V., 32
Muramatsu, Minoru M., 45
Murphy, Elaine, 53
Murphy, Francis X., 32
Murstein, Marjorie Cooper, 41
Nag, Moni, 7
Nam, Charles B., 4
Namboodiri, Krishnan, 13
Nash, A. E. Kier, 51
National Academy of Sciences, 36
National Academy of Sciences, Committee on World Food, Health and Population, 30
National Academy of Sciences, Institute of Medicine, 19
National Academy of Sciences, Subcommitte on Nutrition and Fertility, 30
National Association for Foreign Student Affairs, 53
National Catholic Education Association, 53
National Council of Organizations for Children and Youth, 24

National Council on Illegitimacy, 17
National Population Clearing House, The, 47
National Research Council, Commission on International Relations, World Food and Nutrition Study Steering Committee, 30
National Urban League, 36
Neal, Arthur G., 15, 22
Nelkin, Dorothy, 21
Newman, S. H., 41
New York Times Company, 30
Nickerson, Jane S., 6
Niland, John R., 20
Nordyke, Eleanor C., 51
North, Robert C., 28
Nortman, Dorothy, 15, 39
Nye, Ivan F., 18
O'Hara, Donald J., 15
Okediji, Francis Olu, 44
Olson, David H. L., 17
Oltmans, Willem L., 28
Ominde, S. H., 44
Omran, Abdel R., 41, 51
Operations Research Group, 46
Oppenheimer, Valerie K., 28
Organisation for Economic Co-operation and Development, 12, 18, 36, 39
Orleans, Leo A., 45
Osofsky, Howard J., 41
Osofsky, Joy D., 41
Ostfeld, Adrian M., 24
Overbeek, J., 6
Packard, Vance, 21
Paddock, Paul, 30
Paddock, William, 30
Pakistan Population Planning Council, 47
Pan American Health Organization, 50
Pareek, Udai, 46
Parke, Robert, Jr., 51
Parliament of the Commonwealth of Australia, The, 52
Parry, H. B., 28
Partan, Daniel G., 42
Paxman, John M., 36
Peck, Ellen, 15
Peel, John, 13, 31
Penchef, Esther,
Perlman, Mark, 34
Pestel, Edward, 28
Petersen, William, 4, 5, 26
Pierce, Catherine S., 38
Pilpel, Harriet F., 35
Pinkney, Alfonso, 26
Pino, Frank, 26
Piotrow, Phyllis T., 36
Pitchford, J. D., 34
Pittenger, Donald B., 8
Planned Parenthood Federation of America, Katharine Dexter McCormick Library, 55
Planned Parenthood/World Population, Center for Family Planning Program Development, 39
Plant, Robert, 34
Plender, Richard, 20
Poffenberger, Thomas, 46
Pohlman, Edward, 5, 39
Poleman, Thomas T., 30
Polgar, Steven, 7, 15
Pollard, J. H., 8
Population Council, The, 12, 39, 42, 55
Population Information Program, George Washington University Medical Center, 36, 41
Population Problems Research Council, 47
Population Reference Bureau, 12, 19, 24, 32. 36, 42, 44, 53, 68
Potter, Robert G., 40
Potts, Malcolm, 39
Prachuabmoh, Visid, 48
Pradervand, P., 44
Pressat, Roland, 4, 8
Presser, Harriet B., 39, 50
Preston, Samuel H., 19
Price, Daniel O., 22

Princeton University, Office of Population Research, 54
Prothero, R. Mansell, 21
Prothro, Edwin T., 17
Puffer, Ruth Rice, 19
Queen, Stuart A., 17
Quick, Horace F., 7
Quick, Sylvia, 43
Radel, David, 44, 67
Raisbeck, Bertram L., 35
Ramachandran, K. V., 48
Ramos, Joseph, 50
Randers, Jorgen, 28
Rao, Kamala G., 46
Rao, S. L. N., 40
Rapawy, Stephen, 43
Ratajczak, Rosalinda, 48
Rathbone, R.J.A.R., 43
Rawson-Jones, Daphne, 39
Ray, D. Michael, 6
Reed, Ritchie, 51
Rehling, Louise, 7
Reich, Michael, 31
Reid, Sue Titus, 5, 29
Reining, Priscilla, 5
Repetto, Robert C., 15
Republic of the Phillippines, National Census and Statistics Office, 47
Retherford, Robert E., 19
Revelle, Roger, 6, 29, 31
Rich, William, 15
Richmond, Anthony H., 20, 22
Ricklefs, R. E., 32
Ridker, Ronald G., 15, 51
Riegelman, Mary Ann, 18
Righter, Rosemary, 23
Ritchey, P. Neal, 21
Roberto, Eduardo L., 39
Robinson, JoAnn, 53
Robinson, Warren C., 34
Rock, Vincent P., 23
Rodrigues, Walter, 36
Rogers, Andrei, 8
Rogers, Everett M., 39
Rogg, Eleanor M., 26
Rosaldo, Michelle Zimbalist, 18
Rose, Peter I., 26
Rosen, Robert C., 35
Rosenwaike, Ira, 51
Ross, C. R., 49
Ross, Helen L., 17
Ross, John A., 39, 47
Rowland, Richard H., 48
Ruprecht, Theodore K., 15, 34
Ryder, Norman B., 13
Ryser, Paul E., 16
Sable, Martin H., 50
Safe, Helen I., 20
Sahib, M. A., 13
Safilios-Rothschild, Constantina, 18
Salas, Rafael M., 42
Salkeld, Geoffrey, 39
Samuel, T. G., 20
Sanchez-Albornoz, Nicolas, 50
Saney, Parviz, 36
Saunders, Lyle, 36
Sauvy, Alfred, 29
Sawhill, Isabel V., 17
Schmandt, Henry J., 22
Schmelz, U. D., 26
Schoen, Robert, 19
Schroeder, Richard, 36
Schulman, Sam, 50
Schulz, Barbara S., 15
Schultz, T. Paul, 16, 48, 51
Schultz, Theodore W., 16
Schwartz, Barry, 23
Searing, Marjory E., 43
Seear, B. N., 25
Segal, Aaron, 50
Segal, Sheldon, 39
Selavan, Ida Cohen, 19
Seltzer, Judith R., 52, 53
Seltzer, William, 8
Selvaratnam, S., 34
Senderowitz, Judith,

71

Serrano, Carlos V., 19
Shantokumar, G., 48
Sharma, Prakash C., 54
Shaw, Paul R., 20
Sheps, Mindel, 8
Shiloh, Ailon, 19
Shorter, Edward, 17
Shorter, Frederic C., 8
Shryock, Henry, 8
Sidel, Ruth, 45
Siegel, Jacob S., 8, 24
Sikes, Melanie M., 22
Silvermann, Anna, 16
Silvermann, Arnold, 16
Simmons, George B., 46
Simmons, Ozzie G., 36
Simon, Arthur, 30
Simon, Julian L.,
Simon, Paul, 30
Simon Population Trust, 55
Simpson-Hebert, Mayling, 55
Singarimbun, Masri, 47
Singer, S. F., 29
Siok-Hwa, Cheng, 47, 48
Sivin, Irving, 39
Sly, David F., 23
Smith, Peter C., 47
Smith, Robert S., 34
Smith, T. E., 36
Smith, T. Lynn, 4, 50
Smithsonian Institution, 36, 47
Smithsonian Institution, The Center for the Study of Man, 32
Sobin, Dennis P., 25
Social Issues Resources Series, 53
Sociological Resources for the Social Studies, 53
Sollito, Sharmon, 32
Southern Regional Demographic Group, 51
Speare, Alden, Jr., 23
Spencer, Byron G.
Spengler, Joseph J., 4, 29, 34
Spillane, William H., 16
Spooner, Brian, 7
Stanford, Quentin, 5
Staples, Robert, 17
Stepan, Jan, 35, 36
Sternlieb, George, 23
Stoeckel, John, 48
Stokes, Bruce, 27
Storold, Ellwyn R., 26
Stycos, J. Mayone, 39, 50
Styles, Frederick G., 51
Subbiah, B. V., 32
Suitters, Beryl, 39
Sulbrandt, José, 36
Sun, T. H., 37
Sundquist, James L., 37
Sweden, Royal Ministry of Foreign Affairs, 49
Swedish International Development Authority (SIDA), 18
Swee-Hock, Saw, 47, 48
Sweet, Charles F., 18
Sweet, James A., 25
Sweezy, Alan, 27
Symonds, Richard, 42
Szabady, Egon, 36
Tachi, Minoru, 45
Taiwan Committee on Family Planning, 48
Ta Ngoc, Châu, 32
Tabah, Leon, 34
Taeuber, Conrad, 52
Taeuber, Irene B., 52
Tangri, Shanti S., 34
Tapinos, Georges, 20
Taylor, Philip B., Jr., 50
TEMPO, Center for Advanced Studies, 34
Terhune, Kenneth W., 16
Thomas, Brinley, 20
Thomas, Robert N., 50
Thomlinson, Ralph, 4, 29, 48
Thompson, Vaida D., 37
Thornton, David, 51

Tien, H. Yuan, 45
Tietze, Christopher, 39, 41
Tinker, Irene B., 5, 18, 32
Tirasawat, Penporn, 48
Tomasi, L. M., 21
Toshio, Kuroda, 47
Transnational Family Research Institute, 40, 50
Tranter, N. L., 6
Treshow, Michael, 31
Trewartha, Glenn T., 23
Triche, Charlie W., III, 55
Triche, Diane Samson, 55
Trueblood, Felicity M., 49
Tufts University, Fletcher School of Law and Diplomacy, The, 47
Turchi, Boone A., 16
Turkson, Richard B., 36
Twentieth Century Fund Task Force on Employment Problems of Youth, The, 25
Uche, U.U., 36
Udry, Richard J., 39
UNESCO, Division of Equality of Educational Opportunity and Special Programs, Population Education Section, 54
UNESCO, Regional Office for Education in Asia, 54
United Nations, 13, 18, 42
United Nations, Department of Economic and Social Affairs, 4, 5, 6, 12, 14, 24, 35, 37, 42
United Nations, Department of Economic and Social Affairs, Population Division, 12, 17, 19, 22, 23, 25
United Nations, Department of Economic and Social Affairs, Statistical Office, 6, 12
United Nations, Economic Commission for Asia and the Far East, 14, 19
United Nations, Economic and Social Commission for Asia and the Pacific (ESCAP), 16, 40, 45, 48, 68
United Nations, Economic Commission for Europe, 49
United Nations, Economic Commission for Latin America (CELADE), 50
United Nations, Economic and Social Council, 42
United Nations, Educational, Scientific, and Cultural Organization (UNESCO), 21, 25
United Nations Fund for Population Activities (UNFPA), 37, 42, 47, 68
Universitas Indonesia, Lemaga Demografi, 46
University of Chicago, Community and Family Study Center, 40
University of North Carolina at Chapel Hill, 9
University of North Carolina at Chapel Hill, Carolina Population Center, Technical Information Service, 55, 56, 67
Urban Life-Population Education Institute, 54
U.S. Agency for International Development, 43, 66
U.S. Bureau of the Census, 9, 10, 17, 18, 23, 24, 54
U.S. Bureau of the Census, International Statistical Programs Center, 12, 40, 43
U.S. Bureau of Economic Analysis, Foreign Demographic Analysis Division, 43
U.S. Bureau of Labor Statistics, 25, 26
U.S. Center for Disease Control, 41
U.S. Congress, House Committee on The Judiciary, 21
U.S. Congress. House Committee on Post Office and Civil Service, Subcommittee on Census and Population, 51, 52, 66
U.S. Council of Environmental Quality, 31
U.S. Department of Agriculture, Economic Research Service, 22
U.S. Department of Health, Education and Welfare, Interagency Committee on Population Research, 68
U.S. Department of Health, Education, and Welfare, National Center for Education Statistics, 32

U.S. Department of Health, Education, and Welfare, National Center for Health Statistics, 9, 10
U.S. Department of Health, Education, and Welfare, National Institute of Child Health and Human Development, Center for Population Research, 24, 55
U.S. Department of Health, Education, and Welfare, National Library of Medicine, 56
U.S. Department of Health, Education, and Welfare, Public Health Service, 19
U.S. Environmental Protection Agency, Office of Research and Development, Environmental Studies Division, 32
U.S. Office of Management and Budget, 52
Vaidyanathan, K. E., 19
Valaoras, V. G., 51
van de Walle, Etienne, 6
van der Tak, Jean, 19, 41
Vandiver, Joseph S.,
Van Doren, Charles, 26
Veatch, Robert M., 32
Venkateswara, Rao, 46
Verbrugge, Lois M., 19
Vicker, Ray, 30
Viederman, Stephen, 54
Viel, Benjamin, 50
Vinovskis, Maris, 31
Visaria, Pravin, 42
Vivo, Paquita, 26
Vumbaco, Brenda J., 36
Wagenheim, Kal, 26
Wahren, Carl, 34
Wakstein, Allen M., 23
Walbert, David, 41
Waldron, Ingrid, 32
Walls, Dwayne E., 22
Walters, LeRoy, 33
Ward, Barbara, 23, 32
Ward, David, 23
Ward, Sandra, 47
Ware, Helen, 13, 52
Watson, Walter B., 40
Wattenberg, Ben G., 52
Wax, Murray L., 26
Weinsten, Jay A., 29
Weisbord, Robert G., 40
Weiss, Kenneth M., 7
Welch, Finis, 14, 16
Wells, Robert V., 6
Westoff, Charles F., 13, 14, 51
Westoff, Leslie Aldridge, 14
Whelan, Elizabeth M., 16
Widjojo, Nitisastro, 47
Wilder, Frank, 38
Wilding, Paul, 17
Willett, Joseph W., 30
Williams, Anne, 16
Willie, Charles V., 26
Willing, Martha K., 29
Willis, Kenneth G., 9
Wilsher, Peter, 23
Wilson, Paul R., 21
Wilson, Thomas W., Jr., 29
Wogaman, Philip, 33
Wolf, Bernard, 36
Woods, Clive, 39
World Bank, 12, 23, 33, 35
World Education, Inc., 32
World Health Organization (WHO) 9, 40
World Health Organization, Regional Office for South-East Asia, 45
Worth, George C., 47
Wriggins, W. Howard, 45
Wyon, John B., 46
Wynn, Margaret, 16
Yain, S. P., 45
Yaukey, David, 14
Zaidan, George C., 40
Zeisset, Paul T., 10
Zero Population Growth, 54
Zimmerman, Margot, 41
Zopf, Paul E., Jr., 4